Y0-BBB-125

THE LIBRARY
ST. MARY'S COLLEGE OF MARYLAND
ST. MARY'S CITY, MARYLAND 20686

Missing Chapters

NCTE Committee on Women in the Profession

Jeanne Marcum Gerlach, Chair, West Virginia University
Patricia Bloodgood, Kennedy High School, Bellmore, New York
Deanne Bogdan, Ontario Institute for Studies in Education
Barbara T. Bontempo, SUNY at Buffalo
Lynn Butler-Kisber, McGill University
Judy Prozzillo Byers, Fairmont State College
Margaret Carlson, Conval Regional High School, Peterborough, New Jersey
Mary P. Deming, Georgia State University
Dure Jo Gillikin, College of Staten Island
Sharon Hamilton-Wieler, Indiana University–Purdue University at Indianapolis
Betty L. Powell Hart, Mt. Vernon High School, Evansville, Indiana
Sue Ellen Holbrook, Southern Connecticut State University
Elizabeth Isele, Field Publications, Middletown, Connecticut
Fran Holman Johnson, Louisiana Technological University
Tracey J. Johnson, West Virginia University
Dianne Klein, Bowling Green High School, Ohio
Mary E. Kollar, Woodinville High School, Seattle, Washington
Annie K. Koshi, City College of New York
Lisa J. McClure, Southern Illinois University at Carbondale
Virginia R. Monseau, Youngstown State University
Irene M. Myles, Louisiana Technological University
Shirley A. Rau, Nampa High School, Idaho
Laurie Rozakis, State University of New York College of Technology
Silver Stanfill, Anchorage Community College
Joan C. Tornow, AFCENT International School, Brunssum, Netherlands
Ruth Vinz, Independent School District of Boise, Idaho
Faith Z. Schullstrom, Executive Committee Liaison
Deborah Fox, NCTE Staff Liaison

Missing Chapters

Ten Pioneering Women
in NCTE and English Education

Edited by

Jeanne Marcum Gerlach
West Virginia University

Virginia R. Monseau
Youngstown State University

National Council of Teachers of English
1111 Kenyon Road, Urbana, Illinois 61801

Lines from "The woman in the ordinary" by Marge Piercy are reprinted from *Circles on the Water* by Marge Piercy, copyright © 1982 by Marge Piercy. Reprinted by permission of Alfred A. Knopf, Inc.

NCTE Editorial Board: Richard Abrahamson, Celia Genishi, Joyce Kinkead, Richard Lloyd-Jones, Gladys Veidmanis, Charles Suhor, Chair, *ex officio*, Michael Spooner, *ex officio*

Manuscript Editor: Jane M. Curran

Project Editor: Robert A. Heister

Book Design: Tom Kovacs for TGK Design

NCTE Stock Number **31905-3050**

© 1991 by the National Council of Teachers of English. All rights reserved. Printed in the United States of America.

It is the policy of NCTE in its journals and other publications to provide a forum for the open discussion of ideas concerning the content and the teaching of English and the language arts. Publicity accorded to any particular point of view does not imply endorsement by the Executive Committee, the Board of Directors, or the membership at large, except in announcements of policy, where such endorsement is clearly specified.

Library of Congress Cataloging-in-Publication Data

Missing chapters : ten pioneering women in NCTE and english education / edited by Jeanne Marcum Gerlach, Virginia R. Monseau.
    p. cm.
    Includes bibliographical references.
    ISBN 0-8141-3190-5
    1. English philology—Study and teaching—United States—History.
2. English teachers—United States—Biography. 3. Women teachers—United States—Biography. I. Gerlach, Jeanne Marcum, 1946-   .
II. Monseau, Virginia R., 1941-   . III. National Council of Teachers of English. Committee on Women in the Profession.
PE68.U5M57   1991
428'.007'073—dc20								91-2082
												CIP

For Roger and Paul

Contents

Acknowledgments ix

Foreword by Walter Loban xi

Introduction xiii

Part I: Paving the Way 1

1. Rewey Belle Inglis: A Crystal-Ball Gazer 3
   Jeanne Marcum Gerlach

2. Ruth Mary Weeks: Teaching the Art of Living 30
   Judy Prozzillo Byers

3. Stella Stewart Center: Proceeding under Their Own Power 49
   Sue Ellen Holbrook

4. Dora V. Smith: A Legacy for the Future 69
   Virginia R. Monseau

Part II: Working Together 95

5. Angela M. Broening: Implacable Defender 97
   Dure Jo Gillikin

6. Marion C. Sheridan: A Lifetime Commitment 116
   Sharon Hamilton-Wieler

Part III: Looking to the Future 139

7. Lou LaBrant: A Challenge and a Charge 141
   David A. England and B. Jane West

8. Luella B. Cook: A Teacher's Teacher 168
   Betty L. Powell Hart

9. Helen K. Mackintosh: Expanding the Concept of
   Our World   186
     Lisa J. McClure

10. Ruth G. Strickland: Looking Back, Looking Forward   202
      Tracey J. Johnson

    Afterword by Arthur N. Applebee   227

    Editors   229

    Contributors   231

Acknowledgments

We would like to thank West Virginia University and the Youngstown State University Research Council for providing us with the funding and the library and secretarial help which made this project possible. Specifically, we would like to thank Dwight Burton, Alvina Treut Burrows, James Hocker Mason, J. N. Hook, Walter Loban, Harold Allen (who provided valuable information about these pioneering women shortly before his death in 1988 and whose widow, Elizabeth Allen, offered further information), Stanley Kegler, James Squire, Dianne Monson, Janet Emig, Nancy McHugh, Judith Stitzel, Ruth K. J. Cline, Thomas McCracken, and Rudy Almasy, professors, professors emeriti, and teachers, for their committed support and valuable comments. We would also like to thank NCTE archivist and librarian Carolyn McMahon, and the many other archivists and librarians who helped us garner information about these women. Finally, we are indebted to George Baxter Smith, brother of Dora V. Smith, and to Margaret Carlson, director of the University of Minnesota Alumni Association, for their help on this project.

Foreword

After the American Revolution three Frenchmen observed the emerging United States of America and commented on what they believed to be a new type of human being. However, typical of their times and culture, they focused on the men of the New World, not on men and women. Crèvecoeur wrote that "here individuals of all nations are melted into a new race of men, whose labors and posterity will one day cause great changes in the world.... The American is a new man, who acts upon new principles; he must therefore entertain new ideas and form new opinions." Lafayette found a "delightful equality prevailing everywhere," and he found no peasants similar to what he had known in Europe. Tocqueville wrote two volumes on America, but he expressed no thoughts about any type of woman, new or old. When these eighteenth-century gentlemen spoke of a "new man," they did not envision any new woman. They expected women to continue playing the traditional European roles: housewives, mothers of many children, mistresses, or servants.

Nevertheless, America was producing a new strain of feminine behavior, even before women joined the historical conquest of a larger continent beyond the colonies. Jane Addams and Dolly Madison created some cracks in the ancient molds for women, but history waited for First Lady Eleanor Roosevelt to break those molds. Change in the quality of women's lives was slow. One rebel, Margaret Fuller, foreshadowed the future, but time was necessary for pioneer life, science and industrialization, World Wars I and II, and the slow working of the Constitution to produce what the three French observers had failed to foresee.

The women featured in this book represent not only teachers, but also a new kind of woman in history. Both as teachers and as leaders of others, they believed fervently in a unified nation "with liberty and justice for all." They viewed the field of elementary language arts and secondary-college English as infinitely more than an enterprise to produce "elegantly refined genteel people." Believing that power should reside in a citizenry able to choose between wisdom and folly, they taught language for thinking and literature as the examination of values. Language, composition, and literature were not ends in themselves, but rather means to a much greater end, the strengthening of a free society.

Of the ten women celebrated in this volume, the two whom I knew best, Luella B. Cook and Dora V. Smith, were notable for their joyous personalities. Their lives and activities were ordered, exceptionally free from incoherence and confusion. Their value systems enabled them to sort out and organize quickly the multiplicity of demands upon their time and attention. These value systems placed very high emphasis on all humane, sympathetic relations with everyone who entered their orbits. They implicitly assumed that being a woman was important, but no more so than being human, being an American, being a teacher. From all that I learned from my acquaintance with the other women in this book, the same relaxed, ordered vitality prevailed for them. These are the American women of whom Walt Whitman wrote:

> I am the poet of the woman the same as the man
> And I say that it is as great to be a woman as to be a man.

These are the new women that Crèvecoeur, Lafayette, and Tocqueville failed to foresee.

Walter Loban
Berkeley, California

Introduction

This book is the first historical text to explore in depth the impact women have had on English education. We have chosen to focus on ten women who have made significant contributions to the profession during the first fifty years since the founding of the National Council of Teachers of English: Rewey Belle Inglis, Ruth Mary Weeks, Stella Stewart Center, Dora V. Smith, Angela M. Broening, Marion C. Sheridan, Lou LaBrant, Luella B. Cook, Helen K. Mackintosh, and Ruth G. Strickland.

There are obviously more than ten chapters missing from the history of English education. The profession needs to become more informed about the important work of many other women in language education—for example, women of color, who struggled to overcome barriers of racism as well as sexism. Further volumes always need to be written, and we would hope that another collection of missing chapters will extend the scope of this project beyond the limits we felt necessary for ourselves.

Though there are certainly others who deserve recognition, we have chosen these women because they had a significant impact at a time when women's accomplishments were not widely recognized. In spite of their hard work and achievements, many of the women included here are, at best, only "names" to teachers and English educators working in the field today.

This book, then, is not just a series of biographical sketches about ten women who have made important contributions to English education, but is a way of connecting the work of these women to what is being done in English education today. For example, both Rewey Belle Inglis and Dora V. Smith wrote about the importance of diagnosing and treating causes of error rather than using meaningless drills to help improve student writing. Over three decades later Mina P. Shaughnessy won acclaim for her book *Errors and Expectations*, which addressed the same problem. Smith also spoke of a spiral growth in a child's control over language—a broadening, extending, and refining that takes place from infancy. This "spiral" concept is the basis for what Jerome Bruner was later to call the "spiral curriculum," which repeatedly visits basic ideas, broadening and expanding upon them as a child grows older. Marion C. Sheridan pioneered the use of film in the classroom, just as Helen K. Mackintosh's work foreshadowed today's whole language movement. Because these kinds of connections have not been made, English educators may not be fully aware of how the contributions of these pioneering women influence and inform what we do today. Their ideas and accomplishments are especially significant in light of the contemporary move to create gender awareness in the profession. History shows little consciousness of gender at the time these women were most active professionally.

Though some may argue that we should not separate women from men in discussing professional contributions, it is important to note that scholars in the past have largely ignored the place of women in the history of English education and, therefore, the power of social concepts of gender in the making of that history. These oversights were the result of cultural perceptions of women at the time. In a tape-recorded interview with Robert S. Fay in 1965, W. Wilbur Hatfield said of Rewey Belle Inglis: "She was the youngest president we ever had. She was a very pretty woman. You see a pretty young woman getting ahead pretty fast, you sometimes wonder how much is the face and how much is something else." Though he later admitted he was wrong, this statement reveals that even respected longtime professionals in the field have been tempted to assess the achievements of women in terms of their physical appearance rather than their professional accomplishments.

In this publication we examine how and why these ten women were able to succeed in a male-dominated academic world. This information is valuable to both men and women in the field of English education today. A large percentage of students training to be English teachers are women, who need real-life models to emulate and look up to. This is especially important today, when gender awareness is such an essential part of the curriculum. Since gender studies have become so significant, it is imperative that we consider the contribution of women in English education in order to add to this growing body of knowledge.

As a matter of fact, the idea for this book was born of the frustration we experienced as doctoral students in the early 1980s trying to find information on some of the women included here. However, it was not until 1987, as members of the NCTE Women's Committee (later renamed the Committee on Women in the Profession), that we seriously began to discuss the need for a book which would provide the "missing" information. The committee members voted unani-

Missing Chapters xv

mously at the 1987 Los Angeles Convention to support such an effort. In addition, we received encouragement from several members of the Council's Executive Committee. Heartened by such positive response, we began our research.

As part of our data collection for this publication, we have visited the workplaces of these women, wherever possible, and have found letters, personal papers, awards, and photographs not available through other sources. In addition, we have tape-recorded and transcribed interviews with relatives, colleagues, and former students. Especially exciting is our videotaped interview with Lou LaBrant, who celebrated her one hundredth birthday in 1988. This interview was described at a presentation during the 1989 NCTE Annual Convention in Baltimore, and papers on the other women included in this volume have been presented at various other NCTE conferences.

It is important for readers to note that at the time these ten pioneering women were writing for publication, use of the masculine pronoun to refer to both genders was commonly accepted. In order to preserve the integrity of the quoted material and to avoid distraction to the reader, we have not attempted to alter what now appears to be sexist language. We trust that readers will understand the historical significance of leaving the language intact.

We have divided the book into three parts to provide a conceptual framework for the reader. Part I: Paving the Way focuses on four women who were truly pioneers in English education. Their early work showed remarkable foresight in light of what is happening in the field today. Part II: Working Together recognizes two women who worked to resolve difficulties the profession experienced during and after World War II. Their strong leadership during these hard times stressed the importance of cooperation within the profession. Finally, Part III: Looking to the Future identifies four women who were sensitive to the needs of an expanding world and to the challenges that world presented. Their work foreshadowed what was to come in teacher education, classroom practice, and research. These three serve to establish a pattern of organization which connects the women and their work to significant events of the time.

This publication, then, provides readers with a different way of looking at the history of English education. It not only chronicles the achievements of ten influential women in the field, but it also offers for the first time an exploration of women's contributions to the profession and to NCTE. It reinforces Ruth G. Strickland's 1960 convention theme as the Council celebrated its fiftieth anniversary: "All our past acclaims our future."—*J.M.G. and V.R.M.*

Part I:
Paving the Way

1 Rewey Belle Inglis: A Crystal-Ball Gazer

Jeanne Marcum Gerlach, West Virginia University

> In you bottled up is a woman peppery as curry
> a yam of a woman of butter and brass,
> compounded of acid and sweet like a pineapple,
>   like a handgrenade set to explode,
> like a goldenrod ready to bloom.
>
> Marge Piercy, "The woman in the ordinary"

Rewey Belle Inglis
1885-1967

In 1928 Rewey Belle Inglis transcended both regional and national notions about women's roles in the early part of the twentieth century to become the first woman elected president of the National Council of Teachers of English. Through her active encouragement of women who wished to take risks in her chosen profession of teaching, Inglis helped to transform the women's "sphere," not only in teaching but in professional leadership roles and publishing. Although she worked to help improve the course of women's progress in education, she was equally concerned with the educational needs of a larger audience, an audience of boys and girls and men and women. Therefore, she dedicated part of her life's work to developing pedagogical models which provided both students and teachers with confidence in their own beliefs and ideas; she taught them to value their own voices. In this respect Inglis was a pioneer in advancing the progressive ideals of her day. These same ideals are at the heart of contemporary feminist theory, which emphasizes the valuing of individual experiences.

3

This chapter will focus on the events of Inglis's professional life and will place her individual experiences in a broader perspective in order to provide the reader with some understanding of how her personal educational philosophy echoed the progressive ideals of the 1920s and 1930s and how it was an antecedent of contemporary feminist pedagogy. The impressive record she compiled in over fifty years as an English educator continues to serve as a guide to the history of English education and to document her wide-ranging interests and achievements.

Inglis began teaching high school English in 1915, a time when most educated women gravitated toward positions of teacher or librarian. After a few years of working, however, most of these same women gave up their chosen professions to marry and raise a family. Sacrificing one's career as a teacher was necessary, for the prevailing policy of many state boards of education was that teaching jobs should be filled by the unmarried since a married woman had a husband to take care of her. The only exceptions to the rules were wives whose husbands were mentally or physically unable to earn a living or wives whose husbands were deceased (Woody 1929/1966, 1:512). While most of these laws were revoked in the early 1920s, women continued to be discriminated against by school boards that required them to adhere to certain rules of conduct and appearance both inside and outside the classroom. It is a fact that Inglis never married, but whether or not she chose to remain single in order to teach is not known. However, according to her adopted daughter, Blue Lenox (1989), she refused to sign any statement agreeing to conform to specific social ideals and expectations. Lenox contends that her mother was too independent to relinquish her rights to court, to smoke, or to drink liquor if she so desired.

Inglis was indeed concerned with the absurdity of the rules and regulations for teachers, especially women teachers, but she was equally interested in other educational issues, such as the need for equity in every classroom and the valuing of students' experiences, beliefs, and ideas. In regard to classroom concerns, she knew that "the value of a course so often lies in the way it is taught and the person who teaches it" (1928, 382). Therefore, developing teaching pedagogy and preparing future teachers became two important focuses in her life.

So it was that Inglis was concerned with issues on several educational fronts, and out of her concern grew a lifelong commitment to improve education. But her dedication to the improvement and change of educational practices did not include radical activism;

instead, she labored to enlighten and to empower her family of colleagues and students through her teaching, mentoring, and writing, so that they could work together to ensure democratic educational ideals for all.

At this point it is necessary to remind the reader that the years of Inglis's classroom teaching career (1915–33) were years filled with controversies and debates concerning the teaching of English. Through those years, English was discussed as an intellectual discipline and as a means to the acquisition of knowledge, a socialization process necessary for individual development, and a method for character growth for individual development of democratic citizens. Many educators felt that English education should serve all three purposes, but there were those who believed that it should serve one purpose more than the others. Most educators, therefore, expressed either a traditional or a progressive view of learning, knowing, and teaching.

The traditionalists concentrated on the teacher's role as the initiator of knowledge; teachers transmitted or delivered knowledge, a collection of facts and ideas, to the students through lectures and course readings. Students passively received the information and stored it for later use on examinations and term papers. The ability to recall information and ideas was emphasized. Thus, learning meant receiving information. Knowing was the condition of having received information which could be measured by evaluating students' responses to examination questions.

The progressives held another view of learning, which focused on an activity or process that the school was to induce in each student. Knowing implied making connections; both the teachers and the students were learners. Teaching involved creating contexts for learning, not reporting facts.

Rewey Belle Inglis's life (1885–1967) spanned these years of dramatic change in English education. As Sanford Radner (1960) pointed out, the impact of two world wars, a worldwide depression, an increase in school population, and scientific and technological change resulted in shifts in English teaching pedagogy. First there was concern with teaching English for intellectual and spiritual growth (1910–20); this was followed by a view of English as advancing democratic ideals (1921–25), reappraisal (1926–29), English for emotional growth and practical living (1930–37), reappraisal (1938–41), English for promoting democracy (1942–46), and then English for maturity in an age dominated by science (1947–59). Although Inglis recognized these changes and their impact on teaching English, she remained a progressive throughout her career. She structured her courses, shaped her writings, and focused her work on individual needs both inside and outside the classroom. Her activities during her long life illustrate how she, as a teacher, professional leader, writer/editor, and mentor, worked to create a world where all people's voices are valued.

Inglis was committed to a lifelong teaching pedagogy of a democratic education based on equity; she did not, however, advocate the abolition of differences among individuals. Rather, she supported equity in the sense that it accommodates and nurtures differences between men and women and boys and girls. She encouraged the individual voice and bestowed those around her with confidence in their own values, thoughts, and feelings. Yet equity for Inglis did not mean abrogating or compromising academic standards. She provided her students with challenging lessons which motivated them to engage in critical thinking, as opposed to activities which required only simple recall skills.

While this view of equity is similar to the contemporary feminist critique of the traditional masculinist, patriarchal ways of being and the need for rethinking pedagogy and restructuring educational models to reflect the valuing of the individual experience, it also echoes the teachings of John Dewey and G. Stanley Hall, Inglis's contemporaries, who felt that course work should be structured to meet individual needs and that students should be encouraged to relate their personal and social experiences to school work. Hall said that a child's mental and physical growth occurs in stages and that the onset of the stages varies from child to child; therefore, some children might not pass beyond a given stage because of personal limitations. Thus, it was ridiculous to teach all children the same thing at the same time (Hall 1914). These beliefs helped to pave the way for the development of the progressive movement in education, and over the years they have been developed and reiterated, often in an altered form.

Inglis's views on the value of a democratic education based on equity did not develop overnight. Actually, her parents, Rewey E. (Graham) Inglis and James S. Inglis, instilled within their daughter the idea that her voice was as valuable, as important, and as significant as anyone else's. This type of parental guidance was rare in 1885, the year Inglis was born. Instead of encouraging all their children to express themselves freely, many parents were molding their daughters' spirits in order to teach them to conform to societal expectations of submissiveness and silence, while encouraging their sons to be assertive and speak their minds.

Unlike many parents, Rewey G. and James Inglis taught their daughter that reading good literature would help make her self-reliant and thus exposed her to a vast array of reading materials. Inglis spent much of her time while growing up in Minneapolis, Minnesota, sitting around the fire with her parents reading poetry, short stories, and novels.

Her parents continued to encourage Rewey Belle, as she liked to be called, to speak her mind throughout her public school years in Minneapolis. The Inglises were frequent visitors to the public schools during their daughter's enrollment, for they believed that parents and teachers should work together to ensure their children's success as learners. Inglis recognized her parents' wisdom, and after her graduation from the University of Minnesota in 1908 and subsequent employment as a secondary school teacher, one of her primary goals was to see that her students' parents were informed about their children's education. This same goal remains a priority of many teachers today.

While Inglis advocated parent-teacher communication, she also stressed the importance of student-teacher relationships, believing that positive student-teacher rapport contributed greatly to the success of both the student and the teacher. She once commented proudly that at University High School, where she taught, "one of the most noticeable points of the school is the friendly cooperation between teachers and the students" (1917, 10). Thus, one of Inglis's goals as a teacher was to learn to understand her students' feelings, motivations, and sense of self as each related to the learner's ability to comprehend the material to be studied.

In this respect she saw teaching as an activity where the teacher's primary responsibility was to create contexts for learning, not to deliver a collection of facts and ideas to students through lectures and course readings. This same view is popular among educators and scholars today. Learning, according to James Britton (1970), is the process of an individual mind making meaning from the materials of its experience.

Inglis was fortunate enough to spend most of her teaching career at University High School in Minneapolis, where students were offered alternatives to traditional academic courses. In addition, extracurricular activities were provided in an effort to extend and enhance classroom learning. Inglis described a number of these activities:

> Not all of the benefit of our school to the pupil comes from the actual classroom work. We try to furnish a variety of interests beyond mere book study. For instance, groups of the students are

taken at intervals to visit the various departments of the University, including the agricultural college, the purpose being not only to familiarize them with the University, but also to help them decide upon the kind of work they may wish to take up after graduation. As a result the pupils will be, by the end of the year, better informed about the University than many of the college students. The government class makes weekly expeditions to all kinds of institutions which have to do with civic life; the American history class presented a play illustrating Puritan life, written by one of its members; the Latin classes last year put on in the little theatre a play all in Latin written by the teacher; the German Club gave a German play last year and another this year; the mathematics club studies enthusiastically matters of mathematical interest which are not considered in the classroom; the drawing class is taking up amateur photography; musical interest is represented by the boys' glee club and the orchestra; the literary society in addition to biweekly meetings manages the school monthly and has presented scenes from "Macbeth" and "The Merchant of Venice." (1917, 9)

The students of University High were active participants in activities concerning social, political, and liberal arts issues that were in some ways related to their own interests and concerns. Under the progressives the school's focus was on the needs of the whole child, and the curriculum was designed around those needs.

Following the tone set by the progressives, Inglis encouraged students to use composition, language, and literature as an integral part of their learning. Her classrooms were set up as learning laboratories where students could move about freely and discuss their thoughts and ideas with their peers.

Writing projects included writing plays on social and political issues, publishing school newspapers, writing autobiographies, and making word games. Creative writing assignments were also included. Inglis felt that the purpose of writing was to expound one's thoughts, not merely to show one's ability to use correct grammar and follow mechanical rules. Therefore, she valued and included in her courses assignments which gave the students experience in using such forms of discourse as poetry, letters, journals, and personal narratives. Believing in the value of expressive writing forms, she commented, "We are aware of the genuine, natural tone of the modern child's letter as opposed to the copy-book phrases found in the family heirlooms" (1930, 15). Inglis knew that writing was not simply a service skill or a tool of transcription. Rather, she saw writing as a process fundamental to the lifelong course of connecting and integrating thoughts and ideas. Thus, she did not believe that teaching grammar and mechanics was teaching writing. However, she did acknowledge that there were those among her colleagues who still debated the grammar issue: "In grammar we still come to blows among ourselves on how much and how, but at least in class we do not call on each student in turn to recite a given rule unto the twentieth time, nor do we have them parse every sentence in the first book of *Paradise Lost*, both of which methods have been fairly common within the experience of living man" (15).

Even though Inglis acknowledged the strides her contemporaries were making toward eliminating the idea that teaching grammar and rules of mechanics was not teaching writing, we are still faced with the same rule-based, grammar dilemma today. For example, research by Arthur N. Applebee (1981), Ernest L. Boyer (1983), James Britton et al. (1975), and John Goodlad (1984) reveals that students are spending only a small percentage of their class time working on writing of at least a paragraph in length. Most student writing is limited to grammar exercises or to recording information to be utilized on multiple-choice, fill-in-the-blank, or short-answer tests. Students are seldom asked to engage in expressive writing. In short, students are not writing much, and when they do write, the writing is often poor in quality.

Responses to the current writing dilemma are varied. They include sharp increases in large assessments of student writing on national, state, and local levels, a proliferation of teacher-training programs in writing, a burgeoning of research into all aspects of the writing process, an explosion of developmental courses and programs, and new publications in the fields of rhetoric and discourse theory. However, as English educator James Kinneavy (1983) contends, some of these measures are only "Band-Aid" provisions which affect only some aspects of the crisis. The most promising effort to improve student writing appears to be the writing-in-the-content-areas movement, which emphasizes writing as an expression of one's thoughts, feelings, and ideas synthesized from experience. Proponents of the movement believe that writing, the revision of one's thinking, can be used to assist in making meaning. Writing is a coming to know (Emig 1977). What is interesting here is that antecedents of the current writing-to-learn movement can be found in the philosophy of the progressive educational movement in America and in the classrooms of progressive educators like Rewey Belle Inglis, who agreed that the object of written composition was not only to enable the pupils to understand the expressed thoughts of others, but to help them explore, connect, and integrate their own thoughts in order to make meaning for themselves.

It is also important to point out that the same revisionist views of writing as a complicated, developmental process and as a way of learning are related to contemporary feminist theory, where writing is valued primarily as a linguistic activity to be used for the discovery of one's inner voice or "self." Feminists value the same discourse forms that Inglis valued, including letters, journals, and exploratory essays. Whether or not she knew it, Inglis was ahead of her time in helping to establish a pedagogical model for teaching writing that serves as a precursor to current revisionist and feminist writing theory.

Rewey Inglis felt the traditional methods of writing instruction ignored the way real people write and learn to write and the reasons why they write; likewise, she believed the traditional methods of language instruction were poorly conceived and ineffective in promoting and enhancing students' natural language development. She wrote about how traditional programs which emphasized word meanings, spellings, and grammar rules overlooked whole dimensions of language including language change, language variation, and language functions. Inglis did not deny that the study of language should include the study of grammar, spelling, and word usage; what was needed, she concluded, were more effective approaches to language study: "The children of all people are entitled to good English, but should it be crammed down their throats or rather extracted forcibly from their throats? Can we justify drilling for accuracy on the grounds of inherent right? Is not drill itself the accompaniment of a militaristic, autocratic structure?" (1927, 568).

Inglis felt that teachers used methods of drilling for accuracy because they were confused about what accuracy really meant. The English teacher, according to Inglis, had only two categories—good English and bad English.

> Good is good under any circumstances; bad is bad under any circumstances. It is as if all kinds of clothes were thus divided— evening and semiformal clothes being good; sweaters, overalls, and aprons being bad. If a teacher has no sense for the connotations of words or phrases, or if she is guided by outworn handbooks rather than by recent dictionaries and the best current usage, she is likely to make some distinctly inaccurate pronouncements, or to change the natural and entirely legitimate idioms of children into stilted formalities. (574)

Inglis believed, as did other progressive educators, that students had a right to their own language, and that it was the responsibility of teachers to help students learn about the nature of language and develop a sense of excitement about their language and the study of it. Inglis contended that popularizing language study did not mean drilling for accuracy: "Habits mean drill, drill means repetition, and repetition with some teachers results in a class that is not only comatose but moribund. Interminable sentences without intrinsic interest will nauseate the stoutest stomach" (575). Rather, she felt that students should learn to appreciate and have fun with language while participating in such classroom activities as developing individual language histories; writing puns, riddles, and stories; solving puzzles; and participating in contests. After all, she argued, "Legitimate fun in the classroom is the surest way to combat illegimate fun" (575). More importantly, these kinds of language activities focus on the processes of language and recognize the integrity of individual language development. Here again, Inglis's progressive views about valuing individual voices are compatible with feminist emphasis on the need for classroom pedagogy which provides students with confidence in their own language.

Inglis's claims about language instruction have been debated throughout the twentieth century by both teachers and administrators. In spite of powerful evidence that the drill/memorization approach to language study produces no growth in vocabulary, no improvement in spelling, no greater conformity to standard usage, and no improvement in writing ability, many classroom teachers still use the drill method for teaching language. Furthermore, they often are supported in their choice of methods by administrators who advocate the teaching of "basics" through rules and definitions.

At this point it is necessary to remind the reader that according to Stephen N. Tchudi (1983), there has never been a time in American educational history when parents, teachers, and society have been satisfied with the way students develop and use language. However, history informs us that there have been times during the twentieth century when language study valued and utilized the skills and internalized knowledge of the students. The concern was not on accuracy or correctness, but on the importance of language as it characterizes human ability to think. From the point of view of Susanne K. Langer's "new key," sense data are "constantly wrought into symbols which are our elementary ideas" (1960, 42). The symbol systems are the language through which we represent, study, and understand the whole world.

Rewey Belle Inglis realized that when children learn a symbol system, they learn to operate in it; in language, they use the system to think through talking, reading, and writing about content. Therefore, she was an advocate of language study which focused on helping students to think:

> We have wrangled unconscionably over "Fluency First" and "Accuracy First" even though it seemed evident that Tabitha Timid needed a dose of the "Fluency First" bottle while Harry Heedless needed one out of the "Accuracy First" bottle, and that rather than rap either one on the head with a spoon à la Mrs. Squeers, we might better put on a good steady milk diet of "Purposeful Thinking." (1930, 16)

A look at the teaching philosophy of progressive educators like Inglis can serve as a guide as we seek to change curricula to respond to new conditions.

Just as Inglis's views about student language development can help to balance our concern for the child's need to make meaning through language against our concern for grammar and mechanics, her stance on the teaching of literature can aid us as we debate whether to teach literature for efferent or aesthetic purposes. A true progressive, Inglis advocated the teaching of literature as it fulfilled the needs of the student. She felt that students learned best when they were interested in the literature to be studied, and not when they were forced simply to memorize facts about the text at hand. Her views reflected those of John Dewey, who advocated: "Abandon the notion of subject matter as something fixed and readymade in itself, outside the child's experience, cease thinking of the child's experience as also something hard and fast; see it as something fluent, embryonic, vital" (1902, 16).

Inglis, like her contemporaries Dora V. Smith and Louise M. Rosenblatt, felt that a student's response to a literary work must be spontaneous and personal. She considered such an emotional reaction to a work as an absolutely necessary condition of sound literary judgment. "Literature," commented Inglis, "is a major outlet for a stream of ideas" (Inglis et al. 1958a, 552). Michael Polanyi (1958) built on these progressive views when he contended that all knowledge, if it is to be genuine, must be made personal. In fact, the theme of his book *Personal Knowledge* is that successful learning is engaged, committed, personal knowledge.

In view of her beliefs, Inglis first exposed her students to literature which sprang from their own environment and then moved them on to more unfamiliar realms. For example, she provided her students with American literature selections from their own century with hopes that the works would be more easily understood. She felt that if the students could read rapidly without being distracted by historical background or outmoded style, they would be more likely to determine the significance of the piece as it related to their own lives (Inglis et al. 1952). She argued that teaching unfamiliar, esoteric material, "tends to widen the gulf between 'literature' as taught in the classroom and 'interesting reading' as boys and girls pick it up for themselves" (111).

Although Inglis first exposed her students to literature which was representative of their interests, she later provided them with reading opportunities that would move into more difficult realms and different worlds. She believed that studying the literature of other nations would gradually develop for the student a "conception of humanity as a constant stream flowing between banks of varying beauty and interest." That conception, she stated, "is part of what we call cultural background" (Inglis et al. 1958b, 111).

Inglis, like her good friend and colleague Dora V. Smith, spent much of her life traveling over the world to find literature which would enrich students' lives. She felt that literature was more valuable than the study of foreign languages, history, music, and art because of its power to create an immediate personal, direct, and intimate understanding of the development of world cultures. This understanding, she contended, could serve as a beginning for knocking down blockades to world peace (iv).

This humanistic view of literature education was not only popular in Inglis's day, when teachers were often confronted with the task of teaching literature in the context of maintaining a democratic way of life and eradicating illiteracy, but it remains popular today, especially since we are still faced with the problems of preserving a democracy and eliminating illiteracy. In addition, Inglis's humanistic view of literature encourages the resourcefulness of the student to assess the literary work, to use inner resources, and then to make decisions and act or not act on those decisions. This inner resourcefulness compels students to rely on their own experiences. The traditional methods of teaching literature, where students are asked to identify literary techniques, memorize plot structures, and recall authors' names, does not require them to analyze, synthesize, and evaluate the work in order to connect it more accurately to their own thoughts and ideas. Instead, they are asked to memorize information, store it in short-term memory, and use it for evaluative activities which stress the ability to regurgitate information.

Inglis's views about teaching composition, language, and literature were based on her knowledge of and respect for the past, her keen awareness of the present, and her prognostication of the future. Her knowledge about the history of English teaching in the nineteenth century helped her to realize that a teaching pedagogy emphasizing correctness in writing, rule-based language instruction, and recall/memorization methods of teaching literature did not work.

Therefore, she tried new ideas and methods based on progressive beliefs and ideals; she gave her students frequent opportunities to integrate language into their speaking, reading, and writing activities, believing that students who were active in their own language development were more likely to understand and appreciate language learning. While she admitted that "crystal-gazing into the future might be classed as a light occupation" (1930, 20), she felt it had its values. She knew her present teaching pedagogy not only would influence her students' futures, but would, in all probability, influence the "slants" taken by English teaching in the future. Her concerns, like other progressive educators of the day, were on the needs of her students, and her English teaching was designed around those needs. Equally important, her progressive beliefs, advocating equity as it encourages the individual voice and experiential learning as it encourages students to value self, serve as an antecedent to contemporary feminist theory.

Inglis was indeed a dedicated classroom teacher who was devoted to helping her students receive an education that would enhance their present lives as well as prepare them for their futures. Although she spent most of her classroom teaching career at University High School (1915-30) in Minneapolis, she spent two years (1931-33) teaching at Northrop Collegiate School, a private girls' school in Minneapolis. Her daughter, Blue Lenox, commented that Inglis preferred teaching at University High, but suggested that her mother's experience at Northrop not only gave her an opportunity to learn about private education and how it differed from public school training, but it also provided her with a chance to think about women's ways of knowing (Lenox 1989). That Inglis realized how women's ways of knowing are often different from the traditional, patriarchal ways of knowing is not surprising, since these views are rooted in the philosophy of progressive education. What is surprising is that many contemporary educators are just now beginning to realize the difference between classical or traditional concepts of education, where the valuing of one product over the other requires the teacher to evaluate and judge that product, as opposed to the progressive/feminist view, where the processes of learning are valued and where the teacher functions both as a facilitator of learning and as a learner. *Women's Ways of Knowing* (Belenky et al. 1986) is now used in many college classrooms to help students understand how women's learning and knowing differs from the traditional, patriarchal model developed by W. G. Perry in *Forms of Intellectual and Ethical Development in the College Years* (1970).

Rewey Inglis's decisions about the course of her own life reflect her own independence as a learner. During her career as a classroom teacher, she took time to complete her M.A. in 1923 at the University of Minnesota and to take advanced graduate courses at Columbia University; however, she never completed her Ph.D. According to Stanley Kegler (1988), a longtime English educator and student of Dora V. Smith's, Inglis felt that she did not need what was then primarily a research-based degree, for her career emphasis was on classroom teaching. Kegler noted that Smith agreed with Inglis's reasoning. Inglis's daughter, Blue Lenox (1989) offering yet another reason for her mother's lack of interest in pursuing a Ph.D., explained that her mother was an analytical and an economically minded woman who realized that over a period of years she would earn more from investing her money than she would in spending the same amount of money for the Ph.D., and who therefore opted to invest in stocks. Both Kegler's and Lenox's stories appear to be accurate, for Inglis was more of a teacher than a researcher, and the dividends from her investments continue to be paid to her beneficiaries.

Even though Inglis spent eighteen years as a classroom teacher, she knew that she could influence a larger audience if she became a teacher of teachers. With that in mind, she accepted a position as an assistant professor of education at the University of Minnesota in 1923; thus, she held joint positions, one as a classroom teacher at University High School and one as a professor of education whose primary responsibility was to train teachers to teach English. In addition to training teachers in Minnesota, Inglis taught English methods courses at Harvard University in the summer of 1928 and at the University of Missouri in 1930.

Today's readers might question how Inglis was able to work simultaneously and effectively as a classroom teacher and as a university professor. The answer is simple. University High School was a laboratory school maintained for the purpose of training university students to become teachers. Laboratory schools were usually staffed by university professors who taught methods courses to education majors. This method of staffing provided advantages for all involved—the school, the students, the practice teachers, and the classroom teacher/university professor. Inglis described the situation at University High:

We feel that the high school pupils do not suffer by these conditions. In the first place, the prerequisites for practice teaching include a number of education courses, a great amount of preparation in the particular department involved, including a teachers' course and the maintenance of a certain standard of scholarship. Then, no student teacher takes charge of a recitation hour until he has observed the critic teacher for a week or two and has made out careful plans in advance of the work to be covered. The plans involve method as well as material so that the student teacher cannot go very far astray. Moreover, the critic is always present when the student conducts the recitation except toward the end of the semester when occasional absences of the critic give the student a greater feeling of responsibility. With this careful supervision the teaching is likely to be superior to that of some teachers of one or two years' experience in schools where there is little or no supervision. Then too, as the practice teacher conducts only about one-fourth of the entire number of recitations, the critic teacher is in charge most of the time.

In many ways the practice teachers are an advantage. They can do individual work with students and those who have been absent; they can assist in the correction of written work, the supervision of study classes, the collateral work of department clubs, class plays, etc., so that a greater scope is given to the work than would be possible under one teacher alone. Moreover the presence of one or two wide-awake, observant practice teachers is a decided incentive to the critic teacher's best efforts, especially when that teacher also acts as instructor in the methods course as is the case in the mathematics and English departments. (1917, 10)

Although very few universities still maintain laboratory schools, today's requirements for student teachers remain somewhat similar to those described by Inglis. She noted that in 1913, Minnesota law required thirty-six practice exercises or their equivalent as a prerequisite for a state certificate to teach, and that while the practice teachers were given only three hours' credit for their work, they were required to attend a certain high school class every day for a semester, teach it a certain number of times under the supervision of the regular teacher, give assistance, when needed, to individual pupils, correct papers, and in every way become in touch with the high school situation (10). Presently, most states require seventy-two to ninety-six student teaching hours as a prerequisite for state certification. However, in most cases student teachers receive six to twelve hours of course credit for their student teaching experience. Student teachers are still required to participate in the same kinds of activities that were required of practice teachers at University High.

As a supervising teacher, Inglis created classroom conditions for student teachers to practice the progressive pedagogy she had exposed them to in her university methods courses. Rejecting the idea that learning only occurs in silent classrooms where students sit one behind the other in straight rows of brown wooden desks nailed to the floor, copy notes, and memorize facts for later recitation or testing, Inglis advised her students to move about freely and to discuss their ideas with their peers, with her, and with the student teacher. She encouraged the students to work collaboratively to solve problems through employing high-level critical thinking skills of analysis, synthesis, and evaluation. Inglis, the student teacher, and the students were all learners. Today many teachers, including those who relate their efforts to feminist theory, are encouraging their students to participate in collaborative work. While some educators give credit to Kenneth A. Bruffee (1978) for developing collaborative learning methods, others credit feminists like psychologist Carol Gilligan (1982). The reader has seen, however, that the antecedents for the collaborative learning movement can be found in the classrooms and teaching philosophy of progressive educators like Rewey Belle Inglis.

Since Inglis practiced her progressive teaching philosophy in her classrooms, she was an ideal role model for her student teachers. They were able to see a teacher successfully employ the classroom activities that she had advocated in her methods courses. But Inglis was more than a role model for her student teachers: she was an adviser and a mentor who guided and encouraged them in their professional decision making. While her role as a supervising teacher involved evaluating her student teachers' performances, she was constructive in her criticisms, always focusing on the student teachers' strengths while commenting on the areas that needed improvement.

Even though he was not one of Inglis's students, Walter Loban, a former English educator and professor emeritus at the University of California at Berkeley, remembers how Inglis helped him acquire his first public-speaking engagement when he was a student of Dora V. Smith's, one of Inglis's close colleagues at the University of Minnesota. At the time Inglis was president of the Minnesota Association of Teachers of English, and the group was in need of a speaker for an upcoming meeting. Realizing that Loban needed public-speaking experience, Inglis arranged for him to speak to her group. Loban admits that his presentation was disastrous; he was overcome with anxiety, lost track of his thoughts, and performed poorly. Yet Inglis only commented, "You can do better." Loban was frustrated and vowed never to make another speech; however, several days later Inglis called him into her office and persuaded him to accept another speaking engagement. Loban was reluctant to take advantage of the second opportunity, but Inglis persuaded him to accept, offering to help him prepare his speech. Loban recalls that Inglis was quick to point out the weaknesses of his first speech, but she helped him to find ways to overcome them in his successful second performance. Loban feels that without Inglis's belief in his ability and determination to do well, he might never have made another public presentation (Loban 1988, 1989).

Inglis was committed to the preparation of future teachers of English, for she realized that the continued growth and success of the profession depended on how well teachers were prepared. Consequently, she was equally concerned with the educational needs of practicing teachers. After completing survey research which indicated that 77 percent of the teacher respondents had never taken any courses beyond their undergraduate degrees, Inglis asked, "Can a teacher really teach who never returns to the status of a learner?" She answered her own question: "Our minds, like our last summer's frocks, need refurbishing lest they brand us as antiquated; and though the demands of the body for rejuvenation seem insistent when June days arrive, there is no reason why a not-too-heavy program, a change of scene, a shift in point of view from teacher to learner may not provide rehabilitation for both body and mind" (1928, 380). Remaining true to her beliefs, Inglis spent time each summer teaching English education courses to practicing teachers. In addition, she spent much of her free time during the school year planning and presenting quality inservice workshops to teachers who were interested in enhancing their educations.

Her workshops, including such topics as "Teaching English to Meet Individual Needs," "The Need for Smaller Class Size," "The Need for Newer Physical Plants with Updated Equipment," "Establishing Libraries and Procuring More Books," and "Methods of Evaluation," always emphasized progressive methods as they related to high standards of scholarship. While the topics often indicated a need for change and development, Inglis emphasized the necessity of appraising the present in terms of recent growth and improvement. For example, she admitted the need for smaller class size, but metaphorically reminded teachers, "Better, perhaps, a staggering load than an empty sack" (1930, 14). She agreed that many school districts needed to build new schools, but pointed out that in many towns and cities, schools loomed like "giant silhouettes against a vast expanse of sky, magnificent in contour, dominating the little serf-like buildings clustered about" (14). She acknowledged the need for more libraries with vast numbers of books, but pointed out that "now even the humblest Main Street without a library proportionate to its size is a byword and a hissing to its neighbors" (14). In regard to examinations, she commented:

> We have examined examinations from college entrance to objective tests, with minutest scrutiny and occasional contumely. Our individual views range all the way from the necessity of a brief examination at the beginning of each class period to the total abolishment of any form of examination. Perhaps our only points of real discovery so far are that there is nothing sacrosanct about an examination, and that we know as little about making them as some of our dullards know about answering them. But we are learning. (16)

While we have made significant and lasting progress on some educational fronts, we still must contend with many of the same problems that Inglis wrote about. We currently face debates about the need for smaller class size, more and better libraries, newer schools with more advanced equipment, and alternatives to traditional evaluation methods, but we, too, are continuing to learn.

Inglis saw learning as an activity that continued throughout one's lifetime, and she actively encouraged teachers to continue their educations, whether it be through inservice training, through course work, or through their own writing and sharing of that writing. She saw writing as a way of learning, a way of discovering what one knows or does not know, a view recently popularized by Janet Emig (1977). Just as she believed that writing was an important activity for students to engage in, she felt it was an important activity for teachers, too. After all, how can one who never writes teach writing? Inglis believed that successful teachers needed experience with life, keen observation, and a lively pen—"One can scarcely go bankrupt with those," she commented (1930, 15).

Rewey Inglis was a zealous teacher and a teacher of teachers. She was committed to helping both students and teachers develop and learn to use their knowledge in order to enjoy a more meaningful life. Through her teaching and supervision she helped those with whom she came in contact to solve problems, to gain new knowledge, and, in turn, to help others do the same. Her roles as a classroom teacher and as a teacher educator gained her access to large audiences where she could share her beliefs and ideas with many who would benefit from them.

Inglis truly desired to help others become better educated, but wanted to continue in her own quest for knowledge as well. In an effort to achieve both ends, she chose to become active in the National

Council of Teachers of English. The Council's conventions and publications provided a forum where teachers like Inglis could discuss their ideas and concerns, where teachers could work together to improve English teaching.

And work she did. Inglis wrote articles for the Council journals, attended its conventions, presented convention papers, served on and chaired several of its committees, and encouraged her colleagues and students to become active members in the organization. Equally important, she took the information and knowledge that she garnered from her NCTE activities back to her school and her classroom and shared it with those who were unable to attend the conventions. Her dedication to the Council and to its membership eventually helped her to be elected as the first woman president of NCTE.

Until Inglis's victory in 1928, several women in the Council had been elected to the nominal office of vice-president, but the Council nominating committees had not ignored gender in making their selections for presidential candidates. This time, however, they could not ignore the impressive scholarship and exceptional leadership of Rewey Belle Inglis, even though she was a woman. Nevertheless, there were those who questioned the ability of a woman to lead such an influential organization. W. Wilbur Hatfield, longtime secretary-treasurer of the Council and journal editor, would admit years later in an interview with English educator Robert S. Fay that he, too, had his doubts about Inglis's ability to serve as president. When Fay asked him how much effect Inglis's leadership had on the Council, Hatfield offered these comments:

> Until five years ago or so I thought it was very little. She was the youngest president we ever had. She was a very pretty woman. You see a pretty young woman getting ahead pretty fast, you sometimes wonder how much is the face and how much is something else. I went back and looked at the minutes as far as they were reported in the *English Journal* and more happened in the organization of the Council that year—not more outside the Council, but more happened in the organization that year than most other times, so I was evidently mistaken about that. (Hatfield 1965)

Hatfield's candid comments are representative of much of the thinking during the early part of the twentieth century. Women, many believed, were suited and equipped for such service roles as mother, teacher, or secretary, never leadership roles. Rewey Belle Inglis's active and effective role as president of the National Council of Teachers of English helped to change that thinking.

Wilbur Hatfield was right: he was wrong. Rewey Inglis was more than just a pretty face. No president in the history of the National Council of Teachers of English had done more to stimulate the growth of the Council than Inglis did during her one-year presidency, 1928–29. She brought to the Council humanistic leadership skills and techniques of persuasion and direction without parallel in Council history.

Inglis's skill as a leader was brought to bear upon the Council when she, with the help of good friend and colleague Ruth Mary Weeks, convinced the Board of Directors and the Executive Committee to hold the 1929 annual meeting in Kansas City, Missouri. Never before had the Council met in a city west of the Mississippi River. In order to persuade the Council to take such action, Inglis worked with Weeks and others to secure advance pledges of attendance from one thousand persons ("National Council," 815).

The Kansas City convention, attended by at least that number, was larger than any preceding Council meeting, drawing attendants from all over the nation. Included for the first time were black registrants. Meeting rooms were jammed with teachers and educators who desired to work, to serve, and to grow in English education. The convention program, planned by Inglis, provided something to stimulate everyone's interest: a large exhibit devoted to "home reading stimulators," a general session, special conference sessions, the annual business meeting, and section meetings. The conference sessions, including the Conference on Curriculum, Conference on the Relation of the Library to the English Classroom, Conference for Heads of Departments of English High Schools, Conference on Problems Concerning the College Undergraduate, Conference on the Training of Teachers, Conference on Public Speaking and Dramatics, and Conference on Council Activities in Elementary English, addressed significant issues in English education as they related to the growth of both the Council and the profession.

In her presidential message, "Retrospect and Prospect," Inglis pressed the point that although NCTE was a relatively young organization and had made some mistakes, its members could be proud of its major accomplishments, publications, and pronouncements. She told the members:

> Nineteen years ago the National Council came into being and things have been happening ever since with the increasing speed of a geometric progression. What an infinitesimal period is this nineteen years compared with the one hundred, the two hundreds, and the aeons behind us. As an organization we are still a minor, under twenty-one, perhaps displaying the vagaries and

inconsistencies of the adolescent. We have been accused of not knowing our own objectives. We have, indeed, seen through a glass darkly. Yet when one of our number a few years ago cleared a space in the glass and showed us the composite of our own mind, we recoiled at the horrid image and violently repudiated our own pronouncement that spelling was our most important objective. (1930, 16)

Inglis noted that in addition to changing its views on the place and value of spelling in the curriculum, the Council had made readjustments in its thinking about such issues as the teaching of "Fluency First" and "Accuracy First" as opposed to the teaching of "Purposeful Thinking."

Rewey Belle Inglis asked her audience to consider the history of their professional growth as they continued to expand and create new ideas. She knew that historical knowledge would not only help them to develop an appreciation of the past and of the "stars" in the field, but more importantly, it would help them to understand current educational patterns and innovations. Her message was clear. Knowledge about the past provides one with a perspective on the present and helps one to determine future directions.

In regard to the Council's future directions, Inglis summoned the membership, the Board of Directors, and the Executive Committee to give sincere consideration to developing better advertising for the organization, establishing networking relationships with other organizations, creating a research bureau for research in English, and setting up a teachers' bureau for the teaching of English. She spoke with knowledge, determination, and conviction about why the Council needed to pursue such activities.

First, Inglis believed that the official journals of the Council, *English Journal*, *College English*, and *The Elementary English Review*, were valuable in giving voice to the various interest groups of the organization, but she felt they were "reaching too small a proportion of those persons who are doing the actual teaching of English." Therefore, she stated, "One of the big Council needs is a greater advertising of our organization." Inglis felt this would be a difficult task because

our inherent dispositions make this hard. There is more of the Charles Lamb than the Mary Lyon in our natures. Our training in the humanities makes us either shudder or smile at the blatant half-truths of the born advertiser. But in the interests of our united needs we shall have to swallow our conservatism though it choke us, and outline a consistent and continuous policy of making our name known in order to make our principles operative. (19)

Inglis's second concern was the Council's relationship with other professional organizations such as the National Association of Teachers of Speech and the National Association of Teachers of Journalism. She admitted that each organization had its own special interests, but many of those interests cut across organizational concerns. For example, she commented:

> We cannot escape the responsibilities of speech because another organization bears the main burden. Two horses pulling together move a bigger load than one, but woe to the wagon when one pulls east and the other pulls west. Our brothers of the facile pens may occasionally jar us, but we must not forget that they daily serve and often delight us. The extended palm will do us both more good than the extended fist. (20)

A third issue that Inglis felt needed attention was the problem of the relation between teaching and research. She conceded that the age was one of great research, but questioned whether it was one of great teaching. "But our educational institutions," she contended, "have confused issues by trying to make the same person a specialist in both fields. Only a genius can be that." She explained her position:

> The great microbe hunters have seldom been conspicuous for their "bedside manner," but this personal quality has helped many a child through the whooping-cough and measles. On the other hand, say over to yourself the names of the really great teachers of history or your own experience. Did they spend hours humped over correlations? Many antagonisms between the two fields could be saved if each were given due place and recognition, and persons fitted by nature and disposition for the one were not forced into the other. (20)

Inglis envisioned the future as being one where teachers and researchers could work "independently, yet harmoniously with mutual respect and mutual service" (20). She looked forward to the day when NCTE would become a great bureau for research in English and a great bureau "to which the loneliest teacher in her prairie town can send for help on those issues which loom so large to her" (21).

Inglis might have been doing some "crystal gazing" when she discussed her future hopes for the Council, because her desires have been realized. The National Council of Teachers of English has engaged in extensive advertising campaigns during the last fifty years, and its membership has jumped from 5,000 in 1936 to 57,000 in 1987, with combined journal subscriptions numbering over 115,000 (Maxwell 1987). In addition to stepped-up advertising efforts, NCTE engages in networking activities with such sister organizations as the Modern Language Association. Finally, the Council serves its membership both as a bureau on teaching and as a bureau on research. Classroom teachers from all over the nation can get help with their teaching concerns through convention sessions, publications, and workshops about teaching. The same is true for educational researchers. Of significant importance is the NCTE Research Foundation, which awards grants-in-aid to members whose research on the subject of English, including language arts and related fields, has significance to the teaching or learning of English. In addition, the Council offers annual Outstanding Research awards as well as Excellence in Teaching awards.

Rewey Inglis's presidential address called the Council to action; it challenged the membership "to think, to work, to serve, to grow, to carry on" (1930, 21). Her presidency served as a model of the growth that she advocated. The accomplishments of the Council during her term were numerous, including establishing *The Elementary English Review* as an official organ of the Council, organizing a new committee on elementary school English, developing new membership campaigns, and initiating an annual audit of Council finances. In addition, Inglis began the NCTE President's Book (1929), which consisted of general information about the Council and the duties of the president. Her intent was to make material available to the incoming president which would put him or her more quickly in touch with the office in order to function with more ease and effectiveness. English educator James Hocker Mason (1988) commented that it was this kind of efficiency and hard work that not only helped Inglis lead the Council to adulthood, but that earned her recognition as one of the most influential women in the Council and the profession. She was indeed more than just a pretty face.

Rewey Belle Inglis was a dedicated teacher and an outstanding professional leader. Her respect for individuals and her commitment to lifelong learning helped to shape and enrich the lives of all who knew her. From the beginning of her career, Inglis recognized that teaching offered her an opportunity to support the development of an educational system which fostered the American ideal—an education for everyone based on the valuing of individual voices. Although she set high academic standards in her classrooms, she was sensitive to individual abilities and never belittled a student who made an honest effort to complete an assignment or answer a question. To say that her teaching was child centered is an understatement.

Inglis never lost her passion for teaching, but she had an independent nature that led her to defy convention by entering a profession dominated by men. In 1933 Inglis left classroom teaching to become a full-time textbook writer, editor, and consultant with Harcourt, Brace and World, Inc. After having worked part-time for Harcourt, she recognized that publishing offered women, who had more often written privately than publicly, an opportunity to voice their beliefs, ideas, and experiences. According to her daughter, Blue Lenox (1989), Inglis wanted to "break the mold" that had constrained women for so long. Moreover, she realized that a career in publishing would permit her to reach an even larger audience than she could in the classroom.

Inglis became the senior editor for Harcourt's Adventures in Literature series, including multiple editions of *Adventures in American Literature* (1952), *Adventures in English Literature* (1958a), and *Adventures in World Literature* (1958b). This series, which began in 1930, has gone through numerous editions and today remains a popular text in some classrooms. While there are those who question the value of using only a single text for teaching literature, it must be remembered that until the late 1960s and early 1970s, schools did not provide teachers with alternative reading materials for their students. Even today many classroom teachers are forced to rely on one literature anthology.

Remaining true to her teaching pedagogy, which emphasized the importance of providing students with a variety of reading materials to stimulate both their emotional and intellectual interests, Inglis developed texts which comprised a wide variety of literary genres, including poems, short stories, and plays written by men and women representing various ethnic backgrounds. In addition, the series was among the first to include pictorial essays, color illustrations, maps, time charts, records, and teachers' manuals. As noted earlier, Inglis spent time traveling all over the world to find literature which would appeal to young readers and help them develop an appreciation of how literature works to enhance their lives.

Inglis enjoyed her career as a textbook writer, for it not only freed her from the traditional classroom constraints of teaching all day and evaluating papers and planning lessons all night, but it provided her with a financial security that she had never anticipated. For all that, she never lost her passion for teaching. She returned often to the classroom, sometimes as a guest lecturer, sometimes as a consultant. In addition, she volunteered her time to teaching developmental and remedial English to adults, including illiterate GI's. She had realized early in her teaching career "that those who were advanced in years but burdened with bad language habits usually become discouraged and drop out after a few lessons" (1927, 569). Further, she knew that the high attrition was due in part to the teachers' use of meaningless drills to teach the language skills of reading, writing, and speaking. Therefore, she developed lessons and activities which would accommodate individual learning needs and focused her instruction on the processes of learning rather than on the product.

Inglis was not alone in her efforts, for her colleagues Dora V. Smith and Luella B. Cook were advocating the same teaching methods. Years later, Mina P. Shaughnessy wrote about similar teaching problems in her book *Errors and Expectations* (1977). Speaking specifically about student writing growth, Shaughnessy concluded that student writing errors are individual and must be treated as such. Again, Inglis was at the forefront in recognizing the importance of valuing and respecting personal experience as a basis for all learning.

Besides continuing to accept part-time teaching responsibilities, Inglis remained active in the National Council of Teachers of English, the Alumni Association of the University of Minnesota, which in 1957 made her the first woman recipient of its outstanding alumni award, and the Minnesota Education Association. Moreover, she found time to work for the Republican party, the Presbyterian church, the League of Women Voters, the American Association of University Women, and the Y.W.C.A., serving on the national board of directors. How could one woman do so much so well?

Blue Lenox (1989) contended that her mother's success was due to her overwhelming love for life and her love for people. Lenox described this love as she recalled her own adoption. It all began in 1941, when Inglis invited two girls from war-torn Britain to come to America and live with her for the duration of World War II. Their mother was serving with the civil nursing reserve at Wychemore Hill near London. The girls, Doris Bull, sixteen, and her sister, Elizabeth (Blue) Bull, eleven, had been evacuated to West-Cliff-by-the-Sea in Essex. They arrived in Minneapolis on 2 February 1941, by way of Montreal after crossing the Atlantic in the Canadian-Pacific mail boat named the *Warwick Castle*.

After a few days of orientation to their new surroundings, the Bull sisters enrolled in American schools, Doris at Northrop Collegiate School, a private girls' school where Inglis had taught for two years, and Blue in the Minneapolis public school system. After the war Doris returned home, but Blue had come to love Rewey Inglis like a mother and begged to stay with her. Eventually Blue's biological mother agreed to let her stay, and she became the daughter Inglis never had. Inglis filled her new daughter's life with books, with travel, and, most importantly to Blue, with love.

In 1955, when Inglis was finally able to arrange for a legal adoption, Blue Lenox was a twenty-four-year-old adult with two children of her own. Lenox, noting that hers was one of the first adult adoptions in Minnesota, recalled how the judge reminded her that it was customary to tell the adoptive parents to love and respect the child, but that Inglis had already given her the love and respect she needed. Therefore, the judge told Lenox that it was her duty to love and respect Inglis, her new mother.

According to Lenox, it was easy to love and respect Rewey Belle Inglis, for she was a woman who exemplified the virtues of a gentlewoman until her death in 1967. She was kind, considerate, and caring; she was able to get along with all kinds of people. However, alongside this calm, serene portrait, there existed a woman who was independent, who was actively committed to her own success, to the success of her students and colleagues, and to the success of women in the teaching profession. Inglis dedicated her life to helping her fellow beings come to know and value their beliefs, feelings, and ideas. Her teachings and her writings reflect dedication, leadership, hard work, and achievement in the field of English education.

It is because of these significant contributions that the Women's Committee (later renamed the Committee on Women in the Profession) of the National Council of Teachers of English established in 1989 the Rewey Belle Inglis Award for Outstanding Woman in English Education. This annual award recognizes a woman who has shown excellence in scholarship, research, writing, teaching, and/or service relating to English and the language arts. It is a fitting tribute to Inglis, a woman who knew how to get things done, who advanced the teaching of English, and who was one of the most influential women during the early years of the Council. Rewey Belle Inglis was a woman who respected the past, who was keenly aware of the present, and who dared to gaze into the future—a crystal-ball gazer.

Works Cited

Applebee, Arthur N. 1981. *Writing in the Secondary School: English and the Content Areas*. Urbana, Ill.: National Council of Teachers of English.

Belenky, M. F., B. M. Clinchy, N. R. Goldberger, and J. M. Tarule. 1986. *Women's Ways of Knowing: The Development of Self, Voice and Mind*. New York: Basic Books.

Boyer, Ernest L. 1983. *High School: A Report on Secondary Education in America*. New York: Harper and Row.

Britton, James. 1970. *Language and Learning*. London: Penguin Books.

Britton, James, Tony Burgess, Nancy Martin, Alex McLeod, and Harold Rosen. 1975. *The Development of Writing Abilities (11-18)*. London: Macmillan.

Bruffee, Kenneth A. 1978. "The Brooklyn Plan: Attaining Intellectual Growth through Peer-Group Tutoring." *Liberal Education* 64 (December): 447-68.

Dewey, John. 1902. *The School and Society*. Chicago: University of Chicago Press.

Emig, Janet. 1977. "Writing as a Mode of Learning." *College Composition and Communication* 34 (May): 122-27.

Gilligan, Carol. 1982. *In a Different Voice: Psychological Theory and Women's Development*. Cambridge, Mass.: Harvard University Press.

Goodlad, John. 1984. *A Place Called School*. New York: McGraw-Hill.

Hall, G. Stanley. 1914. *Adolescence: Its Psychology and Its Relations to Physiology, Anthropology, Sociology, Sex, Crime, Religion, and Education*. Vol. 2. New York: D. Appleton.

Hatfield, W. Wilbur. 1965. Interview with Robert S. Fay.

Inglis, Rewey B. 1917. "The University High School." *Minnesota Alumni Weekly* 16: 7-11.

———. 1927. "Popularizing Accuracy." *English Journal* 16 (May): 567-78.

———. 1928. "What Shall I Study? Answers by Expert Teachers on English. Balance Your Rations." *English Journal* 17 (April): 380-82.

———. 1930. "Retrospect and Prospect." *English Journal* 19 (January): 11-21.

Inglis, Rewey B., et al., eds. 1952. *Adventures in American Literature*. New York: Harcourt, Brace and World.

———. 1958a. *Adventures in English Literature*. New York: Harcourt, Brace and World.

———. 1958b. *Adventures in World Literature*. New York: Harcourt, Brace and World.

Kegler, Stanley. 10 June 1988. Interview with Virginia R. Monseau. Minneapolis, Minn.

Kinneavy, James. 1983. "Writing across the Curriculum." *Profession*: 13-20.

Langer, Susanne K. 1960. *Philosophy in a New Key: A Study in the Symbolism of Reason, Rite, and Art*, 3d ed. Cambridge, Mass.: Harvard University Press.

Lenox, Blue. 16 July 1989. Interview with author.

Loban, Walter. November 1988. Interview with author. National Council of Teachers of English Annual Convention, St. Louis, Mo.

———. 18 January 1989. Telephone interview with author. Berkeley, Calif.

Mason, James Hocker. 28 October 1988. Interview with author. Terre Haute, Ind.

Maxwell, John. 1987. Executive Director's Report to the National Council of Teachers of English Board of Directors, Los Angeles, Calif.

"The National Council, 1911-1936: The First Phase." 1936. *English Journal* 25 (December): 805-36.

The National Council of Teachers of English President's Book. 1929. Unpublished.

Perry, W. G. 1970. *Forms of Intellectual and Ethical Development in the College Years*. New York: Holt, Rinehart and Winston.

Polanyi, Michael. 1958. *Personal Knowledge: Towards a Post-Critical Philosophy*.

Chicago: University of Chicago Press.

Radner, Sanford. 1960. *Fifty Years of English Teaching: A Historical Analysis of the Presidential Addresses of NCTE*. Champaign, Ill.: National Council of Teachers of English.

Shaughnessy, Mina P. 1977. *Errors and Expectations*. New York: Oxford University Press.

Tchudi, Stephen N., and Joann Yates. 1983. *Teaching Writing in the Content Areas: Senior High School*. Washington, D.C.: National Education Association.

Woody, Thomas. [1929] 1966. *A History of Women's Education in the United States*. 2 vols. Reprint. New York: Octagon.

2 Ruth Mary Weeks: Teaching the Art of Living

Judy Prozzillo Byers, Fairmont State College

An English curriculum which develops the intellectual, emotional, and creative elements of our youngsters in well-balanced fashion can be planned and taught only by teachers who are themselves keen and sensitive and witty and creative. The art of living—that is the subject that we teach; the art of living! And we ourselves must be the masters of that art.

Ruth Mary Weeks, "Teaching the Whole Child"

Ruth Mary Weeks
1886-1969

With these words Ruth Mary Weeks of Kansas City, Missouri, concluded her presidential address before the twentieth annual meeting of the National Council of Teachers of English in Cleveland on 28 November 1930. When she became the nineteenth president of NCTE, she was just forty-three years old and only the second woman to lead the Council. She was a unique person, with diverse talents and energies channeled into varying roles ranging from poet, public speaker, and both literary and pedagogical critic, to researcher, author, and textbook editor. She spent her daily life, however, as an English teacher from 1909 to 1956, almost half a century. During this long career she formulated a teaching philosophy not only modeled in her classroom, but also internalized as her personal approach to life. By the time she became involved in NCTE during the early 1920s, she had already applied aspects of her teaching philosophy to vocational training and socializing education in America and was in demand on the national lecture circuit for her pedagogical writings in both fields. Weeks spent the last half of her life, however, enthusiastically advocating her teaching philosophy for English instruction across all grade levels. Consequently, "teaching the art of living" has left an impact on the history of education in America with particular emphasis on English instruction, providing a teaching model that is especially applicable for our schools today.

The keys to understanding Ruth Mary Weeks's pioneering contributions to the history of English teaching are found in two testimonies published in *English Journal* seven years apart. They reveal her beliefs and personality. First was her presidential speech, "Teaching the Whole Child," delivered in 1930. Presented to a national audience, this speech was Weeks's first and most advantageous opportunity to proclaim her philosophy of "teaching the art of living" and to outline the components needed for effectively orchestrating this approach in the English classroom. Her speech also established "teaching the art of living" as the underlying theme of the Curriculum Commission, initiated under her presidency (1929–30) "to develop a 'pattern curriculum' that would illustrate the best current practice and thus provide a stable reference point in the midst of the rapidly shifting instructional concerns" (Applebee 1974, 118). Weeks "not only proposed the Curriculum Commission, but also established the machinery and led in the selection of most of the workers on the extensive curriculum-building project" (Hook 1979, 111–12). Chaired by W. Wilbur Hatfield, the commission finalized its work in 1935 with the publication of *An Experience Curriculum in English*, which was not a prescription for a single curriculum to fit the needs of all students, but instead "a pattern that other groups could take as a starting point in developing a curriculum to fit their particular circumstances" (Applebee 1974, 119). The commission concluded that experience "is the best of all schools. . . . The ideal curriculum consists of well-selected experiences" (quoted in Applebee, 119).

Teaching the art of living represented an experiential, child-centered approach to learning, emphasizing the ideals of John Dewey and the progressive education movement, both of which Weeks interpreted and made her own. In a changing society fed by large influxes of immigrants and vast economic imbalances, along with the scars of World War I and the Great Depression, Weeks saw that English instruction in the early twentieth century needed to change to make learning more relevant to life and to make learners more responsible and creative participants in their world. The intellectual, emotional, and creative elements of each child had to be nurtured equally. She thus advocated a teaching approach that would develop "the whole personality for a complete and happy life" (Weeks 1931, 10).

As a veteran teacher, Weeks recognized, though, that the successful teaching of the whole child rested with teachers who were able to bring their vital personalities and resources into the classroom before an atmosphere for learning could be established. From the speaker's platform Weeks warned her English colleagues: "And I say that until we are complete human beings, we are unfit to be school teachers. Lessons are only a part of a good teacher's work. You teach far more by what you are than by the lessons you assign. Your child is your natural copyist, your dramatist in living" (16).

In her second testimony, "Content for Composition" (1937a), Weeks reiterated her teaching philosophy by championing with some reservation the correlation movement to integrate various academic subjects with English for holistic learning. Now that the concept of an activity curriculum had been born, she saw integration as the means of bringing "the world into the English classroom" (299). The Committee on Correlation of the Curriculum Commission, chaired by Weeks, published *A Correlated Curriculum* in 1936, which she edited and in which she continued to advocate a new kind of teacher for a new teaching approach: "A whole teacher teaching a whole child to live a whole life is the new idea. Everything must be fitted into this whole and serve its purpose there. Subject matter in itself is valueless; only as a part of living can it be valuable. To give it some value is the teacher's function; and he does it by making his classroom the scene of living" (297).

Once teachers become masters of the art of living, then they can impart the art of learning or make the classroom the scene of living in two ways: "By organizing the subject matter of his [their] instruction so that its content will be meaningful and by presenting this content through a series of activities in which every child can take an interested part" (297). In other words, correlation translates content into activities and experiences.

Weeks challenged the English educators of America to become new kinds of educators by becoming masters of the art of living. How would a teacher become such a master? Her answer was through individual determination to develop one's "whole living personality." She saw the new kind of educator as eager to become involved in all facets of existence, from making friends in varied walks of life, traveling, reading current books and periodicals, and keeping in touch with current events in art, music, science, cinema, and drama, to becoming involved outwardly in the community and inwardly in personal grooming and fitness. She even advocated regular exercise for both good physical and mental health (17).

Having already taught approximately twenty years by the time she stood before the 1930 national delegation espousing a teaching renaissance, Ruth Mary Weeks was sensitive to the limitations typically placed on those who taught, especially women. She recognized that the very nature of the profession could make them recluses or at least out of touch with much of adult humanity. She outlined various examples from a thousand influences that tended "to hedge in and cramp" each teacher's personality. She criticized as often weak the academic preparation that teachers received in normal schools, which, by sacrificing content to method, limited their range of cultural and social background. Rules and regulations governing the profession prevented teachers from participating in civic and political affairs. Coupled with public isolation, personal lifestyles of teachers further starved their personalities, relegating them to "a life of scant leisure, a constant contact with immature and inferior minds, of comparative poverty, of social isolation, and in the case of women who more and more dominate the profession, of complete biological detachment from life" (16). Weeks told the delegation that in her hometown of Kansas City, a woman accepting a teaching job had to sign a contract saying she would not marry during the year. Weeks compared the signing to "taking the veil" (16).

As a teacher, Ruth Mary Weeks also recognized how easy it was to fall into a rut of stultifying routine. She used herself as an example when she confessed that during 1914 to 1915 she was a victim of such paralysis while teaching at Tudor Hall in Indianapolis. She did not go anywhere, meet anyone, or affiliate herself with any community activity. Later, when a friend labeled her as "not dead but teaching" (17), Weeks was so shocked by the analogy that she learned a valuable lesson, which she imparted to her audience: "Most people die long before their death. It takes effort to keep alive" (17). Thus, educators who master the art of living are determined to have meaningful lives. Automatically their zest carries over into the classroom, where students are inspired by the whole personalities of their teachers. Weeks, therefore, challenged English educators across America to rise to a new level of teaching by rising to a higher level of living. Her words seemed electric.

Just who was this woman who spoke with such conviction—this high school teacher who dared to give her colleagues a pep talk about staying alert and alive in the profession and who emphasized her personal observations and practical experiences? J. N. Hook, in his history of NCTE, hinted at her dynamic personality by calling her an "energetic little woman—'this whirlwind'" in describing her early dealings with the Council (1979, 94). While she had written previously for *English Journal* (1925a, 1925b, 1929) on phrasal prosody and on adapting content and instruction to student ability, it was also due to her energy and spunk that she quickly rose in the Council's leadership. By 1928–29 she was serving on the Editorial Board of *English Journal*.

James Hocker Mason, who wrote his 1962 dissertation on the early years of NCTE and whose interviews with various Council executives are included in Hook's NCTE history, offered two anecdotes about Weeks that give further insight into her personality. At the 1927 Board of Directors meeting in Chicago, she was not only a newcomer but a dynamic female wanting her views recognized, a relatively new phenomenon to the male-dominated executive branch. Realizing her dilemma, she was able to reflect on the occasion jokingly, not taking herself too seriously. As she recalled for Mason, "I believe I was noticed mainly because the hotel was *freezing* and I wore a rather striking silk, fringed, green shawl. I was also young for the Council in those days. It was a small, tight group on the gray side" (quoted in Hook 1979, 94). Laughter was an important component of her teaching personality.

As a further example of Weeks's exuberance, Mason recounted how she encouraged the Council to hold its 1929 annual convention to the west of the Mississippi River, which resulted in expanded membership and status for NCTE. At the 1928 convention in Baltimore, she promised the Council directors that she would personally guarantee six hundred delegates if Kansas City were selected. Since no convention had ever drawn more than four hundred members, her pledge was daring. Convinced by her enthusiasm, the Council leaders took a chance on her, but few really believed that meeting so far west would be successful. A year later on the eve of the Kansas City convention, when Executive Secretary W. Wilbur Hatfield saw the huge ballroom reserved for the opening evening session, he canceled it for a smaller room. The Hotel Baltimore then canceled its extra chairs and staff for the evening. Fortunately, Weeks and the local committee arrived early enough to rectify the situation. Weeks described the frenzy of activity: "Well!!!! Every remaining-on-duty employee of the hotel, the local committee, all Kansas Citians whom I could commandeer, and a lot of early arriving delegates who were angels of God if ever there were such, stripped *every* bedroom, *committee* room, parlor, etc., of its straight chairs. I'm telling you it was some job! But we seated the crowd of 600! Tennyson would have written another 'Charge' had he seen it" (quoted in Hook 1979, 95).

In fact, over one thousand people attended the Kansas City convention from all parts of the nation, including for the first time many black educators and the first black children on an NCTE program, a chorus from Lincoln High School in Kansas City. Mason reflected, "Suddenly in its last year of teen-age existence, the Council changed; some would have it that the Council's 'manhood' dates from the Kansas City convention" (quoted in Hook 1979, 95). Perhaps NCTE did reach "manhood" in Kansas City; if so, a local female teacher was responsible for its record growth. Her publicity skills and determination, mixed with originality and enthusiasm, made the difference. To thank her, the Council "crowned her with a wreath of roses as our Princess Ruth Mary" and elected her NCTE president for the next year ("Kansas City Council Meeting," 61).

Beyond anecdotes, however, a perusal of Weeks's background reveals more fully the genesis for her temperament and beliefs. Hook only alluded to the uniqueness of her background by describing her as "the daughter of a Kansas City, Missouri, socialite" (1979, 94). Actually, Weeks's enthusiasm for embracing an active life came to her almost as a birthright. She was born in Kansas City on 21 February 1886 to Edwin R. and Mary Harmon Weeks, both of whom were outstanding civic leaders and innovators. Her father was only ten years old in 1865 when his family drove fifteen cattle and two covered wagons into Kansas City. As one of the pioneering families in the area, Grandfather Weeks, a Seventh-Day Adventist minister, and his wife fought for the abolition of slavery and the education of black children. They had operated a station on the Underground Railroad in New York before starting west to help bring Kansas into the Union as a free state. Young Edwin helped his father build a school from an old rented house in Westport, an outlying area of Kansas City, that became the first free school for blacks in Missouri ("Weeks, Edwin R."). Grandmother Weeks was also an enthusiastic torchbearer in the bloomer movement for dress reform and the emancipation of women ("Random Thoughts").

Edwin R. Weeks worked so he could attend Phillips Exeter Academy at Exeter, New Hampshire, where he studied physics and the new field of electricity. Through luck and determination he became a nationally recognized pioneer not only for bringing electrical lighting to Kansas City, but also for developing the electrical industry from its infancy along with his friend and colleague Thomas Edison ("Edwin R. Weeks"). Edwin Weeks's electrical innovations were equaled by his strong humanitarian instincts. For forty-five years he was president of the Kansas City Humane Society, which encouraged child welfare along with kindness to animals. He was one of the founders of the Bands of Mercy, an organization that included humane societies across the United States. He was also one of the organizers of the original Kansas City Art Association and School for Design, which supported the first art school in Kansas City ("Weeks, Edwin R.").

Ruth Mary Weeks's mother, Mary Harmon Weeks, likewise made outstanding contributions, hers in the field of education. By the time Ruth Mary was born, her mother had already taught mathematics and English for twenty-one years at the old Central High School in Kansas City. Mary Harmon Weeks pioneered the Parent-Teacher Association of America. Her work for mothers and children, which began in 1889 in Ruth Mary's own kindergarten class, antedated the national organization by eight years, igniting an interest that quickly spread throughout the country (Craven 1941). She organized parent-teacher groups all over Kansas City in churches and clubs, and seeing the need for unification, she founded the state's first Parent-Teacher Association in Kansas City. When the National Congress of Parents and Teachers was formed, she became its first vice-president. After her mother's death, Ruth Mary helped establish two memorials to her mother in Kansas City, the Mary Harmon Weeks Elementary School and the Mary Harmon Weeks Scholarship (Karrell 1932).

In a family of such accomplishments, Ruth Mary Weeks's childhood environment was filled with wide and varied experiences, obviously sowing the seeds for her personal philosophy of mastering the art of living. Her parents not only were models of humanism, but they also influenced her development as a versatile individual. She was surrounded by innovation and participated both actively and indirectly in their pioneering projects. Weeks probably was one of the first children in America to do homework mainly by electricity instead of candle light. Her girlhood home was the first house in Kansas City to be electrically lighted, and the phenomenon attracted many visitors. She was probably also one of the first children to have a lighted Christmas tree, for one yuletide her father rigged electric lights on the tree. People came to see the unheard-of spectacle, and another holiday tradition was born ("Weeks, Mr. and Mrs.").

Weeks's mother and father were friends and confidants as well as parents to their only child, and they worked aggressively at molding her whole personality or what she would later call "the four faces of the human soul: thought, feeling, action, and laughter" (1931, 10). They were especially concerned with kindling her emotional sensitivity through the aesthetic experiences they provided. As Weeks told the 1930 NCTE convention:

> I learned to love sunsets by being taken as a child night after night and summer after summer to the hillside above our country home to watch the sun drop down into the waters of a sapphire lake.... I learned to love religious music by sitting in a half-lighted chapel evening after evening while a choir sang and a great organist played his favorite selections. I learned to love poetry by having it recited to me throughout childhood as an evening lullaby by a mother who could not sing. I learned to love rhythms by dancing and skating and marching to music and experiencing the undiluted physical glow of metric movement. (13)

Intellectually, Weeks excelled in high school and graduated from the same Central High School at which her mother had taught. While in high school she showed the same keen interest in physics that her father had possessed in his youth. But when he saw that she was leaning towards a career in science, he cautioned her that there were no openings for women in science: "It would break your heart to train for something you couldn't use" (Phillips 1956). Heeding his advice, when she traveled east to do her undergraduate work at Vassar College from 1903 to 1908, she majored instead in economics, read Greek, and enjoyed literature.

Vassar was a progressive and outward-looking school for women in the early twentieth century. It continued what Weeks's parents had begun in expanding her whole personality. As she recalled much later, "The theme song of Vassar was how to apply intelligence to life. Every girl thought she had a mission to make the world better . . . and no graduate ever stopped to worry about being unfashionably aggressive" (Phillips 1956).

Ruth Mary Weeks also wanted to make the world better, but in 1908 she was uncertain what her purpose would be. She hoped to make a contribution to the social services beyond volunteerism, the typical lot of many educated, privileged women of her generation. Her parents had proven that the world could be made better by first making the best out of one's own home territory. Following their example, she decided her pioneering work would start in Kansas City as a teacher, since that was the one standard profession available to women. Her vision must have touched the hearts of her senior classmates, because they voted her the William Borden European Fellowship after hearing her open letter to the class in which she stated that she would return to the city where she had been born and reared and would attempt to become a useful citizen ("Ruth Mary Weeks").

In 1908 Weeks began her teaching career in Kansas City at the opening of Westport High School. Except for the five-year period from 1910 to 1915 when she traveled in Europe on her Borden

Fellowship, received her master's degree as a rhetoric graduate fellow of the University of Michigan, and taught at two private schools, Packer Collegiate Institute and Tudor Hall, she taught in Kansas City until she retired in 1956 at the age of seventy. During the summer breaks she attended or taught at numerous summer institutes for teachers sponsored by the University of Chicago, University of California, University of Pittsburgh, University of Pennsylvania, Teachers College of Columbia University, and Missouri State Teachers College. Though trained in economics, she was assigned to teach English at Westport High School because "those in charge," she recalled much later, "wouldn't even let me teach civics, let alone economics. Women didn't have the right to vote then" (Phillips 1956). Weeks continued to teach English throughout the rest of her career. She was on the first faculty of the Kansas City Junior College from 1916 to 1926 and then moved to Paseo High School when it opened in 1926. She served as chair of its English Department for thirty years.

Even though Weeks was not allowed to teach in her first field of economics, she adapted her economics and social training to active involvement in the community. In national recognition for outstanding citizenship, she was listed along with her parents in the 1925 edition of *Who's Who in America*, the only entire family featured. The listing revealed Weeks's diverse personality and interests. Since she favored woman's suffrage, she was labeled a socialist. Her organizational affiliations included such groups as the Association of Collegiate Alumnae, Woman's Trade Union League, Associate Alumnae of Vassar College, Consumers' League, Phi Beta Kappa, Gamma Phi Beta, American Association of University Women, Women's City Club of Kansas City, National Education Association, and Theta Sigma Phi. Later, more expanded lists in other biographical references (*Leaders in Education: A Biographical Directory*, 1941; *Who Was Who in America*, 1977-81; *Who's Who of American Women*, 1958; *Who's Who among North American Authors*, 1976; *Women's Who's Who of America, 1914-1915*, 1976) included additional activities, such as president of the Kansas City Association of High School Women, 1942-43, and a contributor to *Education Review, English Journal, Atlantic Monthly, The Troubadour,* and *The Forum*. She belonged to a female poetry group called The Diversifiers and wrote verse and prose for *The Kansas City Star*. Her main recreation was listed as tramping, a general term for brisk walking and hiking. After her retirement, she was also active in the Kansas City Athenaeum, which her mother had helped to found.

Ruth Mary Weeks was also honored in *Who's Who* for advocating social awareness in learning. At first she focused on the vocational training movement, but soon she expanded her support to adapt social education to all aspects of learning. By 1925 she had published six books and had lectured widely on the relevance of social education.

The summer of 1908, following Weeks's graduation from Vassar, she volunteered at a New York settlement house sponsored by five women's colleges. She was shocked and saddened by the scene, describing it as "a low slum area full of immigrants right off the boat" (Phillips 1956). Quickly she realized that the well-meaning attempts of the college students were futile. She reasoned, "A school was the natural approach to these people" (Phillips). But what kind of school? How would it be organized? What would be its curriculum? These were questions Weeks was determined to answer.

While working at the settlement house, she began to study vocational or trade school concepts and experiments in America and abroad by attending the New York School of Philanthropy. Her investigations led her to realize that even though vocational education was the type of school needed, American educators generally were unaware of its potential. Moreover, she felt both the advocates and opponents of vocational training were too radical in their attitudes. "The supporters of such training," she said, "charge that current academic education is not useful and practical enough, while the opponents say that trade training will overthrow all cultural standards in education" ("People's School"). Weeks became fully impressed with the need for vocational schools to expand employment opportunities and to prevent delinquency not only for new immigrants but also for native-born Americans. She noted:

> There are four thousand Kansas City children between the ages of 14 and 16 who are not in school. Many of these left school after the fifth grade—neither trained for work nor for citizenship. A large proportion of these are idle or in some blind alley occupation of no educational value. Most boys of that age are messengers or do odd jobs. What will become of them when they are too old for such work?
>
> Only 5 percent of criminals have a trade ... the prisons would not be so crowded if the other 95 percent had had the advantage of vocational schools in their youth. ("People's School")

After teaching for a year, Weeks felt she should write a text analyzing and presenting the best curriculum for vocational education. Other books had explained the theoretical side of vocational education. She was concerned with its pedagogy. She engaged the opinions of the leaders of local labor unions and of the American Federation of Labor. Using her Vassar fellowship, she traveled abroad in 1910, visiting the foreign trade schools, sometimes under restriction since in both France and Germany women were not allowed to visit the boys' schools. Fortunately she had wired ahead letters of introduction from prominent educators at Vassar and Harvard to exchange for permits of admission. Most permits were made out to "R. M. Weeks, but it is safe to assume that the authorities issued them without realizing that a woman was to be the beneficiary" ("People's School").

As a result of that year of travel and observation both abroad and domestically, Weeks wrote *The People's School: A Study in Vocational Training* (1912), in which she examined every phase of trade schools for boys and girls, describing the practices of the German, French, and Swiss schools from her own observations. She considered the experiments in vocational education by American city schools as well as those of corporation schools. In conclusion, she presented her attitudes on the best trade schools and described the actual school work in language suitable for general reading. Speaking of her purpose in writing her book, Weeks stated, "I wanted particularly to show the very intimate relation of the trade school idea to various social and intellectual movements. I regard it as being potentially one of the most far reaching means of social improvement" ("People's School"). Hailed as the first American book on vocational training, *The People's School* attracted considerable attention and was later placed on the reading lists for the Great Books Foundation. The popularity of the book resulted in the widespread demand for Weeks as a lecturer at educational conventions ("Entire Kansas City Family").

Ruth Mary Weeks also contributed two bulletins to the emerging field of vocational education. The first, *Making American Industry Safe for Democracy* (1918), was read by Weeks at the convention of the Vocational Education Association of the Middle West in Chicago on 25 January 1918. Recognizing industry as the backbone of our national life, she asked the audience to ponder if American industry is really democratic. "No," she answered, "American industry is not yet a democratic institution; but it is destined so to be, and the problem of public education is to make it safely, sanely and efficiently so" (1918). She suggested two methods of giving young people this training for participation in the responsibilities of democratic industry: "Direct instruction in elementary economics and industrial organization, and indirect impacting of the same material in connection with personal studies" (1918).

The second bulletin, a monograph on vocational education titled *Report of Committee on Teaching Social Science in High Schools and Industrial*

Classes (1921), was written in collaboration with John R. Commons and Frank M. Leavitt. Weeks chaired the committee that issued this report at the Minneapolis convention of the Vocational Education Association of the Middle West on 12 February 1921, contending that all American students should develop some understanding of the social, political, and economic organization of society and suggesting practical activities and lessons for applying the basics of economics across the curriculum (1921, 5). It is ironic that even though Weeks was never allowed to teach economics in the classroom, she helped to formulate how economics should be taught to future generations of Americans.

Ruth Mary Weeks analyzed vocational education as her first step toward linking school and life, formulating her personal teaching philosophy. Next she took a long stride by exploring the entire school curriculum. She had been inspired by John Dewey while studying for her master's degree in rhetoric at the University of Michigan in 1912 to 1913, especially his epoch-making little volume, *The School and Society* (1902). Already sensitive to the growing trend of social education that identified the school as a world in miniature, Weeks recognized that teachers needed more practical guidance in applying the theorems of the progressive education movement to actual classroom settings.

She translated her ideas into a text for educators, *Socializing the Three R's*, published in 1919. Successful teachers of tomorrow, she reasoned, would not simply question the best methods for teaching children how to read, write, and calculate; instead, they would inquire how to help children to survive in society and to create a better world in the process. The principles of democracy fought for in World War I were to be maintained through socializing schooling. Weeks urged teachers and other school officials to increase "materially the time and attention devoted to instruction bearing directly on the problems of community and national life" (1919, 8). All subjects, therefore, were to be reinterpreted and taught through studying contemporary civilization: current thought, changing needs and issues of the day, and application of democratic principles to civic life (165).

Weeks next applied her principles to arithmetic, the least naturalized and socialized of the school subjects. Her 1923 text, *Primary Number Projects*, coauthored with Rosamond Losh, executive secretary of the Kansas City Children's Bureau, specifically analyzed, through extensive examples, how children could learn early number facts in real-life situations. Even though the concepts set forth in *Socializing the Three R's* were generally accepted in the elementary curriculum, Weeks had observed that those teaching arithmetic resisted the progressive changes the most, thus *Primary Number Projects* became a timely, strategic opportunity for enlightening teaching practice for the first two years of instruction in numbers (Weeks and Losh 1923, vii). In the book Weeks expressed her enthusiasm for social education as a partner in any learning: "A man who can live in society! This is the goal of the progressive teacher; social education is the watchword of the hour" (1). She then spent the next thirty years of her professional life adapting that "watchword" to the subject of her daily living and teaching—English. When Weeks became chair of the English Department of the new Paseo High School, she had not only a center for her teaching philosophy, but also a pivotal niche from which she advocated the improvement of English education from NCTE's Executive Committee down to classroom curriculum and pedagogy.

In 1930 Ruth Mary Weeks was elected president of NCTE. Her presidency was marked by the same energy and efficiency she had shown in bringing the annual meeting to Kansas City the year before. Through her dynamic leadership she directed three changes in the internal structure of the Council that expanded it from "a businesslike but rather informal organization" to a corporation that could handle its quickly expanding purposes and services ("National Council," 24). As one of her first tasks, she devised with Rewey Belle Inglis, immediate past president, a compilation of general information about the Council and the duties of the president in the NCTE President's Book, since no such permanent record existed. Their intent was "To put the president more quickly in touch with his office, to render him less dependent on secretarial advice, and to enable him to function with the greatest ease and effectiveness" (NCTE President's Book). In a supplement to the President's Book, Weeks included guidelines for planning annual meetings. Unfortunately, after her tenure nothing more was added to the President's Book by subsequent presidents, despite the request to other presidents: "Please keep it up to date and pass it to your successor."

Her other two changes, however, were lasting. With the support of the Executive Committee, she arranged for the Council to become a not-for-profit corporation so that it could assume responsibility for "its own business transactions" ("Cleveland Council Meeting," 82). Since the incorporation was drawn up by Kansas City lawyers whom Weeks consulted, NCTE was designated a Missouri corporation. Weeks initiated one of the Council's first transactions in its newly incorporated form, "the approval of a contract between the National Council and the *English Journal* providing for publication of the *Journal* as a Council organ, for the maintenance of a joint office, and for the purchase of the

Journal by the Council in the case of Mr. Hatfield's death or his desire to sell the *Journal* during his lifetime" (82).

The 1930 annual meeting at the Hotel Statler in Cleveland, with Weeks presiding, had a socializing undertone to its programming and exhibits, one of which was a model classroom: "An armchair in which to sit and study, a fireplace, a comfortable couch to lend a homey atmosphere, and a stage nearby, is the very least that Little Willie should expect to find in his English classroom today" (Driscoll 1930).

The attendance of well over one thousand educators was even larger than the number at Kansas City the year before, and the programming was the most integrated and lively attempted by the Council. "Most credit for this is due the president, Ruth Mary, who employed in organizing this program the same originality and energy that she displayed in the publicity for last year's convention" ("Cleveland Council Meeting," 54). Weeks's address, which challenged the profession to make English, both its content and instruction, reflect the art of living, climaxed the meeting and set the tone for the first Curriculum Commission.

Apart from initiating this national curriculum study and serving as one of its 175 members, Ruth Mary Weeks's major curricular contribution was analyzing whether correlation as a design for selecting units of content was a virtue or hindrance to any English program. Weeks had intended the national curriculum study to present a guide or model of "HOW an English course should be made, if not exactly WHAT should be its content in every locality" (Bulletin to Workers in the National Council Curriculum Study, included in the NCTE President's Book). After five years of extensive study, in 1935 the commission published its findings in a monograph, *An Experience Curriculum in English*, that basically fulfilled Weeks's initial intent, concluding that "well selected experiences" should compose any English course (Applebee 1974, 119). However, though many progressives championed correlation or integration of subjects, traditionally separated by departmentalization, as the design to make learning relevant to life experiences, the Curriculum Commission, while praising experiments in integration being conducted, had really failed to fully examine them.

Weeks, therefore, chaired a subcommittee of the Curriculum Commission, the Committee on Correlation, which tackled the challenge of compiling and analyzing existing correlation experiments in English pedagogy across the United States. Weeks edited those results into a 312-page report, *A Correlated Curriculum*, published in 1936 as the Council's fifth monograph. While the report encouraged "natural fusions and integrations," it discouraged "some of the ill-considered attempts at correlation made merely because it is in fashion" ("National Council," 19). The report concluded that even though correlation could be conceived "in world pattern, in subject pattern, in experience pattern, and in the psychological growth pattern of the individual being taught," the success of any integration was largely dependent on the creativity of the teacher (Weeks 1936, 4-5).

When Ruth Mary Weeks presented the newly published *Correlated Curriculum* at the 1936 annual meeting in Boston, she equated the true curriculum maker to "a juggler with four balls, each of which he must keep in the air—interest, growth, social vision, and skill" (Weeks 1937b, 192). As always, her emphasis was on teachers' becoming masters of living before they could pass on the art of living to their students. Weeks declared she would remain a "staunch correlationist" despite her reservations that integration could easily be misinterpreted and misapplied by being reduced to narrow themes or taken to such extremes that the components of English, such as literature, would be sacrificed: "But, like the man who exclaimed, 'I can deal with my enemies, but heaven preserve me from my misguided friends,' I am eager to preserve integration from the pitfalls of unwary enthusiasm. Let us by all means make of education a vital pattern. But let it be a rich pattern" (193).

Weeks next turned to creating learning materials that illustrated her own pattern making. During the same year that *A Correlated Curriculum* was published, she produced with Thelma Winnberg Cook and P. H. Deffendall a series of ten units collectively entitled *English through Experience*, in which the English skills of grammar, usage, spelling, and composition were integrated with a wide variety of literature and life themes: "Pilgrimages on Paper," "Reading for Pleasure," "Becoming a School Citizen," "Listening In," "Playing the Game," "Reliving Famous Lives," "Filling the Nation's Market Basket," "Sight-Seeing in a City," "Broadcasting Our Favorite Poems," and "Nature Does It Again." Why did Weeks create such an English text? Her second testimony to her teaching philosophy, "Content for Composition," contains her rationale:

> It has been my lot in the last two years, in looking for a suitable text for adoption, to examine a large number of drill pads and other such texts designed to teach the fundamentals of grammar, punctuation, and usage which have become the bane of so many good teachers by setting up teaching goals quite at variance with the life needs of their pupils . . . what a deadly intellectual blank

they created for the student. . . . Grammar in a vacuum describes almost all of them. (1937a, 298-99)

Likewise, Weeks collaborated with Rollo L. Lyman and Howard C. Hill, both from the University of Chicago, in creating two literature anthologies for the secondary level. Both anthologies, *World Literature* (1938) and *English Literature* (1941), viewed literature as the content of life and were rich in selections that covered the full expansion of literature, from the oral forms, orations, debates, folksongs, and folktales, to the written genres represented in fiction and nonfiction forms, including diaries and letters. These anthologies were natural extensions of the integrated units that appeared as examples of correlation experiments in *A Correlated Curriculum*: "The Living Legacy of Greece and Rome" (138-47), "Cooperative Foreign Literature Courses" (154-56), and "A Survey of the Arts on the Secondary and Junior-College Levels" (163-77). As an introduction to each anthology, Weeks penned an essay emphasizing the importance of reading to unlock life's secrets contained in literature.

Her support of ample and varied literature as important content in teaching the art of living led her to chair two other Council committees that surveyed current uses of available reading materials in English classes across America: the Committee on Present Practice in the Use of Reading Lists (in 1938) and the Committee on Magazines and Newspapers in the Classroom (in 1946). The second committee published its compilation of classroom practices in a report that Weeks edited, *Using Periodicals: A Report on the Use of Magazines and Newspapers in the English Class* (1950).

Despite the wide audience for these publications, it was Weeks's own students, during her ten years at Kansas City Junior College and especially during her thirty years at Paseo High School, who most fully benefitted from her enthusiasm for literature and life. They were at the heart of her pedagogy, using her texts, developing under her modeling, and learning the art of living. Her teaching philosophy even permeated the halls of Paseo High School, which contained watercolor and oil paintings selected by the students (Weeks 1936, 242). She was an outstanding teacher whose reputation for making the English classroom a center of living instead of dullness was so widespread throughout Kansas City that she became legendary. Often described as vibrant, Weeks was best remembered for her "stimulating lectures . . . darting from one economic or historical subject to another," that were attributed to her "great field of knowledge, superior intellect, and the imaginative use of it" (Phillips 1956).

When Ruth Mary Weeks retired on 10 June 1956 after forty-eight years of teaching, *The Kansas City Star* headlined a tribute to her, "No Dullness in Classroom Has Been Teacher's Goal" (Phillips 1956). And when she died thirteen years later, on 13 July 1969 in Kansas City, the city to which she had dedicated her life, *The Kansas City Star* eulogized this "Outstanding Teacher": "Ruth Mary Weeks was a great teacher, as thousands who were her English students at three Kansas City public schools had good reason to know. Her highly personalized instruction was never routine, always lively and marked by a love of literature and language which she wanted to implant permanently in the minds of her young people and often succeeded in doing" ("Ruth Mary Weeks").

Her teaching philosophy, however, reached not only far beyond her locale, but also beyond her life. Even though history and circumstances have revealed shortcomings in the experience curriculum and correlation design of the progressive era, the spirit of these pioneering movements in education, which Weeks reinterpreted as her guide for teaching and living, have remained relevant. Much of the philosophy behind this experiential-integrated approach to learning resurfaced twenty to thirty years later when the Council formulated the NCTE Commission on the English Curriculum, culminating in a five-volume curriculum series, and well into the 1960s, when the Anglo-American Seminar on the Teaching of English held at Dartmouth College in 1966 emphasized the importance of children's activities, especially oral and creative experiences, for holistic learning (Hook 1979, 120–21).

Today in our global society, where knowledge can be stored and retrieved instantly, English teachers more than ever must be masters of the art of living. Most parts of the earth are no longer far removed from a child's reality, for our massive communications systems have shrunk the world and placed it closer to home. Teachers are challenged to make each learner "globally literate." English as the primal content of communication, with the teacher in the center as its supreme model, must be treated as an integrated whole if classroom learning is to remain relevant in our futuristic society. Weeks would have agreed.

As recently as 1986, seventeen years after the death of Ruth Mary Weeks, a former student nominated Weeks to be included in a tribute to outstanding educators who taught in the Kansas City Junior College and Metropolitan Community College between 1915 and 1986. In describing her teacher, Dorothy Varney said: "I first met Miss Weeks in a course in freshman English composition —not always a subject to evoke special enthusiasm. But when I entered the room, I had a feeling that this class would be notable. The teacher was pretty and full of sparkle. She proved to be humorous and liked to shrug and to gesture with her delicate hands to emphasize a point. She always had something encouraging to say about our attempts to write" (1986, 12).

What greater tribute can teachers receive than to be favorably remembered by their students? Of all of her accomplishments, Ruth Mary Weeks was proudest of her students who went on to successful and often creative careers. Many of them became lifelong friends who kept in touch with her years after leaving her classroom ("Ruth Mary Weeks"). They had surely learned well "the art of living."

Works Cited

Applebee, Arthur N. 1974. *Tradition and Reform in the Teaching of English: A History.* Urbana, Ill.: National Council of Teachers of English.

"The Cleveland Council Meeting." 1931. *English Journal* 20 (January): 54–85.

Craven, Elba. 14 February 1941. "Weeks, Mary Harmon: Parent-Teacher Associations Pay Tribute to Founder." *Kansas City Star.*

Dewey, John. 1902. *The School and Society.* Chicago: University of Chicago Press.

Driscoll, Helen. 27 November 1930. "Teachers Open 3-Day Meet on English Study." *Cleveland Press.*

"Edwin R. Weeks: Eighty-Second Birthday." 7 December 1937. *Kansas City Star.*

"An Entire Kansas City Family Listed in Who's Who." 13 March 1925. *Kansas City Times.*

Hook, J. N. 1979. *A Long Way Together: A Personal View of NCTE's First Sixty-Seven Years.* Urbana, Ill.: National Council of Teachers of English.

"The Kansas City Council Meeting." 1930. *English Journal* 19 (January): 57–80.

Karrell, Docia. 14 March 1932. "She Blames 'Giddy Few' for Criticisms of Youth." *Kansas City Star.*

Mason, James Hocker. 1962. "The National Council of Teachers of English, 1911–1926." Ph.D. diss., George Peabody College for Teachers, Nashville, Tenn.; plus a detailed supplement extending the history to 1936.

"The National Council, 1911–36: The First Phase." 1936. *English Journal* 25 (December): 805–36.

The National Council of Teachers of English President's Book. 1929. Unpublished. Supplement issued in 1930.

"The People's School: A Kansas City Teacher's New Book on Vocational Training." 24 March 1912. *Kansas City Star*, 10C.

Phillips, Marjean. 10 June 1956. "No Dullness in Classroom Has Been Teacher's Goal: Ruth Mary Weeks, Educator for 48 years, Retires to Take Up Busy Life of Writing and Civic Work." *Kansas City Star.*

"Random Thoughts." 15 June 1947. *Kansas City Star.*

"Ruth Mary Weeks, Outstanding Teacher" (obituary). 15 July 1969. *Kansas City Star.*

Varney, Dorothy. 1986. "Ruth Mary Weeks." In *In Praise of Teaching, 1915–1986,* by the Kansas City Junior College and Metropolitan Community College.

Kansas City: A Project of the Foundation–Alumni Association, Metropolitan Community College.

"Weeks, Edwin R." (obituary). 18 August 1938. *Kansas City Star.*

"Weeks, Mr. and Mrs. Edwin R." 2 February 1938. *Kansas City Journal Post.*

Weeks, Ruth Mary. 1912. *The People's School: A Study in Vocational Training.* Riverside Series of Educational Monographs. Boston: Houghton Mifflin.

———. 1918. *Making American Industry Safe for Democracy.* Chicago: Vocational Education Association of the Middle West.

———. 1919. *Socializing the Three R's.* New York: Macmillan.

———. 1925a. "Objectives for A, B, and C Groups." *English Journal* 14 (February): 139–40.

———. 1925b. "Bibliography for High-School English for Sections of Differing Ability." *English Journal* 14 (February): 128–36.

———. 1929. "Adapting Instruction to Pupil Ability." *English Journal* 18 (April): 287–94.

———. 1931. "Teaching the Whole Child." *English Journal* 20 (January): 9–17.

———. 1937a. "Content for Composition." *English Journal* 26 (April): 294–301.

———. 1937b. "Pattern-Making in Education." *English Journal* 26 (March): 187–94.

Weeks, Ruth Mary, ed. 1936. *A Correlated Curriculum: A Report of the Committee on Correlation of the National Council of Teachers of English.* New York: D. Appleton-Century.

———. 1950. *Using Periodicals: A Report on the Use of Magazines and Newspapers in the English Class.* Chicago: National Council of Teachers of English.

Weeks, Ruth Mary, John R. Commons, and Frank M. Leavitt. 1921. *Report of Committee on Teaching Social Studies in High Schools and Industrial Classes.* Chicago: Vocational Education Association of the Middle West.

Weeks, Ruth Mary, Thelma Winnberg Cook, and P. H. Deffendall. 1936. *English through Experience.* New York: Macmillan.

Weeks, Ruth Mary, and Rosamond Losh. 1923. *Primary Number Projects.* Boston: Houghton Mifflin.

Weeks, Ruth Mary, Rollo L. Lyman, and Howard C. Hill, eds. 1938. *World Literature.* Our Literary Heritage Series. New York: Charles Scribner's Sons.

———. 1941. *English Literature.* Our Literary Heritage Series. New York: Charles Scribner's Sons.

3 Stella Stewart Center: Proceeding under Their Own Power

Sue Ellen Holbrook, Southern Connecticut State University

> If you are a poor reader, you are not a self-reliant student. Through this planned study and more like it, you can come into your own as a reader and travel under your own power. The whole plan is worth a fair intelligent trial. Do you not agree?
>
> Stella S. Center and Gladys L. Persons,
> *Practices in Reading and Thinking*

Stella Stewart Center
1878–1969

Two photographs of Stella Stewart Center, taken at different times in her life, have a notable similarity. Each depicts her on the left-hand side, seated in half-profile with her eyes cast down on pages she holds in her hands. The earlier photograph appeared in a journal article commemorating the twenty-fifth anniversary of the National Council of Teachers of English ("National Council," 827); the second was printed nearly thirty years later (Sullivan 1965, 7) when Center had taken residence as a reading consultant at her alma mater, Tift College for Women in Forsyth, Georgia. As images of a woman reading, these two pictures are fitting bookends for the career of Stella Stewart Center, for it was one dedicated to the value of reading.

A brief delineation of Center's life will illustrate the place her work has in the history of our profession of teaching English. Center came from a well-established, economically comfortable, white southern family. Her grandfather had been a member of the Alabama state legislature (Sullivan 1965, 6). She was born in 1878 in Forsyth, Georgia, where she also spent the last four years of her life, dying at age eighty-three in 1969, not many days after enthusiastically watching the

49

moonwalk on television (Baykin 1969). Typical of other white women who came of age in the late nineteenth century, Stella Center looked on the teaching of children as a suitable career; indeed, it was almost the only honorable paid vocation and alternative to the role of homemaker. Her education was designed to prepare her for the teaching of English: A.B. from Tift College for Women (in her native city of Forsyth) and George Peabody College for Teachers in Nashville, Ph.B. (bachelor of pedagogy) from the University of Chicago, M.A. from Columbia University's Teachers College, and finally Litt.D. (doctorate of letters) from the University of Georgia ("Our Own Who's Who" 1933, 166).

Although the South was her ancestral home, both the extent and the quality of Center's higher education suggest that in the early twentieth century she would find more career opportunities in the urban Northeast. And so she did: Center spent most of her professional life, from 1914 to 1955, in New York City (Sullivan 1965, 6). From 1917 to 1931 she was an instructor in the program of "secretarial correspondence" of Columbia University, but for many years her principal work was in secondary school teaching at Julia Richmond High School, Walton Junior and Senior High School. John Adams High School, where she was head ("first assistant") of the English Department, and ultimately Theodore Roosevelt High School, where again she was head of the English Department and also director of a reading school ("Our Own Who's Who" 1933, 166; Baykin 1969). From 1936 to 1950 she brought her expertise in reading and her administrative ability to the Reading Institute of New York University, which she codirected with Gladys L. Persons, and extended her teaching energy to adult learners, whom she taught in the institute's evening school (Center 1952, xv). Fourteen years after beginning her career in New York City, Center had become prominent in the National Council of Teachers of English. In 1928 she became second vice-president; in 1930 she cochaired, with Max J. Herzberg of New Jersey, the Council's Committee on Recreational Reading, producing two influential reports; and in 1932 Center became the Council's twenty-first president and the third woman to fill that position. During her career she wrote or edited several educational books for school or commercial distribution, as well as a research study published as the Council's sixth monograph; the topic of most of her published work, like that of her teaching work, was reading.

That reading was the focus of Stella Center's professional life is of historical importance for present-day teachers of English, both in secondary schools and in colleges. In her work we find indexes of her times and our past—four decades of change and challenge for English in America—and noticeable connections with developments in our times.

From its inception in 1911, the National Council of Teachers of English made reading a prominent concern, as the very circumstances of the Council's foundation indicate. NCTE was formed in reaction to the attempt by the National Education Association to impose uniform college entrance requirements on the preparatory schools and thus to control the curricula of the schools. In the case of English, the requirements dictated that students were to know certain literary texts (see "National Council"; Hook 1979; Applebee 1974; Berlin 1987). Those educators who founded NCTE were opposed to standard requirements, not to literary texts. Even so, they were critical of the texts named on the lists. They advocated the addition of contemporary fiction and also a wider range in the type of reading expected of students. Some argued for the value of reading even for students not bound for college.

NCTE's long-standing attitude toward the primacy of reading is reflected in some of Stella Center's work for the Council. Although teachers evidently continued to prescribe traditional texts in school, since 1913 the Council had sought to broaden the reading curriculum, or at least high school students' exposure to books, by publishing a list of books for "home" reading. As cochairs of the Council's Committee on Recreational Reading in 1930, Center and Herzberg undertook the rewriting of this list, first composed by Herbert Bates in 1913 and brought up to date by him in 1923. In the hands of Center and Herzberg, the 1930 pamphlet *Books for Home Reading* expanded from Bates's original eleven pages of recommended fiction, drama, poetry, biography, collections, history and mythology, speeches, travel and adventure, and "other works not classified," to eight times that number. Besides adding many authors and titles to Bates's list, Center and Herzberg streamlined the original categories, listed the title first rather than the author's last name, filled the pamphlet with illustrations from editions of the texts included—many in color—and addressed the pamphlet to students rather than teachers. As a result, the 1930 *Books for Home Reading,* and its revision in 1937, was transformed from a "pharmacopoeia" for teachers to use as if "prescrib[ing] the right medicine" (Report of the Committee upon Home Reading, 4), to one for students themselves to browse through, looking for "books you will like to read" (Herzberg and Center 1930, 4). In 1932 Center and Herzberg inaugurated a separate pamphlet for seventh through ninth graders, entitled *Leisure Reading,* which followed the same enticing format. A revised version appeared in 1938.

For both high school and junior high school students, Center and Herzberg suggested that readers not limit themselves to books that were easy to read or of one kind only, that they give a second chance to a book that bored them when they were younger, and that they form their own program of reading. Center and Herzberg encouraged reading books not as a "school duty" but as "one of life's greatest pleasures" (4).

Although the idea of reading lists was as old as the Council itself, Stella Center's work on the Committee on Recreational Reading exemplified her concern for the reading ability of secondary school students. She became convinced that reading instruction was inadequate: children intelligent enough to do well in secondary school were failing because they had not learned to read, and students were leaving school—graduating or dropping out—with their reading ability sorely undeveloped. It was the force of Center's work that made the teaching of reading, not just the presentation of great books, a subject in the secondary schools. Although her position may not seem unusual now, it was then. According to Dora V. Smith, "She certainly alerted the Council to the fact that reading skills belong in the secondary school as well as in the elementary school and that reading *literature* has a technique all its own. Until that time *reading* was an elementary school subject" (1969, 1–2).

Center's approach to reading and her view of its value to children and adults are evident in several of her publications and convention papers spanning her career. Although wholly without any editorial comment on its theory and purpose, one of the first and most remarkable of these publications is *The Worker and His Work* (1920), which Center edited as part of a series of literature textbooks. It contained a few poems, several illustrations of graphic and sculptural art, and over 150 selections from different sources, largely but not exclusively fiction, all displaying the labor that people perform in the United States and in other countries. The authors were by and large contemporaries, "present-day," as the subtitle says; as an addendum, Center included a brief description of each author, listing place of residence, even the address. Although most of the selections described men at work, some also showed women, such as Edna Ferber's story of Fanny Brandeis (including the motif of anti-Semitism) and Rebecca Harding Davis's *Life in the Iron Mills*, a work on leftist and feminist reading lists today. In general, the selections, although not devoid of tragedy or criticism for the conditions of the laborers, are optimistic accounts of labor—"making a living"—seen as interesting and successful, such as the following poem (Morgan 1920, 37):

> Work!
> Thank God for the might of it,
> The ardor, the urge, the delight of it—
> Work that springs from the heart's desire,
> Setting the brain and the soul on fire—
> Oh, what is so good as the heat of it,
> And what is so glad as the beat of it,
> And what is so kind as the stern command,
> Challenging brain and heart and hand?

A recognizable forerunner of readers in today's composition courses, *The Worker and His Work* is, in its form as an anthology of literary selections, a relatively early example of one method that English educators used to broaden the school reading lists. In the prominence it gave to contemporary writers, Center's anthology shared the Council's emphasis on contemporary as well as traditional texts. The slant of the biographical information served to make the readings seem accessible: these were living people to whom a student might even write a letter, not ancients to be revered. In having one theme, the anthology used a method shared by some other educators who hoped that students would be enticed to read about issues of consequence to them. It is in its particular theme of work, however, that Center's anthology is especially intriguing. Although the perspective was not fully proletarian, the anthology did celebrate workers. The theme reflected the opportunities for jobs and the values of pride, ingenuity, and efficiency in working well that befit the industrial, capitalistic United States before the Great Depression. The choice of such a theme reflected the responsibility of the English teacher, in Center's eyes, to prepare students not only for higher education but also for the world of work. This textbook provides evidence of the shifting emphasis of school from "a 'fitting school' oriented toward college entrance" to "a school for the people, whose chief function would be preparation for life" (Applebee 1974, 46). The generally optimistic tone of the anthology also reflected the attitude of the schools toward industry before the Depression: business was an ally of education, giving English teachers a purpose for teaching literacy (see Tyack, Lowe, and Hansot 1984). As a historical artifact, Stella Stewart Center's *Worker and His Work* does reflect a period of American culture, but textbooks like these were not simply passive mirrors; they were also agents of social change, change that such teachers as Center believed, in the tradition of John Dewey, was social progress.

Twelve years after *The Worker and His Work*, Center affirmed her belief in the power of reading to effect social progress, but in a context very different from the one celebrated by that anthology: the onset of the Great Depression. Her presidential address of 24 November 1932, "The Responsibility of Teachers of English in Contemporary American Life," touched on several matters, among them the English teacher's responsibility for teaching reading as a major means of producing a "thinking" electorate, as cultural enrichment, as a useful activity for nonworking hours, and as a way of promoting world peace and international cooperation. Center urged teachers to exploit the political impact of reading, stating that only recently had "textbooks and courses of study recognized the necessity of teaching boys and girls how to read newspapers and periodicals" (1933, 102). The United States needed, she argued, an electorate capable of weighing speeches, newspapers, and magazines; toward this end, English teachers had a "powerful lever that might accomplish wonders" (103). Furthermore, as she argued elsewhere in her speech, courses in literature might include "literature of liberal internationalism," thus hastening "the day when negotiation and conference instead of war become the chief instrument of foreign policy." By having students read such literature in a time when "tariff walls" were mounting and political leaders were pursuing a policy of isolation, English teachers might be able to develop a "feeling of world solidarity and to create better international understanding" (104).

In a shrewd move, Center also tied the enforced leisure of the Depression to the Council's long-standing attempt to influence students' reading habits through "recreational reading." In the double-edged reference to both the displacement of workers by modern technology and the unemployment rate at the beginning of her address, Center announced, "Economists tell us that no more in this country will there be work for everyone, eight hours a day, six days a week, on a forty-eight-hour schedule. Some wonder if there will be so much as thirty hours a week for each worker. This state of affairs means increased leisure or unemployment, call non-working time what you will, according to your bank balance" (98). Arguing that the worthy use of leisure was one of the cardinal aims of education, Center pointed out that "the history of the past three years has brought home forcibly to us that we are facing an era when time not occupied by work must be productively occupied, if the integrity of American society is not to be impaired. We have been keenly aware in this country of the value of work, but have we given due consideration to the value of the fine activities of leisure in lifting the level of character?" (103). She stressed that besides affecting taste in radio, theater, and motion pictures—all media for leisure time—English instruction "will educate young people to rely on reading as the chief resource of their leisure hours" (103).

Center was right about the growth of "leisure" reading. By 1936 her *Home Reading* list, published the second year of the Depression, already had sold 360,000 copies ("National Council," 14). Furthermore, people increased their use of libraries (which the Council had been vigorously supporting), not just to while away the time with escapist fantasies, but for "serious" reading, as they sought to understand political and social issues and to find ways to earn money (Tyack, Lowe, and Hansot 1984, 41).

Stella Center's presidential address presented reading as essential in the wide context of American life. In 1934 she began to make it essential for success in education. In her work for the Reading School of Theodore Roosevelt High School in the Bronx, Center was dedicated to helping children who could not read well, training unemployed graduates and former teachers as auxiliary remedial staff, using the latest scientific educational methods, formulating a philosophy of reading instruction, and struggling to offer reform without completely damning her own profession.

Although city schools took the blows of the Great Depression later than rural schools, by 1932 even teachers in New York feared losing their jobs, and some were in fact put out of work despite the rise in enrollments and retention rates of secondary students (33–38). The Roosevelt administration intervened by hiring men and women on relief to provide or assist with instruction in programs intended to supplement the regular curriculum of the public schools (93–131). Most of the supplemental programs lay in adult education or in preschools and primary schools (131), but Theodore Roosevelt High School did become an early site of a New Deal experiment. The elimination of illiteracy was the government's premiere mission in instruction (131), and at Theodore Roosevelt the Department of English had gathered proof that well over half of the entering students were deficient, or "retarded," readers (Center and Persons 1937, 3–14; Center 1952, 283). Therefore, according to Center, in December 1934 the high school division of the board of education assigned approximately thirty young men and women who were on relief to the Department of English at Theodore Roosevelt, funding them with money from the Civil Works Administration (later to be titled the Works Progess Administration) to provide remedial instruction in reading. The resulting "Reading School," which Center and Persons planned and supervised, was the first project of its kind in New York's public high schools (Center and Persons 1937, v, 15; Center 1952, 283).

Today, visitors coming to Theodore Roosevelt High School move through a medley of Latino accents and signs in Spanish (recalling perhaps the television program "The Bronx Zoo"), but in the 1930s different immigrant populations occupied the neighborhood and poured into this Bronx public school, a school that to Stella Center seemed to be a microcosm of the "new order" in American society. Jews and Italians predominated, although numerous other ethnic groups were also present among the school's 7,000 girls and boys (Center and Persons 1937, 4). Most were not college-bound students but registered in the "commercial course," and for many English was a second language: besides Yiddish and Italian, Center cited home languages of Hungarian, Albanian, Turkish, Armenian, and Russian (19).

During the course of the project, Center and Persons enrolled a total of 500 students in the Reading School, each term basing their selection of students on data about the students' mental ability (through the Terman Group Test of Mental Ability) and reading level (primarily through the Stanford Reading Tests). The students substituted the Reading School class for their regular English instruction. Although the focal activity was reading, the students did write compositions (which Center described as "practically illiterate" at first) and received "instruction in every branch of English" (20). Small class size (no more than five students per teacher, instead of the regular forty or more), individual attention, and homogeneous grouping were three of what were then innovative methods used in the Reading School. The class was conducted as a "studio-laboratory," or workshop, as we would say today.

The premise of the instruction was that all pupils could improve their reading ability if teachers could "galvanize their will to learn" and used the right materials and methods. Center and Persons were again *au courant* in their view of materials and methods. They followed the "types approach" (see Applebee 1974, 56), that is, dividing written material into different types according to purpose; moreover, instead of just the "classics," students also studied "work-type" reading. Teachers were to infer individual students' latent interests in order to suggest books that would attract the students in a stimulating, not escapist, program of leisure reading, considered as essential to progress as the work of the studio-classroom itself. The readings were graded, but potentially difficult vocabulary was not to be perceived as inappropriate—how else would students expand their own vocabularies? Silent reading was stressed because of its efficiency. Visual dysfunctions were to be corrected, ocular mechanics to be understood.

Several graphs and photographs display how important this scientific approach was to the experiment. It was a thoroughly corrective model: the students chosen were those who tested most deficient. Whatever barriers stood in the way were to be recognized and, insofar as possible, remedied: physical disability, cultural dislocation, behavioral disorders, family problems, "faulty habits."

Comprehension was the immediate aim: a series of gradually more difficult and longer passages were set forth programmatically, with score cards for the students to fill out, timing themselves and writing in the answer to the "target," that is, the purpose of the reading. Piqued interest and enjoyment were important, but as means of galvanizing the will to learn, not as ends. Hard work was expected and valued. With patience, practice, and generous guidance from supportive teachers, hard-working pupils were expected to see themselves making progress, thus raising their confidence level as they systematically raised their reading level until they had achieved the ultimate aim of the instruction, an educational aim based on William Heard Kilpatrick's theory of progressive self-direction: "to put the individual in a fair way to traveling under his own power" (Center and Persons 1937, 20, 138).

Following the policy of the federal educational projects, the Reading School had to be supplemental, not integrated into the regular curriculum, and it had to be staffed only by people on relief (Tyack, Lowe, and Hansot 1984, 98–131); therefore, the thirty auxiliary instructors funded by the federal government were the sole teaching staff. Center's description of her staff reveals the effect of the Depression on college graduates: many of these instructors had taught in public and private schools before the Depression; the majority had majored in English, journalism, public speaking, or related subjects, but others had degrees in education, sociology, science, law, French, or German. They were "adaptable" and "interested," but they did not know what methods to use or how to prepare materials, let alone how to diagnose reading problems and write case histories for the sake of the experiment. The solution was a mandatory daily conference of one hour (or staff meeting, we might say now) throughout the entire time of the project, during which hour the staff was able "to set forth the objectives of the work, to discuss methods of teaching, to examine teaching materials, to give instruction in the preparation of teaching materials, to discuss all the problems of the classroom, to keep the fundamental philosophy of the course constantly in the focus of attention, to hear reports of committees, and to create a unity of purpose among the teachers" (Center and Persons 1937, 15). In praise of a staff that evidently found the experiment's demands daunting, Center stated, "Their greatest contribution to the work has been their attitude toward the boys and girls under instruction; they have established and maintained a spirit of friendliness in the classroom, an indispensable attitude in remedial work" (16).

The formidable organizing power that made Stella Center a successful Council president is evident in the description of bringing the Reading School into reality. Moreover, those of us who hire adjunct faculty in composition these days, or who have retrained retrenched faculty, will appreciate Center's view of her staff, her solution to the problem of their inexpertise, and the value she placed on their attitude in the classroom.

In evaluating the results of the Reading School experiment, Center and Persons came to some harsh conclusions about democratic education, not as an ideal but in its enactment. Seventy-five percent of the students who finished the experiment made progress, but in some cases "not sufficient progress to overcome all retardation"; that is, students raised their reading levels but not always to that appropriate for their grade levels. Insufficiency was especially true for those beginning in the lowest level. Furthermore, Reading School students did not inevitably transfer their gains to their other subjects; despite improvement in reading comprehension, some still did poorly overall. To Center and Persons, these results did not imply that federal funds had been wasted, that the methods of the Reading School were faulty, or that some students did not belong in school. They argued, very much as basic writing teachers argue today, that no concerted effort existed outside the Reading School to enable the transference of power; that traditional English instruction was wholly geared to the college-bound population; that the later remediation begins, the less likely it is to overcome "retardation"; that the Reading School students were the greatest risks of all the students; and that professional services were necessary to ameliorate the remedial students' complex problems. They contended that remediation was not undemocratic, that it belonged in secondary schools if they were to fulfill their mission, that teachers and schools must face their responsibility for their students' failure:

> Reduced to its simplest terms, this problem of the retarded pupil who is thrown into water beyond his depth and allowed to sink or swim is a problem in humanity. It is destructive of the self-respect and morale to which every person is entitled, to subject him to repeated failure. If, as so many teachers say, they can do nothing for the low-ability groups, then it is scarcely honest to open the

school doors to them and make the gesture of offering education. It is extremely wasteful in time and energy and that commodity called the taxpayer's money. The efforts of these boys and girls to measure up to the impossible ought to be a challenge to their teachers to solve the vexing problem of what to give them and how to give it. The larger measure of failure is on the side of the teacher and the school. (91)

Reflecting a long-term trend of increased retention in high school and not just the dim prospect of finding work during the mid-1930s, Roosevelt High School had in all four of its grades pupils who might earlier have dropped out. In general, there were more students in high schools and more older students. As Center and Persons extended their testing (with the Iowa Silent Reading Test) to the whole student body at Roosevelt, it became apparent to them that students who could not read at their grade level were being passed along from junior to senior high school and graduating from high school. According to their data, 64 percent of the first-term entrants were deficient in reading skill, "large percentages" of students in each grade were performing below the norm, and 38 percent of the graduating class "were below standard" (14). To Center, these findings meant not only that something was wrong with English instruction, but that the schools were allowing students to graduate even though they could not read well enough to learn the material that they were supposed to have been taught. The view that public schools have become largely a holding place for youth, rather than an educative place, is very much with us today.

Center and Persons's *Teaching High-School Students to Read* presents a remarkable chapter in the history of English. Although it has not become a landmark study, it ought to be paired with Mina P. Shaughnessy's *Errors and Expectations* (1977) as two compassionate, yet disciplined, heroic accounts of English teaching during periods of enormous cultural stress in the United States.

At the end of the federal experiment at Theodore Roosevelt High School, Center and Persons took their methods and commitment to New York University, opening a Reading Clinic in the Division of General Education. The clinic (eventually renamed the Reading Institute) was meant to be a pilot program, but lasted for fifteen years. Among its divisions was a Reading School, consisting of a Lower School for school-age children and an Upper School for young adults (aged fifteen to twenty-five). As with the federal project at Roosevelt, Center and Persons grounded their methods in science and the psychology of learning (using Rorschach tests and the Thematic

Apperception Test, for example, and even recommending consultations with endrocrinologists) and their approach in the conviction that "children are entitled to develop within the framework of their inalienable rights"—that is, whether a superior student or an inferior student, whether physically or emotionally troubled or not, a child lived "in a literate civilization, and the obligation to read rested on him heavily. And the obligation to teach him to read rested on his teacher" (Center 1952, 293).

In Center's retrospective account of the Reading Clinic, which she codirected with Persons, and the Reading School, where for fifteen years she supervised teachers and taught in the evening program for adults, it is clear that her faith in the educability of all children and the preeminence she gave to reading never wavered:

> Most of the difficulties and complications that children endure could be avoided. That observation may seem platitudinous, but so much is at stake it can not be repeated too often if the repetition could bring about action that might lessen the woes of childhood. The welfare of children is determined largely by the intelligence and unselfish affection of parents, and by the professional skill and generous service of the teaching profession. . . . It is a fortunate thing that attention today is centered on reading, but . . . a teacher of reading must be concerned with everything that concerns a child—his physical well-being, his intellectual development, his emotional maturity, his social relationships, and his moral sense . . . . The Reading Clinic with its various services was designed to be a pilot institution, to demonstrate that what was done for a small group of students should in time be done for all boys and girls, if they are to achieve their complete maturity. Perhaps when the country awakens to the realization that children are its most valuable asset, barring none, perhaps funds for their needs will be provided, even though it means spending less on what is useless and destructive. (298)

The asperity with which Center criticized government spending and the compassion she had for children must appeal to us in our time.

On the other hand, Stella Center's reliance on IQ tests and other scientific methods (the endocrine treatments may remind us of the Ritalin prescribed in more recent days to quell hyperactivity) and such photographs as students practicing "rhythmical eye movements" may disturb some of us today. However, we should remember that progressive teachers of the 1920s–30s welcomed science. The "mismeasure of man," as Stephen Gould was to say, had yet to be perceived. In general, Center seems to have been an early and lasting enthusiast of technology and advances in scientific knowledge: in her presidential address of 1932 she even forecast optimistically the advent of television (and so it is fitting that television brought her the moonwalk just before her death). In her 1947 report titled "The Council's Awareness of Reading," she pointed out that besides long-standing concern for the aesthetics of reading, for motivating people to read, and for comprehension, the NCTE convention was seeing a new interest in physiological, psychological, and even psychiatric aspects of reading, such as the relation of vision to reading efficiency and emotional blocking, which was proof, Center declared, that the Council was seeking a scientific basis for sound procedures in teaching basic reading skills (142). It seems likely that Center would be fascinated by our recent research on writing and reading anxiety, including the use of protocols (see, for instance, Rose 1985 and Selfe 1986), and by the various uses to which both learning-disabled and all other students may put computers.

The current feminist impetus in English has made us sensitive to gender-related topics in our research and classrooms. Center's work indicated her sensitivity to one topic still of interest. Although she discussed both boys and girls at Roosevelt High School, the bulk of the data, including the case studies, had to do with boys. The frontispiece to *Teaching High School Students to Read* also depicted a boy reading. Although *Practices in Reading and Thinking* was addressed to girls and boys, the chief examples of why we must read and the "true story," complete with photograph and reading graphs, were of boys. We may infer that the majority of the problem readers Center saw were boys, not girls. Indeed, in her account of the Reading Institute at New York University, she confirmed this fact and attempted to explain it: "The Clinic had a preponderance of boys; yet that fact must not be construed as a reflection on their intelligence.... In the United States, boys are subjected to a great deal of pressure by their parents, a procedure that often defeats itself. Boys have more sensitiveness than they are usually credited with having" (Center 1952, 285–86). In Center's day, secondary schoolteachers did have a new population of older boys in their classrooms, for more boys were going to secondary school than in the past (see Scharf 1980, 72). In noting that boys had more difficulty with reading than girls did, Center voiced an observation made by others as well, both earlier and later and even today (see Segel 1986). Why females seem to be better at reading, and at English in general, is a topic, or as Ann Fausto-Sterling would say, a myth, about gender of importance to us now, when the image of English as a "feminine" subject is being reinforced by the increasing proportion of women not only majoring in English and teaching writing but receiving doctoral degrees as well.

During the first four decades of the twentieth century, of course, the interest in the academic performance of boys and young men was bound up with larger issues of gender, prestige, and money: belief in the ill effects women's tutelage had on male development, desire to raise the status of the teaching profession by diminishing its association with women, and preference in a time of job scarcity and retrenchment for hiring and retaining men rather than women, be those women married or single. Today our emphasis is on enhancing the status of women. We are newly concerned, for instance, with pay equity, appropriate role models, and such problems as managing a career along with a marriage. As we review the history of our predecessors in English, we will do well to remember that when Stella Stewart Center entered her profession, a female career teacher not only was routinely paid less than a male teacher for comparable work but was expected to remain single. In 1920, 90 percent of female teachers were single; in 1930 the figure was 80 percent (Scharf 1980, 75). Yet although women teachers were supposed to be single (in some states, the contracts demanded this condition), a prevalent image of the spinster schoolteacher was derogatory precisely because she had not married. Married women made their inroads in the midst of arguments at the expense of their unwed sisters: it was "normal" for women to marry, and it was a normal woman who was wanted in the classroom, not a twisted old maid deprived of sexual and maternal fulfillment (see Scharf 1980, 79–83). Under such a conception of the female gender, it cannot have been easy for a single woman in the 1930s to have held on to her dignity and self-esteem, let alone to her job.

Stella Center, a single woman, does not give us many images of herself in her publications. Only through Barbara Sullivan's story in the *Tift College Bulletin* do we see a woman who frequently traveled abroad, collected and inherited antiques and art, lived in graciousness, and enjoyed visits with long-term women friends. However, Center's view of what teachers should be is abundantly evident. The classroom was a place of work: "The atmosphere of the Clinic was serious and at the same time cheerful. Everybody worked and demonstrated daily the therapeutic value of work. There was no sentimentality; there was no coddling; work was assigned and work was done" (Center 1952, 293). Teachers were responsible, along with parents, for the welfare of children and were to be concerned with "everything that concerns a child," but teachers were not ersatz parents: they had "professional skill" and gave "generous service" (298). That Center valued her work and her colleagues is clear in this rare autobiographical moment in her retrospective account of the Reading Institute:

> The fifteen years I spent as director of the Reading Clinic and the Reading School of New York University telescoped into a brief span experiences that represented chronologically many times that number of years. It would be dishonest to claim a record of uniform successes. The work was difficult, the hours usually twice as long as a normal working day; the schedule permitted few vacations or holidays; the demands on my sympathy and emotions were at times excessive; yet perspective prompts me to express gratitude that I had an experience allowed few teachers. I recall with appreciation those members of my staff who were steadfast in their belief in young people's possibilities and who cheerfully undertook the seemingly impossible, assured that the impossible is often surprisingly possible where young people are concerned. (291-92)

Perspective prompts us to reflect on Center's professionalism in a time when women's work was blatantly devalued and spinster teachers were cruelly mocked.

Stella Center's work for NCTE included significant initiatives in publication. Through a letter-writing campaign, she herself raised the funds to make possible the publication of Sterling Leonard's *Current English Usage* (Smith and Squire n.d., 15). This fund-raising marked a shift in policy that Center engineered. Instead of distributing free copies of publications to members, an act that prohibited the publication of anything lengthy, under Center's initiative the Council negotiated a contract with an outside publisher for commercial distribution; Council publications then became available for a price (15). This new publication policy allowed more extensive publication and brought revenue to the Council.

Furthermore, as Council president, Center defended, on radio and in the newspaper, the perspective on language that Leonard's study promoted ("Usage Study," 160-61; "Current Usage," 594). Its view of language was in step with her own modernity. She welcomed the automobile, the talking picture, and the radio, for instance, because she believed humans could and should put machines to good use in building a community: "Our teaching of correct usage must recognize the influence of the language practices of the travelling majority, touring this continent and converting it into one vast neighborhood" (Center 1933, 101). Language was part of her vision of the United States: "If the social unification of America is to be accomplished, it must be done by travelers who are articulate and who can communicate effectively. The chief instrument of social adjustment and integration is the language of the group used acceptably" (101).

The social integration of minorities such as Jews, Italians, and other recent immigrants from Europe was, as demonstrated by Center's work at Theodore Roosevelt High School, a challenge she tried to meet. Whether she ever worked directly with black students and teachers goes unmentioned. Center did, however, preside at the first NCTE annual convention in which racial segregation became an issue and not just a fact. Although the details of the decision are not clear, in the unpublished account of the 1932 Memphis convention by Dora V. Smith (who was there) and James Squire, once Center was alerted to the "local mores," that is, Jim Crow laws that prevented blacks from entering a hotel for whites, as the convention hotel was, Center's solution was to invite black teachers "in the area to hold a separate meeting and to select any four of the regular convention speakers that they would like to hear" (Smith and Squire, 6). With our present-day consciousness of the history of black and white race relations in the United States, we may indeed feel troubled by the spectacle of segregated teachers listening, separate and unequal, to Center's call for teachers to become "responsive to the forces that dignify human life and contribut[e] to the social progress of a world changing, we hope, for the better" (Center 1933, 108) and her charge to teachers to direct "the forces and trends in contemporary American life" and not to live "remote in academic seclusion, preoccupied with traditions only" (107).

Incomplete though her vision of social unification in America's "vast neighborhood" may have been, Center did believe firmly in the principle of a "cross-section of American society" in the classroom (see Center and Persons 1937, 3; Center 1952, 298). Throughout her work on reading, she made it quite clear that however difficult English instruction had become and however complex the problem of eradicating illiteracy might be, English teachers were failing to use methods and materials that would increase the chances of the less-able students to develop their ability to read and therefore to become educated. The force of Center's reiterated pronouncements suggests strongly that she was at odds with others in her profession whose philosophy of learning was not based on Center's work ethic. She was at odds, too, with those who did not share her view of how the teacher could fulfill the purpose of enabling students to "proceed under their own power," a phrase and its variants repeated often in her writing: "The amount of reading retardation in schools, colleges, and universities has slowed up learning and resulted in a policy of educational appeasement to be deplored.... It is unfortunate that 'Reading is fun' was for many years the slogan of the schools. The implication of the slogan ignores the fact that reading is an art whose mastery requires patient practice and study and analysis" (280–81). For Center, a child became self-reliant and successful in school, leisure, and employment by developing the ability to comprehend different kinds of discourse, to think and judge, to converse about issues. It was an ability to be developed as a skill and set of habits. Reading is thinking, she said again and again. Today, as we emphasize the other half of verbal literacy, "writing is thinking" is the more familiar cry, and the argument is against reducing literacy to a set of skills, to practice in Standard Written English. Center would agree: she wanted a "correlated" curriculum in which spelling and punctuation, for instance, were important, not as isolated skills but as aspects of reading as it converged with writing.

Of all the convictions that made up Stella Stewart Center's philosophy of English teaching, one that may seem so obvious that we neglect to attend to its implications is this: "The point which is dazzlingly clear in the whole problem is that the high school has found no way to educate the boys and girls who cannot read" (Center and Persons 1937, 90). The materials of education require one to read; therefore, unless schools change the vehicle of instruction to a nonliterate medium, to become educated in school and college, one must be a competent reader. Today, particularly in the colleges, we may speak about being "invented by the university" (see Bartholomae 1985; Bartholomae and Petrosky 1986), that is, learning the ideational and rhetorical conventions of academic discourse in order to become members of its "interpretive community." This is an epistemological theory different from Center's view of learning to comprehend the purpose of different types of readings. Nevertheless, there is a point of agreement in the two convictions not shared by expressionist schools of thought: those who cannot participate in the discourse of school are forever excluded from the power its discourse brings.

Today, when long-standing racism and new waves of immigrants challenge the attitudes and resources of our public schools and institutions of higher education, when in some states English teachers cannot find jobs and college writing programs hire masses of underpaid adjuncts, when the "functional illiteracy" of high school graduates, athletes, and a whole underclass of workers is the subject of public service advertising, when elitist education is more elite than ever, when drug dealing has surpassed gum chewing as a common problem, when universities have large remedial reading and writing programs that by state mandate give no credit, when women continue to do devalued "women's work"—today, Stella Stewart Center's work on reading is more than a dated piece of history. It is a reminder that our foremothers in English studies have long labored hard to realize a school for the people and to foster a sense of dignity in the profession of teaching. It is unending labor.

And with all due respect to the forefathers of English, it is the foremothers whose chapters must be witnessed by teachers of reading and writing today, whether professors in English departments or in English education programs or secondary school teachers or aspirants to the teaching profession. For throughout the twentieth century, women have dominated the field of schoolteaching, and they have come to dominate college composition. Most of what these women do is ephemeral; it lies, for good or for ill, in the practices of the classroom, sometimes remembered, always influential in one way or another, but transitory and unrecorded. We cannot read their chapters. Stella Stewart Center's publications and records allow us to recognize her leadership, her talent for organization, her philosophy of learning, her methods, her contribution to the efforts of the National Council of Teachers of English. They also give us a glimpse of her teaching. For although the two photographs that show Stella Center seated alone in repose, reading, are indeed fitting bookends for the career of a woman dedicated to the value of reading, her full significance to us may be brought out by another image, this one a verbal description by Eleanor Baykin, a journalist who had been Center's student as well as a Reading Institute teacher under her supervision: "As a teacher, Dr. Center was an electric current. I shall never forget hearing her give a lesson to some slow readers on a paragraph in her book, *Experiences in Reading and Thinking*, describing a nail-making machine. She made the production of the stream of bright nails an exciting event. A brilliant and distinguished woman" (1969). Nails, not Shakespeare; "slow" readers, not honors students; but "electrical" all the same to those students and the teachers she trained. In practice as well as in theory, Stella Stewart Center taught students "the art of reading so that they can proceed under their own power to acquire an education" (Center 1952, xix). As we learn to read her history, so may she teach us.

Works Cited

Applebee, Arthur N. 1974. *Tradition and Reform in the Teaching of English: A History.* Urbana, Ill.: National Council of Teachers of English.

Bartholomae, David. 1985. "Inventing the University." In *When a Writer Can't Write: Studies in Writer's Block and Other Composing-Process Problems,* edited by Mike Rose, 134–63. New York: Guilford.

Bartholomae, David, and Anthony Petrosky. 1986. *Facts, Artifacts, and Counterfacts: Theory and Method for a Reading and Writing Course.* Upper Montclair, N.J.: Boynton/Cook.

Baykin, Eleanor. 25 January 1969. Letter to Robert F. Hogan, executive secretary of NCTE.

Berlin, James A. 1987. *Rhetoric and Reality: Writing Instruction in American Colleges, 1900-1985.* Carbondale, Ill.: Southern Illinois University Press.

Center, Stella S. 1933. "The Responsibility of Teachers of English in Contemporary American Life." *English Journal* 22: 97-108.

———. 1947. "The Council's Awareness of Reading." *English Journal* 36: 141-42.

———. 1952. *The Art of Book Reading.* New York: Charles Scribner's Sons.

Center, Stella Stewart, ed. 1920. *The Worker and His Work: Readings in Present-Day Literature Presenting Some of the Activities by Which Men and Women the World Over Make a Living.* Philadelphia: J. B. Lippincott.

Center, Stella S., and Max J. Herzberg. 1932. *Leisure Reading.* Chicago: National Council of Teachers of English.

Center, Stella S., and Gladys L. Persons. 1937. *Teaching High-School Students to Read: A Study of Retardation in Reading.* New York: Appleton-Century-Crofts.

———. 1942. *Practices in Reading and Thinking.* New York: Macmillan.

"Current Usage Results Broadcast." 1933. *English Journal* 22: 594.

Herzberg, Max J., and Stella S. Center. 1930. *Books for Home Reading.* Chicago: National Council of Teachers of English.

Hook, J. N. 1979. *A Long Way Together: A Personal View of NCTE's First Sixty-Seven Years.* Urbana: NCTE.

"The National Council, 1911-1936." 1936. *English Journal,* 25: 806-36.

"Our Own Who's Who." 1933. *English Journal,* 22: 166.

Rose, Mike, ed. 1985. *When a Writer Can't Write: Studies in Writer's Block and Other Composing-Process Problems.* New York: Guilford.

Scharf, Lois. 1980. *To Work and to Wed: Female Employment, Feminism, and the Great Depression.* Westport: Greenwood.

Segel, Elizabeth. 1986. "'As the Twig Is Bent . . .': Gender and Childhood Reading." In *Gender and Reading: Essays on Readers, Texts, and Contexts,* edited by Elizabeth A. Flynn and Patrocinio P. Schweickart, 165-86. Baltimore: Johns Hopkins.

Selfe, Cynthia L. 1986. "Reading as a Writing Strategy: Two Case Studies." In *Convergences: Transactions in Reading and Writing,* edited by Bruce T. Peterson, 46-63. Urbana: NCTE.

Shaughnessy, Mina P. 1977. *Errors and Expectations: A Guide for the Teacher of Basic Writing.* New York: Oxford University Press.

Smith, Dora V. 1969. Letter to Robert F. Hogan, Executive Secretary of NCTE, February 10.

Smith, Dora V., and James R. Squire. "The National Council of Teachers of English, 1911-1968." Unpublished draft of an article prepared for a *Dictionary of Education.*

Sullivan, Barbara. 1965. "A Great Lady Comes Home." *Tift College Bulletin,* January, 6-7.

Tyack, David, Robert Lowe, and Elisabeth Hansot. 1984. *Public Schools in Hard Times: The Great Depression and Recent Years.* Cambridge: Harvard University Press.

"Usage Study Gets Wide Publicity." 1933. *English Journal*, 22: 160–61.

4 Dora V. Smith: A Legacy for the Future

Virginia R. Monseau, Youngstown State University

Dora V. Smith
1893-1985

Such a daunting task—attempting to summarize the career of Dora V. Smith. How does one accurately portray in a single chapter this remarkable woman who has left such an indelible mark on the English teaching profession? Perhaps the best way is the simplest—to discuss Dora V. Smith the professional, whose work foreshadowed many of the current trends in English education, and Dora V. Smith the person, whose indomitable spirit energized all with whom she came in contact. Reading what she has written, talking to those who knew her well, and listening to her tape-recorded voice as she discussed teaching, teachers, and students reveals a woman whose personal qualities are inherent in her professional philosophy. In his introduction to *Dora V. Smith: Selected Essays*, Robert C. Pooley wrote:

> Important as she is as researcher and author, it is Dora V. Smith the person who delights all who knew her. Possessed of a happy, outgoing nature, a genuine and all-embracing liking for people, a loyal and unselfish giving of her time and energy to friends and students, she has a radiance that attracts and holds admirers. But beneath this genial exterior there is a firm and staunch character, strong of mind and powerful of will, eager to form principles and convictions and to fight for them with energy and determination. She has done much because she knows how to get things done. (D. Smith 1964, vii)

And so this chapter will focus on Smith's "knowing" and "doing," connecting her work to much of the research and scholarship being done in English education today, and on her "being," suggesting a true symbiosis of the personal with the professional.

69

In order to appreciate fully the evolution of Dora V. Smith's career, it is necessary to start at its beginning, a teaching position in Long Prairie, Minnesota, where she taught English and history from 1916 to 1917 after graduating Phi Beta Kappa from the University of Minnesota. Three years later, in 1919, she earned a master's degree in English from the same university, titling her thesis "A Study of the Use of Accident in the Novels of Thomas Hardy." Nine years later, in 1928, she earned her doctorate, also from the University of Minnesota. Her dissertation, "Class Size and the Efficiency of Instruction in English," examined a topic on which she was to write prolifically in ensuing years. Smith was teaching at the University of Minnesota's University High School at the time, and she used as her research subjects the students of Rewey Belle Inglis, who was then the English Department chair at the school. During the 1920-1921 school year Smith taught at St. George's College in London, England, followed later (1928-1929) by a stint at Lincoln School of Columbia University, where she taught such noteworthy students as Winthrop Rockefeller and the Guggenheim children. She then began a teaching career at the University of Minnesota which was to last until her retirement in 1958.

Dora Smith's parents came to Minnesota from Scotland, and she attributed much of her interest in English to them. In a 1968 interview with Robert Boyle of the University of Minnesota Department of Radio and Television, she commented, "We had access to a good many things that had been written for children, and somehow it seemed a normal part of life to enjoy books and literature." This interest grew throughout her education in the Minneapolis public schools and directly influenced her decision to pursue her three academic degrees—B.A., M.A., and Ph.D.—in English and English education.

A "progressive" in the truest sense of the word, Smith believed that the child should be at the center of education, and her inaugural address upon beginning her presidency of the National Council of Teachers of English in 1936 soundly reflected her beliefs. Titling her speech "American Youth and English," she discussed our true mission as English teachers, as she saw it: "to build a meaningful program" by always keeping in mind the needs and interests of our students. Deploring uninformed criticism of English and English teaching, she began her speech with words that may sound all too familiar to us today:

> It is a wholesome experience to be teaching English when all the world questions what we are doing and why we are doing it. There are those who believe us so far behind the times in our purposes and our program that it will take us fifty years to catch

up with a modern era. On the other hand, there are those who tremble lest we have thrown ancient standards to the winds, who warn us that boys and girls will never speak and write as they used to do until we return to the parsing and analysis of former days; and they will never read as they are reputed once to have read in the halcyon days of fifty years ago until we restore the minute analysis of a few great classics.

In the midst of this attack and counterattack upon our platform it is of supreme importance that we, as individual members of the National Council of Teachers of English, should know where we are going and be able to justify our course; that once having chosen the way, we may keep our vision clear despite the smoke screens of emotional criticism which tend to blur the path. (1937, 99)

At the end of her speech she reminded her audience that education "can be achieved only by taking boys and girls where they are and building gradually toward where we want them to be. . . . Forced development has never yet brought sturdy maturity" (112).

Dora Smith's interest in and knowledge of all facets of English teaching—language study, composition, reading, literature, and curriculum development—are evident in her writing and in her speeches. Though she was always true to her progressive philosophy, advocating active, experiential learning, she never sacrificed excellence and high standards to the gods of educational reform.

In her discussion of language development Smith echoed the ideas of people like Jean Piaget and John Dewey. For example, in her essay "Growth in Language Power as Related to Child Development," she emphasized that children search for meaning in their experiences as they interact with their environment (1964, 17). Her idea relates closely to Piaget's contention that children maintain what he calls "equilibrium" through interaction with their environment, forming the basic structures which contribute to intellectual development. Smith stressed that learning must have a relationship to life: "Defining lists of words on the blackboard, filling in blanks in exercises, and writing themes on topics which have little relationship to what is going on at the moment in school or at home can never be a substitute for development in the classroom of a wealth of opportunities for exploring the world in which children live and for stimulating them to thought and discussion concerning it" (17). Smith's comment is obviously similar to that of Dewey and other progressives who advocated active learning through experience, and it is remarkably akin to the philosophy behind today's whole language movement. In his book *What's Whole in Whole Language?* Kenneth Goodman asserts that in whole language programs, "what happens in school supports and expands what happens outside of school" (1986, 8). Smith recognized the importance of this kind of language learning over sixty years ago.

Smith's stance on the role of formal grammar instruction in language study is also very clear. In "The Problem of Teaching Grammar," written in 1947, she commented on the importance of teaching English usage by continuous practice in what she called the "thought method," as opposed to the grammatical method of teaching, and cited the following example from a study as support:

> Suppose the sentences were: "All my life I have wanted to be a doctor. They do so much good in the world." The thought groups said, "A doctor cannot be 'they.' We must change 'they' to 'he' or revise the first sentence to read 'doctors.'" The second group approached the error in the same way, but learned in addition that "doctor" is the antecedent of the pronoun "they." Pronouns agree with their antecedents in number and gender. "Doctor" is singular. "They" is plural. The pronoun must be "he." The explanation, by the way, shows clearly what poor sentences can result from this kind of attack, for one would scarcely say, "All my life I have wanted to be a doctor. He does so much good in the world." (1964, 252-53)

Smith reported that the longer students were removed from instruction, the greater was the superiority of the thought approach, where students really had to understand the meaning of the sentence. Claiming that for some students grammatical science is actually a stumbling block to the mastery of language, Smith felt that only superior students profited from such study.

To further support her position, Smith pointed out one of the reasons why grammatical science affects usage so little: "In Latin, one must know the case of the nouns in order to get the meaning of the sentence. In English, one must get the meaning of the sentence in order to find out the case of the nouns: and after one has the meaning why should he bother to do so?" (265). She emphasized that we must get out of the clutches of Latin grammar and become students of our own language to see how it works.

That Dora V. Smith recognized and was writing about this problem in the 1940s is interesting in light of the fact that little progress seems to have been made in grammatical instruction since then. By and large, schools still prescribe traditional grammar, assuming it will help students become more precise users of the English language. Yet high school teachers, college professors, and employers continue to complain that young people do not know how to use the language well. A look at the English classroom may reveal, as Smith saw years ago, that students are getting little practice in classes where they sit passively listening to the language of the teacher. In calling for a reexamination of the relationship of sentence structure to meaning rather than to a set of prescribed rules based on another language, Smith was ahead of her time and a member of a small minority of educators with similar views.

True to her professional spirit, Smith obviously kept up with developments in the field of language instruction. In 1964, six years after her retirement, she wrote "Should We Pay Any Attention to the New Linguistics?" (1964), an essay about the role of the new linguistics (structural and transformational grammar) in classroom instruction. Because the new grammars were developed directly from an observation of English, Smith felt they helped students better understand how words work together to form sentences. She used as an example the fact that word order is used to convey meaning in English: "John hit Mary" is quite different from "Mary hit John." In the same way, "an awful pretty dress" is different from "a pretty awful dress." Traditional grammar, she pointed out, had little or nothing to say about word order because relationships in Latin are indicated by inflectional word endings. Because the English language is dynamic rather than static, Smith believed usage cannot be looked upon as a matter of right and wrong. Rather, it is a matter of what is acceptable and unacceptable at particular times and in particular circumstances.

Further evidence of the progression of Smith's thinking on the matter of language instruction is her discussion of dialectal differences, an issue that gained importance in the 1960s. Though she saw the necessity of helping students adjust to the language of the school and to society's accepted norms, she also stressed the importance of accepting the dialect or usage of their community. In this way students could become aware that they habitually vary their speech patterns, depending upon their audience, and that they must add the dialect preferred in school to their repertoire.

It is not surprising that Dora V. Smith's writings would reflect the ideas of people like Piaget and Dewey, for they were her contemporaries. What is remarkable, however, is that she also touched upon concepts that have only recently been "discovered" by modern theorists. Still discussing language growth, she turned her attention to writing, emphasizing that error is individual and must be treated as such. She commented on the importance of diagnosing and treating the causes of error rather than using meaningless drills to help improve student writing (1964, 53). Over three decades after Smith's essay was written, Mina P. Shaughnessy won acclaim for her book

Errors and Expectations, which addressed the same problem. At the end of her introduction to the book, Shaughnessy stated, "A teacher who would work with BW [basic writing] students might well begin by trying to understand the logic of their mistakes in order to determine at what point or points along the developmental path error should or can become a subject for instruction" (1977, 13). Dora V. Smith was evidently doing this very thing years before.

As a progressive, Smith saw composition as a means of socialization—of enriching the experience and broadening the interests of students (whom she always referred to as "boys and girls"). In 1927 she published a book in collaboration with Edward Harlan Webster entitled *Teaching English in Junior High School*. The title is a bit deceiving, if we think of "English" as encompassing literature, composition, and grammar. This book is entirely about the teaching of writing, and the social aspects of composition teaching are discussed in nearly every chapter, with one entire chapter devoted to and entitled "The Group Method." In the preface to the book the authors wrote:

> The group method supplies the machinery for socializing within a class period all the compositions that the children write in and for that period. This method provides in the interpretation of composition—as the little theater does in dramatic presentation—an opportunity for an intimate, close relationship between the entertainers and the entertained. It produces a friendly spirit of cooperation and helpfulness rarely found in procedures that require the attention of the whole class. Its value in producing just the right atmosphere for reading and discussion makes it an indispensable adjunct to nearly every lesson in literature and composition. (Webster and Smith 1927, v)

Webster and Smith described a classroom where writing assignments grew out of natural situations, like the children's discussion with their parents of some of their early childhood experiences. They demonstrated the importance of socialization, as the students divided into small groups and read their compositions to each other, commenting upon one another's papers and selecting the best essays to be read aloud to the entire class.

What is so remarkable to the modern teacher of writing in reading this book is that over sixty years ago Webster and Smith were advocating methods of teaching composition that are being rediscovered by theorists and teachers today. Though this realization reinforces the old axiom that "there is nothing new under the sun," it does give cause for wondering why such obviously sensible methods have not been more widely used by English teachers over the years.

We speak today of the importance of audience and purpose in writing. Webster and Smith, though they did not use these exact terms, were essentially talking about the same things. They could very well have been the forerunners of modern theorists like James Moffett, who goes a step further in stressing the importance of socialization in the writing class, where he sees conversational dialogue as verbal collaboration, which goes hand-in-hand with cognitive collaboration to promote awareness of problems like egocentricity in writing (1968, 73).

In a 1960 essay, Smith wrote about teaching language as communication, lamenting the fact that not enough writing was being done in the schools. She suggested that instruction in formal grammar took up valuable time that would be better spent by having students do more writing. To support her claim, she cited a report from the Modern Language Association which stated that research clearly indicated no correlation between the understanding of grammatical science and effectiveness of expression or correctness of usage. To underscore her point about the absurdity of substituting "formalities" for practice in real communication, she gave the example of a tenth-grade honor student who was required to write 137 sentences containing adverbial clauses. Said Smith, "Apparently, if twenty sentences are enough for the average pupil, the gifted, who must be taught to work hard, need 137 to establish the pattern!" (1964, 256).

It is obvious that Dora V. Smith would be entirely at home in today's composition classroom. Her advanced ideas and modern methods would fit well into today's discussion of rhetorical strategies and collaborative discourse. As early as 1932, in an article entitled "Teaching versus Testing in Composition," she was calling attention to the problems that existed in the teaching of writing:

> It is generally conceded that the teaching of composition with its attendant burden of paper correcting has to its credit more nervous breakdowns in the teaching profession than any other phase of instruction in English. Quantities of red ink, obliterating whatever of sense or of human value the content may originally have had, bear witness on the part of boys and girls to a naive and blissful unconcern for the mysteries of comma and semicolon. At the same time, they speak with tragic forcefulness of hours of discouragement and toil among teachers conscientious and self-sacrificing in their earnest effort to improve the writing of the pupils entrusted to their care. . . .
> What I should like to propose to you . . . is that this situation exists because composition as it has been practiced in the past has been for the most part a *testing* rather than a *teaching* process. The teacher announces a topic or finds one in the experiences of boys

and girls, and sends them home to produce a composition.... The technique [is] the same in every instance: to test the pupils' ability to write without the assistance of the teacher, to analyze the results, and to reprove the pupils *afterward* for what they did not know, instead of preventing by one's own preliminary teaching the errors which one knew in advance were bound to occur. Everybody is testing composition. Whose business is it to teach it? (1932, 22)

She went on to point out that "the procedure is vicious for many reasons," stating: "In the first place, it ignores the essential factor of composition, the stimulation of thought, the provoking of ideas, the putting them together into an organic whole.... In the second place, it violates all the known laws of how men learn" (23).

Not one to offer criticism without suggesting a remedy, however, Smith then described an alternative assignment to "How I Spent My Summer Vacation" which enticed students to create an advertisement for the summer camp they attended (a common summer pastime in Minnesota) and had them vie with each other for the best-written, most pictorially vivid ad. In the process they discussed sensory words, colorful verbs, and well-placed adjectives, resulting in a piece of writing created and completed in the classroom by interested students who were proud of their work. Smith obviously understood the importance of creating authentic rhetorical situations which enabled students to write with authority.

Dora Smith wrote many articles on various aspects of composition, and her foresight is equally apparent in her discussion of literature. She frequently wrote about reading interests, suggesting that teachers pay more attention to the psychology of childhood and adolescence in selecting books for children. Writing in 1939, she described a 1928 study which revealed that only one-fourth of the students understood the average classic that was required reading in high school (1964, 105). Yet teachers persisted and still do persist in presenting these books to students. Smith observed that from the fifth grade on, the great "divorce" begins between the normal interests of childhood and the prescribed course of reading. She emphasized the need for teachers to understand adolescent longings and how students seek books to satisfy them. "Above all," she stated, "they need to understand how inadequate to the normal needs of the junior high school, for instance, are the emotional patterns of *Evangeline* and *The Man Without a Country*" (101).

Smith also wrote frequently about literature as aesthetic experience, where she leaned strongly toward reader-response theory in her views. As G. Robert Carlsen commented: "She looked at literature as a transaction taking place between the work and the reader so that the reader was every bit as important as the work. Louise Rosenblatt had just written the first edition of *Literature as Exploration*, echoing the philosophy that Dora V was presenting in a more concrete form" (1984, 28). Smith herself underscored the importance of personal reaction in reading: "Appreciation begins within," she wrote. "It is both emotional and intellectual. It is determined largely by the experiential background of the individual which makes it possible for him to enter into the aesthetic experience with enjoyment and understanding" (1964, 107). Smith claimed that teachers approached the literary experience backwards, giving students a term like *simile* and asking them to look for examples in the text. She saw this technique as promoting facility in what she called a "literary stunt" rather than increasing appreciation for the work of literature. "Books are not written to illustrate literary techniques," she commented, "but to bring intimate revelation of human experience" (108).

Dora V. Smith had a strong interest in books for children and adolescents. In 1936 she wrote of her disenchantment with the narrowly prescriptive curricula of America's schools, suggesting improvement in the teaching of literature:

> . . . we can begin by determining to approach literature as it is approached by intelligent, cultured people in everyday life. We can put pleasure in reading first; we can aim constantly at enjoyment and the development of hunger for more. We can test the success of our program by the desire of boys and girls to continue more reading of the same sort under their own direction. We can associate books with ever-widening interests and increased understanding of human nature and experience . . . and relate literature to the limitless interests of life itself. (Quoted in Applebee 1974, 132)

In her search for the best in children's literature, Smith traveled the world for an entire year in 1956, looking for books that would accurately depict the cultural heritage of children from different lands. She explained in her interview with Robert Boyle that "there are a great many good books today which reveal children of different countries to each other. . . . a child in India is revealed in a piece of fiction to American children, and in that piece of fiction children discover that the child in India is not very different from themselves" (D. Smith 1968). During her sabbatical year Smith opened the first book fair in Turkey and was responsible for introducing American books to children in Pakistan, India, China, and countless other countries.

Even after her retirement in 1958 Smith continued her interest in children's literature, publishing *Fifty Years of Children's Books* (1963), a pleasant, chronological trip through children's literature from 1910, "Moral Tales from Earlier Generations," to 1960, "Children's Books in a Bursting World." Interspersed with illustrations from various works of children's literature, this is an admittedly personal evaluation of what Smith considered "significant" literature for children. Her purpose in writing the book was to bring "happy recollections and a few new facts to those who have enjoyed a lifetime of reading and [to encourage] those new to the field to taste its joys" (vi).

Dora Smith's work with children's literature naturally led to her interest in literature for adolescents. As Arthur N. Applebee pointed out, the first serious professional attention to adolescent literature came from Smith's concern that literature teachers gave too little thought to the literary interests of high school students (1974, 155). She believed that it was unfair to students and to their teachers to send out from the colleges and universities people trained only in Chaucer, Milton, and Browning. In an effort to do something about this problem, she instituted the first course in adolescent literature at the University of Minnesota, aiming to supplement the training in the classics given by the English Department. This course may well have been the first of its kind ever offered at any college or university in the country.

Stanley Kegler, a former student of Smith's, described how she would come into the Saturday morning class with her assistant behind her, each lugging a huge cart full of books to be used in her lectures and as part of her hands-on instruction. "There would be a hundred people in this room. [They] would be clamoring for books. Then at the end of the hour people were expected to take some of the books home, read them, and bring them back the following week. And they did. They were all willing. She left with an empty cart, usually" (1988).

Smith had extensive booklists for both her children's and adolescent literature classes, containing titles of novels, short stories, poems, plays, essays, and biographies. Part of her list was divided into "Books for Boys" and "Books for Girls," a questionable distinction today, but a seemingly logical one at the time. The list also contained special sections entitled "Biography of Women" and "Life Stories of Famous Women," perhaps indicating an effort on her part to help students see that achievement knows no gender boundaries.

Though Smith had organized her adolescent literature course by 1930, it took a decade for her program to generate interest. The 1940s, however, eventually saw the development of this new literary genre, and more attention was paid to the need for such a course. In the 1950s

Dwight Burton, one of Smith's students, became a leader in the movement to legitimize adolescent literature, devoting considerable attention to the genre during his editorship of *English Journal* (Applebee 1974, 155). Stephen Dunning, one of Burton's students, continued to promote interest in adolescent fiction, writing a pioneering dissertation on the adolescent novel in 1959.

Back in the days of Dora V. Smith, adolescent books were commonly called "junior novels," a term which may have contributed to some of the poor attitudes toward the books. Certain words do carry negative connotations, and in the case of "junior novel," the implication was that these books somehow fell short of the "real" novel and were therefore to be taken less seriously. While it is true that many of the adolescent novels written during the 1940s and 1950s were rather shallow and formulaic, it is also true that there were exceptions, such as Maureen Daly's *Seventeenth Summer*, Esther Forbes's *Johnny Tremain*, and Florence Means's *The Moved Outers*. In spite of the fact that Smith encountered resistance from critics about the nature of adolescent literature, she continued to promote the genre because she believed in its importance to the adolescent's social adjustment and psychological development. If she were still alive today, she might be delighted to see that the genre now referred to as "young adult literature" has come a long way and has a bright future. As excellent authors create works of quality and sophistication for young adults, more and more people are beginning to view this genre as a body of literature with value beyond its sociological or popular appeal.

Dora Smith may have been one of the first people to see the connection between the teaching of literature and the teaching of reading. As today's whole language approach takes hold, the teaching of reading moves closer and closer to what Smith envisioned. And she was anything but reticent about her views. In a 1955 article she openly criticized Rudolf Flesch and his highly acclaimed book, *Why Johnny Can't Read and What You Can Do about It* (1955). In her rebuke, entitled "What Do We Want 'Johnny' to Do? To Pronounce Words or to Read?" Smith condemned Flesch's phonetic approach to reading instruction, charging him with being uninformed and sloppy in his research. She summarized her criticism by referring to an article appearing in the *London Times Educational Supplement* on 14 August 1953 ("Backward Readers") that attributed retardation to a process of "barking at print." Smith called this "a very apt description of the method Dr. Flesch is advocating. When such children reach the modern school, we think they can read, but they can't. They only make noises at print" (D. Smith 1955, 16).

Over and over again in her writing Smith emphasized the importance of reading for meaning. We hear in her words the voices of contemporary theorists like psycholinguist Frank Smith, who declares that reading is not a sound activity: "Phonics works if you know what a word is likely to be in the first place," says Frank Smith (1985, 54). "Readers can recognize words and comprehend text without decoding to sound at all. . . . We recognize words in the same way we recognize all the other familiar objects in our world . . . 'on sight'" (55). Smith goes on to say: "It is not necessary to say what a word is to comprehend its meaning. Quite the reverse, often it is necessary to comprehend the meaning of a word before you can say what it is. In other words, *meaning* is directly related to the spelling of words rather than sound. How otherwise could we be aware of many spelling mistakes?" (56). Clearly Dora Smith would agree with Frank Smith, deploring the fact that "the child is not asked whether he knows the meaning of the words, but he is merely to learn to sound out the letters . . . . sounding out each separate letter in a word is bound to interfere with the process of seeing the word at a glance and getting its meaning instantly" (D. Smith 1955, 13).

One of Smith's major concerns was that teachers were ill-prepared to recognize and deal with student difficulties in reading. In a presentation to a discussion group on remedial reading at the University of Minnesota (1936), she cited six major developments in the field of reading which she felt were "vitally related to classroom method":

1. the relationship of experience to meaning
2. a growing recognition of the value of extensive as opposed to intensive reading in the development of word meanings
3. the importance of motive in reading
4. the utilization of natural cross-curricular course materials in determining solutions to reading problems
5. attention to individual differences
6. the importance of teacher education in keeping abreast of developments in the field of reading research

Smith addressed individual aspects of these six developments in articles she wrote for various journals over the years. In one, "'Lose Not the Nightingale'—A Challenge and Counter-Challenge," she commented on the often-unchildlike nature of the reading curriculum:

> It is true that in numbers of schools in recent years there has been imposed upon children a curriculum most unchildlike in

nature, dealing in many instances with the means of life and not with its ends, encompassed on the north, south, east, and west by food, shelter, clothing, transportation, and communication—with the things of the spirit all but completely forgotten. I have myself visited schools within the last six months where boys and girls are in danger of spending the six years of the elementary school reading about nothing save the fire engine, the creamery, the grocery store, the railroad, the Indians, the Pilgrims, and the Dutch—no one of them a ruling passion in adult life any more than among children, and few of them calculated to give that hunger for more, without which lifelong association with good books is impossible. Not a bookshelf but has its *Story Book of Things We Use,* but on how few do we find *Winnie the Pooh,* whose ineffable spirit of joy in life burst forth in murmuring murmurs to himself "in a singing sort of way." The older boys and girls know Hans Brinker because he "teaches something about the Dutch," but they are on less familiar terms with Tom Sawyer, who (Heaven be praised!) correlates with nothing but a good time! (1938, 8)

The reading curriculum was not the only point of concern for Dora V. Smith, however. She spent most of her career studying and writing about the overall English curriculum in America's public schools. Her views about the teaching of literature, composition, and language were no doubt formed and strengthened by participation in various studies of English teaching over the years, one of the best known of which is her 1933 study of high schools. In her monograph *Instruction in English,* Smith analyzed 156 courses of study from 127 cities in 35 states. She had visited seventy schools that she felt offered an exceptional mixture of content and method. At the time of her survey, Smith found a mix of traditional and progressive approaches in teaching. Though the yearly list of college entrance texts no longer dominated English courses, as they did before 1900, 50 percent of the schools still presented a list of classic texts for study. Smith's research disclosed:

> Literature of English authorship takes an overwhelming lead in the classics taught in American high schools. *Silas Marner* ranks first and *Julius Caesar* second. . . . *The Idylls of the King, Ivanhoe,* and *The Tale of Two Cities* [sic] compete for third place. Five of the titles are dramas, and all of them are Shakespearean. Eighteen of the 30 titles are from English literature, 7 from American literature, 2 from other foreign sources and 3 from a combination of all. ("English Monograph," 408)

Comparing her results with a study done in 1890, Smith found that only one or two titles had vanished from the list of college entrance texts (1934, 114). The study revealed that although preparation for college was at the bottom of the list of objectives for courses of study, teachers were still teaching to college demands, in spite of the supposed movement away from such pedagogy. In her conferences with teachers throughout the country, Smith learned that they continued to labor under the fear of college requirements, real or imagined (Applebee 1974, 125-26).

Reading the results of Dora V. Smith's studies, we might ask, How far have we really come in half a century? Just as Smith and others struggled to introduce American and world literature into the narrowly prescriptive curricula of the time, so we struggle today to include literature by women and minorities and literature for adolescents in the courses of study still dominated by the classics. College entrance examinations still loom large on the educational horizon, and professional accountability is frequently questioned by those who believe the English teacher must keep alive our "literary heritage."

In a 1940 article entitled "Problems of Articulation in the Teaching of English," Smith explained why the curriculum must change to fit the times and the student population:

> In 1890 high-school pupils represented largely professional and clerical classes. Today an influx of boys and girls from laboring and industrial groups makes our enrolment [sic] more truly representative of the population as a whole. In 1890 four-fifths of the pupils in high school were preparing directly for college. Now only one pupil in seven has such an ambition. (147)

Addressing the curriculum controlled by college entrance requirements, she continued:

> The problem of articulation begins with the establishment of a philosophy of education which centers attention upon the growth of the pupil and not upon the attainment of standards set from without. . . . conditions prevail in some school systems which indicate that both the nature and needs of boys and girls are forgotten in an effort to secure the approbation of those who direct instruction in the institution to which these pupils will be promoted. (147)

In the same article Smith called for more articulation between college/university faculty and high school teachers, citing the frequent complaint, "If we didn't have to teach what they should have been taught . . . we might get something done!" (154). "The purpose of any such movement," she continued, "is not to give one institution a chance to make known its wants to another but to give both of them an opportunity to study co-operatively the stage of development reached by the pupil and the reasonable next step in standards" (154).

How pleased Dora V. Smith might be today to see the strides that have been made in university-high school articulation and the countless benefits that have accrued to students.

Having directed the work of NCTE's Commission on the Curriculum, organized in 1945, Smith further demonstrated her foresight and steady conviction in a 1958 article, written the year of her retirement. Entitled "Re-establishing Guidelines for the English Curriculum," it addressed the public anxiety evident in the age of Sputnik about the quality of education in American schools:

> Advice for curriculum makers is the cheapest commodity on the market. We are besieged these days from every direction by critics of the schools . . . "Import Europe's school system," we are told. "Aim your program at the gifted and let others get what they can—or get out." "Look at Russia. Get some of her order and discipline into our schools." . . .
> It never was more important to keep one's head in the language arts than it is right now. Educational systems are rigorous. They cannot be imported wholesale from other countries. The United States has attempted a program of universal education up through the secondary school which has long been the envy of other nations around the world. In fact, the whole story of comparative education in the last twenty years is one of gradual progress in the direction in which we have moved further than any other country. We need to strengthen the faith that is in us and move forward to perfect what we have begun, not cast it aside for a worn-out pattern. (318)

In some ways we are faced with the same kind of criticism today, at a time when the "mediocrity" of America's schools is being decried and the curricula being questioned. Some would even like to see the kind of standardized curriculum that Smith spoke so firmly against.

Though the American educational system has historically seen a swinging of the pendulum back and forth between traditionalism and progressivism, the question remains, How much progress have we really made? Certainly we have made great strides in the teaching of composition and in articulation programs, and reading instruction is improving with the whole language approach. But formal grammar is still being taught in isolation in many schools, and literature classes are still largely teacher centered and dominated by the classics.

In addition, some significant obstacles to effective English programs pinpointed in Smith's studies still have significance today. The most serious problems included poor teacher training, heavy teacher loads, inadequate book supplies, and time-consuming extracurricular programs (Applebee 1974, 127). We need only look at the findings and recommendations of current studies to see that these problems still exist today in American schools, along with others indicative of the times.

Class size, too, continues to be the subject of heated discussion. When Smith did her dissertation research from 1925 to 1927, she found that class size was not as significant a factor in student learning as were the methods used by the teacher. Similarly, a recent analysis of existing research on class size, conducted by the NCTE Task Force on Class Size and Workload in Secondary English Instruction, concluded that "class size by itself, especially in English classes, is not the primary determinant of learning, but that *class size, when combined with mode of instruction, is a powerful determinant of learning*" (W. Smith 1986, 2). Though NCTE has advocated a class size of twenty to twenty-five students and a maximum workload of one hundred students per teacher per day, most classes and workloads exceed these numbers; and teachers are forced to find ways to deal with larger classes, just as they did in Smith's day. If anything, history tells us that progress in education is slow; and, of course, to some, "progress" is a relative term. But if we think of progress in terms of Smith's philosophy, we see that much of today's successful reform and innovation is based largely on the principles and theories that Smith advocated and in which she truly believed.

While Dora V. Smith was at the forefront of education nationally, she was also actively involved in innovative programs in her own state of Minnesota. In 1941 she initiated the first Children's Book Institute at the University of Minnesota, which soon became an annual event. In November of each year, to celebrate Children's Book Week, parents, teachers, and librarians from various parts of the state would gather for a series of meetings and book exhibits at which children's authors, teachers, librarians, and parents would discuss ways of guiding children's reading and of keeping up with the best books in the field. Smith presided over the institute, with local parent and teacher organizations assisting with promotion and planning. In charge of the book exhibit was a committee of University of Minnesota students from the library school, the Child Welfare Institute, and the Department of English Education. Table decoration and book arrangement were done by another committee of art education students.

Meetings were arranged so that the elementary school parents and teachers attended the afternoon session and the dinner, and the high school parents and teachers attended the dinner and the evening session. Approximately eight hundred people took part in the first institute in 1941, with similar interest being shown in ensuing years.

In addition to directing the fall institute, Smith also coordinated the annual Spring Conference on the Language Arts at the University of Minnesota. This was a two-day affair, again directed toward local teachers and librarians. The program consisted of small-group and large-group discussions on such issues as interdisciplinary learning, techniques of group discussion, and reading in an age of mass communication. Among the discussion leaders were such people as Luella B. Cook, Dwight Burton, and Harold Allen, along with other Minnesota teachers and librarians. The conference culminated in a general meeting, with Smith presiding, where reports and summaries of group discussions were given (Dora V. Smith papers, University of Minnesota Archives).

That Smith was doing all this work locally while at the same time directing and participating in national studies, teaching classes, writing for publication, and supervising the work of countless master's students and doctoral candidates suggests a woman undaunted by hard work and impervious to criticism. But her career was not without its difficulties. On 6 April 1950 the following headline appeared in the *Minneapolis Tribune*: "'U' Professor Barred from Speakers' List; Denies Link to Reds." The professor in question was Dora V. Smith. She had been invited to speak at a teacher-training program in Washington, D.C., during the Joseph McCarthy era, so the list of speakers was checked with the House Un-American Activities Committee. Smith's name had somehow made its way onto a list of people involved in "subversive investigations"; therefore, officials announced that she would be dropped from the list of speakers. As it turned out, the superintendent of Washington schools later admitted that the list of prospective speakers had been checked with the Un-American Activities Committee by phone, and someone had apparently misunderstood Smith's middle initial ("Dropping of 'U' Professor"). The committee maintained a listing for Dr. Dora B. Smith, who was a correspondent for *The Daily Worker*, the New York City Communist newspaper. Obviously English educator Dora V. Smith had been mistaken for the Dora B. Smith with the Communist leanings. Ironically, Smith had initially declined the invitation because the engagement conflicted with her Children's Book Week celebration at the University ("'U' Professor Barred"). After more than a year Smith managed to clear her name, but not without anguish on the part of a woman who prided herself on an honorable reputation.

In spite of difficulties such as this, Dora V. Smith enjoyed national and international reknown. In demand as a speaker even early in her career, she received far more invitations than she could accept. And she was loved and respected for her personal qualities as well as for her professional expertise. A wonderful tribute to Smith is an *English Journal* article written by her former student Richard Alm in which he captured the essence of Smith in a way that only one who knew her well ever could, particularly in relating one of the favorite stories about her:

> Dora V's students knew that God kept a careful eye on her, especially when she was behind the wheel of a car. It was commonplace for her to drive down Nicollet Avenue, grandly pointing out to passengers various items in the store windows. Our favorite story deals with her driving five of us to downtown Minneapolis to a meeting of the Minneapolis English Club. Driving on the inside lane with two lanes of traffic on her right, Dora V. leaned over and said to Dwight Burton (now at Florida State University) seated next to the door, "Dwight, would you please ask those cars to let me turn right on the next corner?" She then went back to the conversation she had interrupted assuming Dwight would do as she asked and that the other drivers would cooperate. He did, and they did. (1984, 30)

Discussing Smith's efficiency, Alm stated: "Dora V. could be businesslike. When she telephoned one of us, she usually spoke her piece and then hung up. We had to be particularly adept to get in a word of our own. Most often, we had to call her back to give her our message. It wasn't a lack of courtesy; she was just being efficient" (30). According to Alm, Smith was too busy to think much about money, either:

> Money was never a problem for Dora V., but it was never much of a concern, either. In the late 1940's, when she was an established national leader in English education, the members of the University High English Department were horrified to learn, by accident, how low her salary was. There was no malice toward Dora V. She was a woman, and the College knew that she lived with her mother and sister and was not likely to move anywhere else. When Walter Cook became Dean, he was horrified, too, and substantially raised her salary. Although Dora V. faithfully attended and appeared on the program of the NCTE Convention every year, she never asked the University of Minnesota to underwrite any of her expenses.
> Over the years Dora V. wrote most of her publications for love, not for royalties. (32–33)

Alm's reminiscences not only demonstrate Smith's dedication and unselfishness, but also reveal commonly held attitudes toward women in the profession at the time—attitudes which Smith and others did not seem to question. Yet in spite of such inequities, Smith and the other women included in this volume managed a degree of success quite unusual for their time.

In discussing Smith's career, many of those who knew her commented on her appearance, which gave her a "presence" difficult to forget. G. Robert Carlsen recalled: "I always remember my first methods class in Burton Hall. She came in, a tall, imposing woman with a mass of white hair and that kindly face. Though they did not look alike, she had the same kind of presence that was Eleanor Roosevelt's" (Alm 1984, 32).

But there was no "Franklin" in Dora Smith's life. According to Stanley Kegler (1988), when asked once why she had never married, Smith replied that she had never found a man who interested her very much. At a time when few women had such illustrious careers, there might well have been a choice involved between family and profession. Those who knew her, however, felt Smith never indicated that she consciously made such a choice. According to her former student Dwight Burton, "She was completely career-minded, the prototype of the career woman" (1988). Kegler believes that the lack of a husband and family gave Smith a kind of freedom she would not otherwise have had, explaining: "She would spend a day or two out of town almost every week traveling somewhere, and this was not on airplanes. She would ride a train from here to Chicago, Kansas, and other places, conduct an afternoon workshop, catch a late evening train, and teach an eight o'clock class on Saturday morning back here" (1988).

A professional in every sense, Smith expected the same of her students, encouraging them to attend professional meetings, even sometimes lending them her car to make the trip. Kegler recalled:

> We felt terribly privileged. We'd go to the National Council of Teachers of English meeting, and Dora would introduce us to everybody.... There I was, 26, 27 years old, working on my M.A., and I was meeting all the people who were really big names in the field.... The only thing that was difficult with Dora was when you appeared on the program. She'd introduce you to someone: "This is Stan Kegler. Stan is working on a master's degree. He's speaking tomorrow at 9:30 in room such-and-such." Dora roped them all in—Angela Broening, Stella Center—and they'd all come and sit in the front row ... and you'd be so nervous—absolutely frightened to death! ... You were just like her child. She was showing you off. (1988)

Smith's nurturing kindness extended even further. She once loaned Betty Jane Reed, her secretary and graduate assistant, the down payment on a house so that Reed could move her mother and sisters to Minneapolis from Pittsburgh after the death of her father. Reed recalled: "It was typical of Dora that she agreed to take a second mortgage on the house—in fact *offered* to. . . . One day she appeared very embarrassed and told me her attorney told her she should at least *look* at the house, so we drove out and she took a quick walk around just to satisfy her attorney" (1988).

It is tempting to speculate on how Dora Smith managed to be so successful in a profession largely dominated by men. Burton (1988) indicated that she was one of three women out of one hundred faculty at the University of Minnesota's College of Education. Smith's brother, George Baxter Smith (1988), spoke of how she would come into the University Faculty Club when there were no women there, and she would appear to be on an equal basis with everyone else. Reed, doubting that Smith ever thought of herself as a successful woman in a man's world, commented that she "just went ahead doing what she felt needed to be done" (1988).

This statement seems to characterize Dora V. Smith well. Never self-conscious about her professional role, she seemed secure in her knowledge and ability. Kegler described her as "sex blind" in her dealings with colleagues and students. In addition to her intelligence, energy, and drive, he felt that her success was due in part to her fine character. Calling her "probably the most perfect human being I have ever been privileged to know," he spoke of how she always managed to keep herself above the fray where politics were concerned, being involved in controversy, yet emerging unscathed, without enemies (1988).

It is no wonder that this hard-working, much-respected woman was the recipient of so many honors and awards. In 1957 she received the W. Wilbur Hatfield Award for long and distinguished service to the teaching of English in the United States. That same year a scholarship was established in her name at the University of Minnesota. Theodore Blegen, dean of the Graduate School, praised Smith's energy and dedication in announcing the scholarship:

> I rise to pay a tribute of gratitude and affection to a gallant lady . . . I speak of a human dynamo whose energy can bowl one over and leave one breathless. There is an absurd rumor afloat. People say that Dora Smith is to retire. This of course is ridiculous. We may indeed read about her retirement some time, but we know her too well to be fooled by any such report. The next day will carry a story about a Dora V. Smith book fair, with a dinner and an assemblage of local authors, in darkest Africa.
>
> Then, before long, one will read of a Dora Smith expedition to the moon to introduce the children of the moon to some of the brighter products of American and Minnesota authors. (1957)

In 1958, the year Smith officially retired after forty-one years as professor of English education, she was honored three times in one day: as one of ten teachers selected during the centennial year as "Maria Sanfords of Today," as Minnesota's Teacher of the Year, and as a retiring faculty member from the University of Minnesota's College of Education. Assistant Dean of Education Marcia Edwards, in a retirement tribute to Smith, fondly recalled "the time Dora went home and to bed with the flu—and took the dictaphone along so she could finish a research report and an article while waiting for her temperature to come down." Edwards also spoke of the time Smith "went to a photographer to have an official picture taken for a national program, and on reminding the photographer that she wanted to look intelligent in this particular picture, received the answer, 'Madam, we leave that to the subject.'" Edwards concluded her speech by saying, "To honor Dora V. Smith is to honor all good teachers—she is their symbol" (1958).

In 1961 Smith received a special commendation for outstanding achievement as a University of Minnesota graduate. Civic leader Viola Hymes, a former student of Smith's who was also honored on that occasion, wrote in a letter to her former teacher:

> That I was presented the Outstanding Achievement Award at the same time it was presented to you is to me as high a tribute as the receipt of the Award itself.... You have been the kind of teacher who, I am sure, has influenced the lives of thousands of students who have had the privilege and opportunity of studying with you. As one of those who have been so privileged, I want to take this special occasion to express my deep appreciation to you not only for teaching me how to teach English, but for sharing with me your compassion for and understanding of our fellow human beings. (1961)

This compassion and understanding was at the heart of Dora V. Smith's philosophy of an education for everyone in a democratic society. Her work in all aspects of English education reflects this philosophy, as does the work of many of the "Smith legacies" who hold or have held positions similar to hers in colleges and universities throughout the country. Dwight Burton and his student, Stephen Dunning, now retired from the University of Michigan, did much to advance the cause of English teaching and were especially influential in the cause of adolescent literature during the 1950s. Another student of Burton's, James E. Davis, continues to take a leadership role in the Council and will ascend to the position of Council president in 1992. G. Robert Carlsen, now retired from the University of Iowa, was mentor to such Council leaders as Ken Donelson, Ben Nelms, and Ruth Cline, among others. Add to this list other luminaries, such as Walter Loban, who wrote the foreword to this book, Richard Alm, whose research on Smith has proved invaluable, and the countless others who can be so proud of calling themselves one of Dora Smith's "descendants."

In his book *A Long Way Together: A Personal View of NCTE's First Sixty-Seven Years*, J. N. Hook described the ribbon-cutting ceremony which opened the new NCTE headquarters in Urbana, Illinois, almost two decades ago:

> On May 13, 1971, Dora V. Smith cut a red ribbon, an act symbolizing the official opening of the Council's new home.... It was appropriate that Smith—the beloved "Dora V."—cut the ribbon. She was the senior surviving past president; she had begun writing for *English Journal* almost fifty years earlier, in the 1920's; she had served on uncounted Council committees and had given countless speeches across the country; she had guided research projects and for more than a decade had headed the Curriculum Commission. Some of her academic offspring had followed her in major Council roles.... No one else present on that brisk, sunny May morning could claim so many professionally illustrious descendants as Dora V. (1979, 260-61)

We may never know how proud Smith was that morning, but we do know how proud she *should* have been.

Just a few years later, in 1975, Dora Smith entered a nursing home when her sister Jean, with whom she had lived for many years, suddenly passed away. Smith had become rather frail and needed constant care. In a letter to NCTE Executive Secretary Robert F. Hogan, Smith's brother explained: "She is not able to write and has little interest in reading although she is strong and well physically" (G. Smith 1975). Unfortunately, her health declined over the years, and her mind became less and less sharp. She no longer recognized her former friends and associates when they visited her. A poignant account of such a visit was given by Walter Loban: "Since she gave no indication of knowing me, I said who I was and that I'd come from California. 'Oh, yes,' she said, 'I have many friends out there. I go there fairly often.'" Subsequent mention of her former students and even her brother and sister elicited no comment. "Dora said, 'I had brothers. It's strange I don't remember them.'" But when Loban began to talk about professional matters, she seemed to become more alert:

> I expressed my appreciation for all she had taught me and told her that I still use her ideas and philosophy in my classes at the

University of California. She looked right at me and said, "Oh so much time has passed. I doubt that those ideas could be so useful now." Surprised, I remonstrated and said that my colleague, Grace Maertens, felt the same way about what she had learned from Dora. Dora replied quite clearly, "That's nice of you both." . . . When I said goodby, she nodded pleasantly, and I thought: Dora V. could easily be turning back to her desk or to her next appointment, and I could be descending the steps of Burton Hall. The walk back to Nicollet Mall is long, but I decided I needed time to think about the riddle of time and personalities, for I felt exactly as if the year were 1932, half a century ago. She hadn't really changed, nor had I. Despite what has happened to each of us, our essential natures haven't altered. I really didn't know whether to be dismayed or reassured, and I still don't. (1982)

Upon reading Loban's account, Constance McCullough, Smith's former student and colleague, responded in a letter to Loban: "The miracle is that her personality is not changed one whit. She is the same lovely, outgoing, great-spirited person" (1982). When Dora V. Smith passed away on 28 January 1985, less than a month before her ninety-second birthday, she remained gracious and courteous to the last, "even to a 'thank you' and a smile to the nurse who was with her when she died" (Reed 1988).

But it is on the life of this remarkable woman that we focus today and on her many contributions to the field of English education. And in remembering these contributions we cannot overlook one that needs to be emphasized strongly—Dora V. Smith's status as a role model for the women and men teaching English today. She was working at the time in a field largely dominated by men, yet in her efficient, unassuming way she commanded the respect of all who knew and worked with her. She was tireless, dedicated, and accepted nothing but the best—because that was what she always gave. She was a woman who paved the way for those of us who follow. We owe it to Dora V. Smith and to ourselves to carry on her tradition of excellence as we work to make our own contributions to the history of English teaching in America.

Works Cited

Alm, Richard. 1984. "Dora V. Smith: Teacher, Leader, Legend." *English Journal* 73 (March): 30–37.

Applebee, Arthur N. 1974. *Tradition and Reform in the Teaching of English: A History.* Urbana, Ill.: National Council of Teachers of English.

Blegen, Theodore. 29 November 1957. "For Dora V. Smith." Speech delivered at Books for Children Luncheon, Minneapolis, Minn.

Burton, Dwight. 25 August 1988. Telephone interview with author.

Carlsen, G. Robert. 1984. "Teaching Literature for the Adolescent: A Historical Perspective." *English Journal* 73 (November): 28–30.

Child Welfare Institute. Papers. University of Minnesota Archives.

"Dropping of 'U' Professor as Speaker Is Laid to Phone Error." 6 September 1950. *Minneapolis Star*.

Dunning, Stephen. 1959. "A Definition of the Role of the Junior Novel Based on Analyses of Thirty Selected Novels." Ph.D. diss., Florida State University, Tallahassee.

Edwards, Marcia. 15 May 1958. "Recognition for Dora V. Smith." Retirement tribute, College of Education, University of Minnesota, Minneapolis.

"English Monograph." 31 March 1934. Survey of Secondary Education Series. *School and Society* 39, no. 1005: 408.

Flesch, Rudolf. 1955. *Why Johnny Can't Read and What You Can Do about It.* New York: Harper.

Goodman, Kenneth. 1986. *What's Whole in Whole Language?* Portsmouth, N.H.: Heinemann.

Hook, J. N. 1979. *A Long Way Together: A Personal View of NCTE's First Sixty-Seven Years.* Urbana, Ill.: National Council of Teachers of English.

Hymes, Viola. 5 July 1961. Letter to Dora V. Smith.

Kegler, Stanley. 10 June 1988. Interview with author, Minneapolis, Minn.

Loban, Walter. Spring 1982. Personal account of visit with Dora V. Smith, Minneapolis, Minn.

McCullough, Constance M. 13 June 1982. Letter to Walter Loban.

Moffett, James. 1968. *Teaching the Universe of Discourse.* Boston: Houghton Mifflin.

Reed, Betty Jane. 1 July 1988. Letter to author.

Shaughnessy, Mina P. 1977. *Errors and Expectations.* New York: Oxford University Press.

Smith, Dora V. Papers. University of Minnesota Archives.

———. 1932. "Teaching versus Testing in Composition." *English Bulletin* 24, no. 6–7 (March): 22–26.

———. 1933. *Instruction in English.* Office of Education Bulletin no. 17. National Survey of Secondary Education Monograph no. 20. Washington, D.C.: Government Printing Office.

———. 1934. "Highway *versus* Detour in the Teaching of English." *English Journal* 23 (February): 109–18.

———. 1936. "The Relationship of Remedial Reading to the Problems of Teaching." Paper presented at the Men's Union, University of Minnesota, 27 March.

———. 1937. "American Youth and English." *English Journal* 26 (February): 99–113.

———. 1938. "'Lose Not the Nightingale'—A Challenge and a Counter-Challenge." *American Library Association Bulletin* 32 (January): 7–13.

———. 1940. "Problems of Articulation in the Teaching of English." *College English*

2 (November): 145–55.

———. 1955. "What Do We Want 'Johnny' to Do? To Pronounce Words or to Read?" *Minnesota Journal of Education* 36 (September): 13–16.

———. 1958. "Re-establishing Guidelines for the English Curriculum." *English Journal* 47 (September): 317–26, 338.

———. 1963. *Fifty Years of Children's Books*. Urbana, Ill.: National Council of Teachers of English.

———. 1964. *Dora V. Smith: Selected Essays*. New York: Macmillan.

———. 3 May 1968. Interview by Robert Boyle, Department of Radio and Television, University of Minnesota, Minneapolis.

Smith, Frank. 1985. *Reading without Nonsense*. 2d ed. New York: Teachers College Press.

Smith, George Baxter. 17 July 1975. Letter to Robert F. Hogan, executive secretary of NCTE.

———. 12 September 1988. Telephone interview with author.

Smith, William L., chair, and the NCTE Task Force on Class Size and Workload in Secondary English Instruction. 1986. *Class Size and English in the Secondary School*. Urbana, Ill.: ERIC Clearinghouse on Reading and Communication Skills and National Council of Teachers of English.

"'U' Professor Barred from Speakers' List; Denies Link to Reds." 6 April 1950. *Minneapolis Tribune*.

Webster, Edward Harlan, and Dora V. Smith. 1927. *Teaching English in Junior High School*. New York: World Book.

Part II:
Working Together

5 Angela M. Broening: Implacable Defender

Dure Jo Gillikin, College of Staten Island

Angela M. Broening
ca. 1899-1972

It was Thanksgiving afternoon of 1944, with Angela M. Broening presiding at the first fullfledged annual meeting of the National Council of Teachers of English since the attack on Pearl Harbor in 1941. Two thousand English teachers had gathered for what undoubtedly would be the most provocative business meeting in NCTE history. They were in Columbus, Ohio, ready for a confrontation between one of their standing committees, the Committee on Newspapers and Magazines in the Classroom, and the *Reader's Digest*. They had been reading about the conflict in *English Journal* and in the national press, and now they eagerly awaited a discussion of the question posed in the left-wing magazine *PM*: "'Is there any justification for the criticism that the *Reader's Digest* uses its reputation as a reprint magazine for propaganda purposes or for the criticism that the articles on science and other subjects of human interest are wings to carry propaganda?'" ("Propaganda Study").

Broening was set to perform her final duties as thirty-third president of the Council. However, instead of a peaceful, orderly conclusion to her year in office, she was caught up in a political showdown that her cousin, William Broening, a former mayor of Baltimore, might have appreciated, for he "was highly praised during his administration for establishing the first high quality professional school boards and for allowing them to operate without political interference" (Sargeant n.d.).

On this afternoon of 23 November 1944, Angela Broening was faced with a meeting that could put the organization she was supposed to defend into a long legal battle. Her ultimate challenge

97

was to protect NCTE and to do what her conscience bade her. Unfortunately, she could not support the report of the Committee on Newspapers and Magazines. She did not want it published without reservation for fear that the *Reader's Digest* would "sue the Council and do it irreparable harm" (Hook 1979, 141). To leave office with such a legacy is no president's wish. For months she had been trying to resolve the issue. Consensus, not conflict, had always been her goal. She had begun her career by team teaching at George Washington Elementary School in Baltimore, Maryland. Later, as vice-principal of that school, and then as chair of the English Department at Baltimore's Forest Park High School, Broening would consult with all of the people with whom she was working, be they students, teachers, or advisers.

She had done her best to work out a compromise between the NCTE Committee on Newspapers and Magazines and the *Reader's Digest*. But she was learning that there was nothing as immovable as individuals adhering to a principle, especially when they represented political extremes. When there were at least three sets of principles at stake—hers as implacable defender of NCTE, the committee members', and those of the *Reader's Digest* editors—conflict flourished, and the fight was a very visible one.

Most important to Broening in formulating her position had been her scholarly training at Johns Hopkins University, at which she had earned her Ph.D. in the 1920s. This day she needed all of her expertise from the three fields in which she had done graduate work—English, education, and psychology. Her dissertation, *Developing Appreciation through Teaching Literature*, which was published by Johns Hopkins University Press in 1929, clearly stated her strategies of seeking consensus: "By the trial and success, sometimes error, method the author-experimenter learned how to arouse and hold these pupils' attentions through reading aloud to them and telling them stories about the things they liked to do, the people they liked to know, the places they wished to see, and the feelings they were unable to express" (1). Certainly this whole conflict and the attempt at its resolution had been one of trial and error. It remained to be seen whether her leadership during the preceding year would be vindicated. The words that she had used in her dissertation to define *appreciation* may have come back to her during the term of her presidency: "emotionalized insight," "an idea with a glow, an understanding with a cause" (5–6). Emotion, radiance, and dedication were invigorating as long as they were balanced with insight, an idea, and a basic understanding.

In the days and hours before the business meeting, Angela Broening must have been reviewing how the whole controversy had begun. More than likely she considered the stresses and strains on the NCTE leaders as they participated fully in the war effort. English was vital to the war effort, to the survival of the democracy. Indeed, when the government had called on the Council for its help, Broening was in the forefront in responding. She chaired the committee that prepared *The Teacher of English and the War Savings Program*, which consisted of two units for high school English classes and which was requested by the War Finance Division of the Treasury. Broening also chaired a committee that produced a pamphlet for the Office of Price Administration. Its purpose was to "interpret O.P.A. through English classrooms" with lesson plans and bibliographies so that students would understand "the need for rationing, price-fixing, and rent control" and "to teach the public through school children how to read directions on application forms and ration books" ("United" 463). In November 1942 *English Journal* had published excerpts from Broening's remarks at the Baltimore spring conference on "The Role of the Teacher of English in Wartime," reprinted under the title "English in War and in Peace," in which Broening urged English teachers to have students "open their books, read aloud, and linger with energy on the words which reveal what America is really fighting for and why every boy and girl, man and woman, *must do whatever is needed from each individual to win this war and to secure the peace*" (676).

The dispute between NCTE and the *Reader's Digest* began in 1943 and involved John DeBoer, past president of NCTE and assistant editor of *English Journal*, and W. Wilbur Hatfield, editor of *English Journal*. Perhaps it was DeBoer's zeal to support the war effort, his opposition to "the evils of big business," and his favoring of "many causes distinctly left of center" (Hook 1979, 100) that led him to challenge the loyalty of one of America's most successful magazines. He entered NCTE into the fray with *Reader's Digest* in February of 1943, when he alerted *English Journal* readers "who use or recommend" the magazine by reprinting in his "Summary and Report" column allegations against the *Digest* which had been made by "the left-wing newspaper *In Fact*" in its issues of 16 November and 7 December 1942. Certainly the charges were alarming. If Paul Palmer, then an editor of *Reader's Digest*, had indeed, as *In Fact* stated, "sponsored the publication of numerous antidemocratic articles by Laurence Dennis, outspoken proponent of fascism and admirer of German National Socialism" (DeBoer 1943a, 106), and if the paraphrased "direct quotation" attributed to *Reader's Digest* publisher DeWitt Wallace by George

Seldes, editor of *In Fact*, was accurate, namely, that he was "in favor of a limited victory over Hitler, which would leave him to police Europe, and of some American fascism" (106), then there was serious cause for concern. However, the political gulf between *In Fact* and *Reader's Digest* left considerable room for doubt.

For its part, the *Digest* flatly denied the accusations in the next issue of *English Journal*. In DeBoer's March column he relayed the information that the *Reader's Digest* editors had labeled the *In Fact* accusations as "baseless falsehoods" and "that they will gladly trust the judgment of teachers of English who read the magazine, and their fairness and ability in evaluating the material" (1943b, 167). In the June pages of *English Journal*, two more opposing articles continued the dispute. Herbert A. Landry's article, "Teaching Reading with the *Reader's Digest*," explained the origins and motivations for a practical program for improving reading. To implement this program, *Reader's Digest* editors had called upon former NCTE president Stella Stewart Center and Gladys L. Persons, directors of the New York University Reading Clinic. In September 1941 a sixteen-page supplement entitled "Reading for Pleasure and Profit" had accompanied the school edition of the *Reader's Digest*. This supplement "included reading and vocabulary exercises designed to improve general reading ability of secondary-school pupils." In his assessment of this program, which had used control and noncontrol groups, Landry asserted, "Pupils in whose classes the reading-improvement program was used increased their competence in reading at twice the normal rate" (324). J. N. Hook, in *A Long Way Together: A Personal View of NCTE's First Sixty-Seven Years*, noted that a year after this article was published, Landry started working for *Reader's Digest*, and he even speculated that Landry was working for *Reader's Digest* at the time of the article's publication (1979, 139). However, such allegations did not refute the information in Landry's article about the effectiveness of *Reader's Digest* in improving reading. Hook's challenge to Landry's motives comes close to implying that Stella Stewart Center had been either used or co-opted by the *Reader's Digest* team. Hook's implications further indicate just how volatile the *Reader's Digest* affair remained some twenty-eight years after DeBoer's first column.

Immediately following Landry's positive article in *English Journal* appeared Samuel Beckoff's "The Rainbow," which presented several serious charges against the *Digest*. It probably was this article to which Angela Broening referred when she accused her opponents of unscholarly work. Beckoff made his charges, however, after he established the overwhelming success of the *Reader's Digest*, with its "circulation of five millions and a possible reading public of forty millions" (325). The magazine's incredible success amazed Beckoff when it was considered "in the light of a nation at war, newsprint shortages, increased operating costs" (327). That Beckoff was not an entirely unbiased writer is evidenced by the title of his article, "The Rainbow." Apparently bothered by the fact that the *Reader's Digest* was making money in wartime, Beckoff wrote: "It has long been rumored that there's a pot of gold at the end of the rainbow. As each successive issue has come forth in its cover of ever changing colors, there has been noticed a corresponding change in policy" (327).

Had Beckoff focused only on policy, his article might have been less biased. But Beckoff went on to question whether "the *Digest* was still (1) a digest, (2) reliable teaching material, (3) liberal in thought and expression, and (4) contributing substantially to the war effort" (327). His assertion that the *Digest* was not a "digest" of previously published material but more and more the work of its own "roving" editors has some basis in fact—"a total of forty-four authors wrote directly for the *Digest* in 1942" (328). Where Beckoff most seriously failed in his attack, however, was his question, "Is the *Reader's Digest* liberal in thought and expression?" (328). This question is a most vital one in the whole controversy between NCTE and the *Reader's Digest,* for it assumed that the magazine must be liberal according to Beckoff's definition: "First, liberalism, as understood by this writer, is defined as a forward-looking, progressive, pro-labor, pro-minorities, pro-democratic, pro-Four Freedoms philosophy of social, political and economic action" (328). Was it mandatory during World War II that all magazines be liberal? Beckoff further skewed his case by stating that the *Digest* published predominantly from such nonliberal magazines as the *American Legion* and *American Mercury,* when it had also reprinted seven articles from *The New Yorker* and fifteen from the *Saturday Review of Literature.* Beckoff also objected to senior editor Paul Palmer's use of articles from Laurence Dennis and Harold Lord, whom he labeled as fascists. In addition, Beckoff objected to William Hard's "American Unlimited" for "lambasting labor, the New Deal, and many of the aims which were later to be adopted by the United Nations" and Jerry Kluttz's "To Washington: An 'E' for *In*efficiency," which was "highly critical of the New Deal, of the conduct of the war, and palatable to most isolationists and anti-Wilkie Republicans" (329). When Kluttz published an article favorable to labor—"Pity the Federal Worker"— Beckoff wondered why the *Digest* had not "digested" this for its readers. He pointed out that in its South American edition, the *Digest* "contains no anti-Roosevelt, no anti-New Deal, no anti-labor, no anti-interventionist articles" (329), but he failed to see that U.S. readers were in the best position to support the government or to cease buying the *Digest*. Beckoff further charged that the *Reader's Digest* published anti-Semitic articles, yet his emotionally dominated article concluded with the statement, "It is perhaps Christianity's last big chance to establish the brotherhood of man on earth" (330).

The ultimate question was whether magazine publishing should continue as usual during the war or whether no criticisms of the government were to be permitted in publications. In short, was censorship justifiable in war time? Was the country which was fighting for the Four Freedoms to forgo them in war time? The incongruity of Beckoff's article is best represented by his last paragraph: "We sincerely hope that the *Reader's Digest* will reconsider its course and return to the true American concept of freedom of the press, the concept that included the obligation on the part of the press to print the whole truth—the truth that will make men free and keep men free" (330). What freedom of the press was Beckoff granting to the *Digest*? By choosing to publish Beckoff's article in *English Journal*, was editor Wilbur Hatfield in any way sanctioning its contents? Or did he leave it up to his readers to make their own judgments, as readers of the *Digest* did? In the late 1980s and early 1990s a similar censorship debate rages in Congress, on campuses, in the arts, and in the media over "how to use freedom of expression more assiduously in pursuit of a society free of prejudice and intolerance of all kinds" (Fanton 1989).

Such was the intensity of the controversy that was boiling during the last days of Angela M. Broening's NCTE presidency. That John DeBoer and Wilbur Hatfield were on the other side of the argument and that both were members of the Executive Committee kept the whole matter stewing until it was boisterously resolved in Columbus.

The issue had spread from the pages of *English Journal* and entered the Council itself when DeBoer made a motion at the August 1943 Executive Committee meeting, which was passed, asking the "Committee on Newspapers and Magazines, chaired by Helen Rand Miller, to investigate the usefulness and soundness of the *Reader's Digest* as a teaching aid in the war situation" (Hook 1979, 139). In February 1944, one year from the time the first *English Journal* article was published, Broening read the committee's report and "considered the report biased," as did most members of the Executive Committee since they felt it should be revised "in the interest of objectivity of statement and of proof" before the Board of Directors meeting in Columbus (140).

The *Reader's Digest* editors apparently heard of the committee's report and offered to confer with the Council leaders. A session was arranged at the May Executive Committee meeting to bring together the *Reader's Digest* representatives, Council leaders, and Helen Rand Miller, chair of the Committee on Newspapers and Magazines in the Classroom. The *Reader's Digest* presented its case, and according to Broening's minutes, the *Digest* "agreed to supply headnotes and titles that would give the 'correct impression' of each article's contents and to use cross references to articles supporting other points of view than those of *Reader's Digest* authors" (141). This compromise promised a balanced view without an admission of previous bias and thus seemed to serve the interests of both sides.

The Executive Committee, perhaps recognizing the "irony of a Council committee attempting to challenge the editorial policy of a commercial magazine when the Executive Committee has no constitutional right or privilege of influencing *The English Journal* which is listed as an 'Official Organ' of the NCTE," voted at the May 27th meeting that the committee's study of *Reader's Digest* was concluded (141). However, when the members of the Committee on Newspapers and Magazines realized their original report had not proved its case, they took further action. Wilbur Hatfield and John DeBoer, two of their advocates on the Executive Committee, lobbied for funds to finish the study of the *Reader's Digest*. A mail ballot to the entire Executive Committee in July 1944 resulted in continued funding for the study. In effect, the Executive Committee had flip-flopped on its May 27th vote.

In a 10 July 1944 communiqué to the NCTE membership, Broening cited two responsibilities of the Committee on Newspapers and Magazines: "(1) To develop standards for selecting magazines and newspapers for classroom use; and (2) to project plans for a unit on how to teach the reading of periodicals so as to immunize youth against prejudiced views of authors or of editors in any subject in any periodical." Had the committee been willing to adhere to the last of these two delegated duties, then the public, national conflict might have been avoided, but the committee apparently believed that it would be difficult for the average young reader to overcome the authority and popularity of *Reader's Digest*, particularly when it was presented as a classroom source. On the other hand, Broening clearly considered that it was the teacher's responsibility to teach students to distinguish fact from opinion as they read, to identify propaganda techniques, and to recognize unstated assumptions and logical fallacies. Today, with some of our best colleges and universities having severe problems of their own with students' racist and sexist remarks and acts, we can sympathize with the dilemma facing Angela Broening and the Committee on Newspapers and Magazines. Combatting prejudice without engaging in censorship is not an easy task. Broening, in her July 10th charge to the committee, felt she had the best pedagogical approach and planned to stick to it.

Despite the unacceptability of the committee's report to the Executive Committee, the study was leaked to the press. Two newspapers, the left-wing *PM* in New York and the Chicago *Sun*, both owned by Marshall Field, published parts of the committee's report in their issues of 10 September 1944, making the NCTE-*Reader's Digest* dispute public.

In addition to the criticism from the NCTE Committee on Newspapers and Magazines, the *Reader's Digest* was under attack from other sources as well. First, there were publishers that took exception to the *Reader's Digest* reprint policies, most notably the *New Yorker*. In a February 1944 letter to its contributors, the *New Yorker* editors said they would not renew their contract with *Reader's Digest* because of its farm-out policy: "Nowadays a large proportion of [the Digest's] contents is frankly original with the Digest and not presented as reprint material; and of the stuff that is presented as reprint material, much actually originates in the offices of the Digest and then gets farmed out to some other magazine for first publication. The effect of this (apart from spreading a lot of money around) is that the Digest is beginning to generate a considerable fraction of the contents of American magazines" (quoted in "Digest in the Doghouse," 84). So serious was the problem that "Administration circles have been flirting with the idea of an anti-trust action aimed at the Digest's policy of sewing up reprint sources with exclusive contracts" (82). These allegations were of serious concern to NCTE members and to all educators because "more than 700,000 copies . . . [were] sent each month to high schools and colleges" ("Teachers Council," 82). Members of Franklin D. Roosevelt's administration formed a second group that was critical of the *Reader's Digest*. They took exception to the magazine's unfavorable articles about New Deal actions and statements. A third group of critics were Communists and readers of such left-wing publications as *PM* and *In Fact*, whose political position was diametrically opposed to that of the *Reader's Digest*. It was the allegations from *In Fact*, which *Newsweek* described as a "scantily circulated muckraking sheet" ("Digest in the Doghouse," 82), that had been reprinted by John DeBoer in *English Journal*.

Angela Broening, anticipating a showdown at the convention in Columbus, was prepared to fight for her principles, despite the police outside the hall and the lawyers and newspaper reporters within. Ever ready to serve the Council, she was in a political hot seat. As president of NCTE, she had to do what was best for it according to her own judgment. She could not simply accept the standing committee's unfavorable report on a popular magazine with a readership numbering in the millions. Not only did she believe the charges were unproved, but she also had to safeguard her organization against a potential lawsuit. To Broening, what was best was to present both sides of the conflict and to provide a balanced view. She had done her best to resolve the issue within the Council. Now that the issue was before the public, she was even more strongly determined to deal with it fairly, appealing to reason and avoiding the rhetoric of a political point of view.

The Board of Directors session began on that Thanksgiving afternoon in Columbus in 1944. Angela M. Broening had presided over only three agenda items before she reached the fourth item—the Committee on Newspapers and Magazines, the stick of dynamite that she hoped to prevent from exploding. Looking out into the hall, she observed that committee chair Helen Rand Miller and Joseph Gallant were distributing copies of the committee's report to the delegates. Broening insisted that all copies be retrieved, refusing to let the unproved report be presented at the meeting. Then she called on Harold A. Anderson to present "the true facts" in the conflict between the Council's Executive Committee and the Committee on Newspapers and Magazines and between the committee and the *Reader's Digest*.

After months of striving for a compromise and of insisting on a report that would stand up to legal charges, Broening now had no choice but to repudiate publicly the standing committee. Once she took the floor, the conflict became what the *New York Times* called "'a free-for-all' fight between the executive committee of the council and members of the magazine and newspaper committee" (Fine 1944a, 25).

The concern of the Committee on Newspapers and Magazines, as expressed in its report about the *Reader's Digest* (which was printed in the *New York Times*), was that "if there is even one article in an issue that spreads suspicion or distrust among groups of people or countries that need to work together now for the interests of all, it is betraying instead of extending the brotherhood of man" (25).

Broening must have been seething over this statement, which completely ignored the concessions that the *Reader's Digest* had made in the May meeting with the Committee on Magazines and Newspapers and the Executive Committee. The committee was taking a stance which left no room for compromise: either the *Reader's Digest* would publish only articles that met with the committee's approval, or it could not be used in the schools. It must be remembered that this was 1944, with World War II in full swing; it was a time of legitimate fears about the effects of propaganda. The *Digest* well may have published articles expressing views that the committee found highly objectionable. However, was there such a clear and ever-present danger in these views that it justified, in effect, censoring the *Reader's Digest*? If NCTE accepted the committee's report, it would be considered as censorship, and the effect on the *Reader's Digest* would be seriously detrimental. Broening forcefully pointed out that the committee had published the report without the Council's approval: "'I've been accused of pigeonholing the report,' she shouted, banging on the table. 'I didn't want it to be published the way it was written. . . . It is unscholarly, undocumented, full of libelous statements that would wreck this council if it got out of our hands'" (25).

Referring to passages in the committee's report which "pointed out that The *Digest* had been accused of being anti-Semitic, anti-Negro, anti-labor and anti-Roosevelt" (25), Broening cited the Executive Committee's response: "We asked for documentation, for proof of every damaging statement made, but we did not get it." Broening was well within her prerogatives when she insisted on specific evidence to substantiate the allegations. "Just bringing together negative statements about The Reader's Digest without evidence does not give the executive committee a basis for deciding whether we should continue this study," she declared (Jones 1944).

To the committee's expressed concern that the *Reader's Digest* "is used widely in the public schools as a teaching medium, and often is used as a textbook substitute, according to the investigating committee" (Jones 1944), it was further noted, probably by Broening, that the report was "remiss in not making overt recommendations and in advising classroom use of the Digest at the discretion of individual teachers" ("Teachers Council," 82). Indeed, preparing for this very problem, the program committee had scheduled a session for the following Friday afternoon entitled "Demonstration: How to Teach High-School Students to Use Newspapers and Magazines in Dealing with Controversial Questions."

Responding to the standing committee's charge that she or the Executive Committee had been swayed and co-opted by "a great commercial interest," Angela Broening stated, "it was a 'damnable lie.'" Undoubtedly under a strain from the many months of dispute brought by this issue, not to mention the hours of work spent preparing for the NCTE annual meeting, Broening was determined to have her full say. Despite the acting chair's plea to sit down, she continued, citing "her family's record for fairness" (Fine 1944a, 25). Then Broening flatly stated what she suspected lay behind the whole attack on the *Reader's Digest*: "The Communist press has put me in an incredible position" (25). Appalled at the events, she asked, "Is that the way to treat the president of the National Council of Teachers of English?" (25). [For discussion of another encounter involving the NCTE and the Communist Party, see chapter four of this book, "Dora V. Smith: A Legacy for the Future."]

Broening then distributed copies of the fifty-five-page report that she had presented that morning to the Executive Committee, which authorized her to provide copies to the Board of Directors ("Columbus Meeting," 105). Her report consisted of three parallel columns presenting excerpts from the committee's findings, her scholarly critique of the report, and the *Reader's Digest*'s refutations. Broening asserted that the committee "had failed to examine the reliability of the critics and the validity of the criticisms" ("Teachers Council," 82).

Since NCTE was unable to come to closure on the issue in the afternoon, a midnight session was called for that evening, with Angela M. Broening as chair. Before closing the afternoon proceedings, she insisted upon a vote of confidence, but that, too, was postponed for consideration later that night. At this midnight session, after heated, confused debate, the controversy was resolved, thanks to some strategizing in the interim. Since the three-year term of the Committee on Newspapers and Magazines ended once the annual meeting concluded, a way out of the conflict presented itself. According to Lou LaBrant, who later became NCTE president in 1954, concerned Council members had met because "they were afraid that the Council itself would be split. Because whenever political matters are involved, there is that tendency, and we didn't want that to get into the Council." There was also concern for Broening, "a president whom a great many people admired and felt affection for" (quoted in Hook 1979, 141–42).

As soon as the meeting opened, and without an opportunity for more than a few words of discussion, a supporter of Broening's made the following motion, which was passed: "*Resolved*, That we ask the Executive Committee to appoint a new Committee on Magazine Study to examine and pursue the materials already discovered as far as those seem usable; that they be empowered, however, to go further in the study of this magazine or other magazines used by high-school people; that they report to us, the Directors, next year, and that the committee consist of persons not now on the magazine or on the Executive Committee" ("Columbus Meeting," 105–106). Lou LaBrant and other concerned members of the Council then acted on their strategy; when LaBrant moved to lay the motion on the table, it was quickly seconded (Hook 1979, 142). When Broening asked for discussion of this motion, it was ruled out of order by the parliamentarian. When the motion passed, it took the two factions—the Executive Committee and the Committee on Newspapers and Magazines—out of the fray. However, when the *Reader's Digest*'s legal representative, Arthur Garfield Hays, offered the assistance of the *Reader's Digest* to the new committee, shouts of "Out of order!" from the delegates carried the day, but not before Hays had a chance to throw in some disruptive words about "the smearing that we have received." The vote was almost unanimous in not letting Hays speak, for he was not a member of NCTE. This silencing of the *Reader's Digest* representative pleased Helen Rand Miller, the chair of the Committee on Newspapers and Magazines, who declared, "This is a complete victory for us" (Fine 1944b, 21).

Amazingly, the *Reader's Digest* was also pleased with the results of the midnight session, as attested by Albert Cole, its general manager: "We are, of course, pleased with the action of the directors in repudiating the preposterous report of its magazine and newspaper committee in discharging that committee." He continued: "We note that a completely new committee will consider the character and value of all magazines used in public schools and The Digest for one welcomes that inquiry and offers its fullest cooperation" (21).

Although the convention was not over, Angela Broening had won the day. There would be no legal suit against NCTE by *Reader's Digest*, and the delegates, with only one dissenting vote, had given her the vote of confidence she had demanded (21).

Twenty-eight years later, in 1972, Robert C. Pooley, a member of the 1944 Executive Committee, wrote Angela M. Broening's obituary for *Elementary English*. Surely he was remembering Broening as she was that November day and night in 1944. Angela Broening, he wrote, was "an implacable defender of what she considered right and good for English, her voice, vibrant with sincerity, ringing out at meetings of the Board of Directors and the Annual Business Meetings. At such times she would protest against or strongly defend ideas before these bodies with all the force of a vivid personality. Yet with this earnestness she preserved a sense of humor and could yield with graciousness when over-ruled" (629).

Before her presidency, Angela Broening had served the Council in several important capacities—as second vice-president in 1939 and as first vice-president in 1943—but none was as important as her appointment in 1937 to chair a new committee to continue the work of the previous Curriculum Commission, which in 1935 had published a report entitled *An Experience Curriculum in English*. The original Curriculum Commission had been appointed by the Executive Committee in 1929; its intent was to create "a pattern that other groups could take as a starting point in developing a curriculum to fit their own particular circumstances" (Applebee 1974, 119). Broening's task was to translate this report into action because "Something had to be done about the English curriculum: youth, society, and educational theory—all were changing faster than school practice" (Broening 1939, v). This statement from the preface to *Conducting Experiences in English* remains true today, for we are always caught up in change. In 1939, when the report was issued, the enforcement of compulsory education had caused turmoil in public school education and the need for change; today's conflict appears on the college level with the enactment of open admissions. Broening's preface demonstrates the similarities with today's issue: "With the enforcement of compulsory attendance laws, all kinds of children were attending school and staying on to graduate. Scientific measurements were disclosing a wide range of differences among pupils previously considered alike" (v). Today, reader-response criticism (evidenced by teachers mandating journal entries on works read) seems so new; however, this 1939 report, under Broening's leadership, emphasized these two key points in reader-response criticism: The student reader "takes as much of the book as he can, rewriting it, as it were, in the imagery of his own experience" (Applebee 1974, 122); and such an activity may "foster a 'natural, vital discussion of the experience shared by the author'" (122). It is my contention that the best literature unit which Applebee singles out for praise in *Tradition and Reform in the Teaching of English* is one used by Broening, first in her *Developing Appreciation through Teaching Literature* (1929) and later in *A Guide to Children's Literature* (Bamberger and Broening 1931).

Broening's reasonable success with the Curriculum Commission project and with her acclaimed textbook series inevitably led to her being appointed as associate director of the new Commission on the English Curriculum (1945–63) and as chair of the Production Committee, which produced the third volume in the curriculum series, *The English Language Arts in the Secondary School*, in 1956.

Angela M. Broening's forty-eight years as an educator divide essentially into these four categories: teacher, administrator, author, and editor. During these years she was based in the Baltimore Public Schools, first as teacher and then vice-principal of George Washington

Elementary School, as supervisor of libraries, supervisor of geography, and supervisor of junior high school English, and as head of the English department at Forest Park High School (the position she held when president of NCTE); from 1946 on she served as associate director of the Bureau of Research, Baltimore Public Schools, and in 1953 as director of publications in the Division of Public Information and Publications, Baltimore Department of Education.

Broening was the sole author of one book and numerous articles. Her dissertation, *Developing Appreciation through Teaching Literature*, was published as a book in 1929 after eight years of research. The object of her study was "How to teach literature so that boys and girls will love it and voluntarily read it for the satisfaction of the literary experience it affords" (2). Her operating definition of appreciation was "emotionalized insight: an idea with a glow, an understanding with sympathy, a laugh with a cause; a sob with sincerity" (5-6). Equating appreciation with enjoyment, she located it in seven areas: intellectual, physical, technical, humorous, social, aesthetic, and ethical. To measure appreciation and to demonstrate that it could be developed through literature, she used the principle of judging the best of four versions from Abbott and Trabue's "A Measure of Ability to Judge Poetry" (1921) and also from her own 1923 unpublished master's essay, "Correlation of Ability to Judge Poetry and Certain Other Measures," although she chose prose because her fifth, sixth, and seventh graders read more prose than poetry. This technique involved revising the literary works "to throw into relief the literary merit of the original" (Broening 1929, 8) and to spoil plot consistency, consistency in characterization, poetic justice or truth to human experience, sentiment, and imagery. Once she had established the criteria, Broening then had to find ways of conditioning the growth of appreciation. Teachers found the third chapter of the book, "Experimental Factor," most useful because it illustrated exactly how appreciation was developed in literature. The four segments on "Sea Poetry," "The Pirate in Literature and in Life," "The Awakening of Spring: An Arbor Day Play," and "A Trip to Bookland via No. 22 School Library" are role models combining the methods of organizing by unit and theme. To read this literary list of what boys and girls in the fourth, fifth, and sixth grades read in 1929 is to make 1990 teachers weep for the days that are no more. Of Broening's eleven positive conclusions, these two stand out: "(9) That given a professional attitude, a 'hot interest' in literature, and access to the materials and sources developed by the author-experimenter, a good teacher can produce growth in literary appreciation" (77–78) and "(10) That it is the obligation of instructors in methods courses in the teaching of children's literature and the makers of courses of study to provide teachers with sources of materials and suggestions, based on experience in teaching, as to ways of presenting these materials so that children will grow in ability to develop appreciation of literature" (78). During the sixty years since the 1929 publication of Broening's book, undoubtedly teachers of English have believed in and practiced her proven premise that we can teach appreciation of literature.

That same year, 1929, Broening began to coauthor books. With Mary S. Wilkinson she wrote *Adventures in the Library: Magic Keys to Books*. In 1931 she coauthored with Florence E. Bamberger, her former education professor, *A Guide to Children's Literature*. Broening, at that time an instructor in education at Johns Hopkins University and assistant director of the Bureau of Research, Baltimore Public Schools, identified action, human interest, and imaginative appeal as three elements children desire in their reading. Direct discourse, colorful description, names for everything, funny-incident humor, and sincerity were further cited as ingredients that children prefer in their reading. Chapter three of the work provided valuable assistance on "The Preparation of a Unit in Literature," with subsequent chapters presenting discussions and sample units of "Poetry in the Elementary School," including a reprint of the "Sea Poetry" segment from Broening's 1929 book, "Fairy Tales, Myths, and Legends," and "Animals in Literature and in Life." Broening's sister, Mary L. Broening, an elementary school principal, prepared with Helen Neer the unit on "Experiencing Spring in Life and Art."

In 1936, Angela Broening expanded her work on the library by jointly publishing with Frederick Law, Mary S. Wilkinson, and Carolina Ziegler *How to Use the Library: Practice Exercises in the Use of the More Important Library Tools*. The same year also saw the publication of another coauthored book in the same vein as the library book, *Reading for Practice: Exercises for Remedial Reading and Library*, which was for grades seven through twelve.

The following year Broening shifted from practical exercises to coediting with other department heads in the Baltimore Public Schools *English As You Like It*, two textbooks for ninth and tenth graders. At this time Broening was head of the English Department at Forest Park High School in Baltimore. The title succinctly reflects her pedagogical predilections from the beginning of her career to its close: consensus in the enjoyment of learning. The introduction to the two texts cites, not Shakespeare, but an anecdote from a football hero as the source for the title. "When asked what he meant, he explained that he had not only learned to speak and to write more effectively, but had also *enjoyed the learning"* (v). To ensure that the selections offered pleasurable learning experiences, Broening and her coauthors pretested their selections. "The thousands of high school boys and girls who cooperated in making these units helped the authors to *infuse fun* into the game of learning to speak and to write correctly and effectively" (v). In demonstration of this emphasis on pleasurable learning, both textbooks began with a unit on storytelling, with the ninth-grade book treating the topic in the context of "Wishing to Be Somebody Else" and the tenth-grade text in the context of "Buried Treasure." The final units of each textbook focused on research; the ninth graders were exploring "The Lure of the Middle Ages," and the tenth graders were "Discussing Interesting People."

Broening followed these publications with *Conducting Experiences in English*, the Curriculum Commission report prepared for NCTE in 1939. In 1944 she continued her textbook work by coediting *Competence in English I*, which was "261 pages of material for testing, drilling, and testing again." Published in wartime, the preface validated the worth of the book to ninth and tenth graders by pointing out that members of the Army and Navy had studied the book to master the essentials of language.

The jewel in Broening's textbook crown was the three-volume series *Best-liked Literature*, which was published in 1947. As references for the text, Broening cited *An Experience Curriculum in English* and *Conducting Experiences in English* (Broening 1939), both of which were prepared by NCTE and based on consensus. In the note to students at the beginning of the texts, Broening assured them that these selections were "the reading preferences of boys and girls of your age in two hundred communities scattered over the United States." To emphasize this point, she further stated that "no selection appears within the covers of *Best-liked Literature* unless it has been read, approved, enjoyed, and recommended by the many pupils who have co-operated in choosing the materials." The units in these three volumes continued to reflect Broening's preferences: storytelling and humor; for example, volume three opened with "Enjoying a Good Story" and included works by Agatha Christie and Edgar Allan Poe. The unit on humor included Stephen Leacock, P. G. Wodehouse, and James Thurber. Of particular interest to the members of the Committee on Women in the Profession is Broening's inclusion of such notable women as Marie Curie, Susan B. Anthony, Henrietta Szold, and Clara Barton in a unit called "Some People Worth Knowing" in the second volume of the series.

At the same time that Broening was editing textbooks, she worked full-time in the Baltimore public school system. For fifteen years she served as director of publications, editing, designing, and writing "curriculum guides, books or pamphlets for student use, annual and research reports, and bulletins to parents, teachers and students" (Everett 1968).

As an administrator, Broening was vice-principal of an elementary school, head of an English department, director of publications, president and vice-president of NCTE, and also president of fifteen other organizations, notably the National Conference on Research in English. As a teacher, she was a visiting instructor and a workshop or conference consultant at seventeeen universities during her summer vacations. She taught in the Baltimore Public Schools, first in the elementary grades and then in high school.

As a result of her substantial contributions to education through her teaching, her organizational service, and her editing and writing, Angela M. Broening is a role model. Her mother, Mary Kyne Broening, set her on her career in words when she assigned Angela, one of seven children, the specialty of letter writing, which she practiced by writing to out-of-town relatives. Her sisters also influenced her career. She taught with at least two of them; one persuaded her that she had to be with young people all day if she wanted to get to know them.

Broening understood the ever-changing nature of education and put it into action democratically. Her penchant for reaching consensus by consulting with everyone concerned is her best legacy to today's educators, whether women or men. It was her way of uniting enjoyment with learning. Her focus on how children learn and her belief that knowledge should be built on experience guide us still.

However, Angela M. Broening will be best remembered for those November days in 1944 when she was the "implacable defender" of sound scholarship, of reasoned judgment based on evidence, and of the organization she served so well—the National Council of Teachers of English.

Works Cited

Abbott, A., and Trabue. 1921. "A Measure of Ability to Judge Poetry." *Teachers College Record* 22 (March): 1, 5.

Applebee, Arthur N. 1974. *Tradition and Reform in the Teaching of English: A History.* Urbana, Ill.: National Council of Teachers of English.

Bamberger, Florence E., and Angela M. Broening. 1931. *A Guide to Children's Literature.* Baltimore: Johns Hopkins University Press.

Beckoff, Samuel. 1943. "The Rainbow." *English Journal* 32 (June): 325–30.
Broening, Angela M. 1929. *Developing Appreciation through Teaching Literature.* Johns Hopkins University Studies in Education, edited by Edward F. Buchner, no. 13. Baltimore: Johns Hopkins University Press.
———. 1934. "Factors Influencing Pupils' Reading of Library Books: A Baltimore Book Survey (1931–33)." *Elementary English Review* 11 (June): 155–61.
———. 1939. *Conducting Experiences in English.* New York: Appleton-Century-Crofts.
———. 1942. "English in War and in Peace." *English Journal* 31 (November): 676.
———. 10 July 1944. Letter to NCTE Council members, 1–12.
Broening, Angela M., et al. 1936. *Reading for Practice: Exercises for Remedial Reading and Library.* New York: Noble and Noble.
———. 1937. *English As You Like It.* 2 vols. New York: Harper.
Broening, Angela M., et al., eds. 1944. *Competence in English I.* New York: Harper.
———. 1947. *Best-liked Literature.* 3 vols. Boston: Ginn.
Broening, Angela M., Frederick Law, Mary S. Wilkinson, and Carolina Ziegler. 1936. *How to Use the Library: Practice Exercises in the Use of the More Important Library Tools.* New York: Noble and Noble.
Broening, Angela M., and Mary S. Wilkinson. 1929. *Adventures in the Library: Magic Keys to Books.* Baltimore: Department of Education and the Enoch Pratt Free Library.
"The Columbus Meeting." 1945. *English Journal* 34 (February): 105–106.
DeBoer, John. 1943a. "Summary and Report." *English Journal* 32 (February): 106–110.
———. 1943b. "Summary and Report." *English Journal* 32 (March): 167–70.
"Digest in the Doghouse." 21 February 1944. *Newsweek*, 82, 84.
Everett, Sherbourne. 30 September 1968. "Dr. Angela Broening: Constantly Active." *Baltimore Sun*, B1.
Fanton, Jonathan F. 28 December 1989. Letter to the editor. *New York Times*, A20.
Fine, Benjamin. 1944a (24 November 1944). "Teachers of English Embroiled over Class Use of Reader's Digest: Report Accusing Magazine of Biases and 'Pressure' Causes a Battle Royal in the National Council at Columbus." *New York Times*, 25.
———. 1944b (25 November 1944). "New Inquiry Is Set on Reader's Digest: Teachers of English, After a Noisy Session, Give Fresh Group a Year's Task." *New York Times*, 21, 6.
Hook, J. N. 1979. *A Long Way Together: A Personal View of NCTE's First Sixty-Seven Years.* Urbana, Ill.: National Council of Teachers of English.
Jones, Bill. 24 November 1944. "Magazine Report Debated at Parley." *Columbus, Ohio, Citizen.*
Landry, Herbert A. 1943. "Teaching Reading with the Reader's Digest." *English Journal* 32 (June): 320–24.
Pooley, Robert C. 1972. "In Memoriam: Angela M. Broening." *Elementary English* 49 (April): 629.
"Propaganda Study Scares 'Digest' Staff: Teachers Group Analyzes Magazine

for 'Planted' Articles." 10 September 1944. *PM*.
Sargeant, Jeanne B. N.d. "The Woman behind the Publications." Department of Education, Baltimore Public Schools (?).
"Teachers Council Bans Own Report in Hot Feud over Reader's Digest." 4 December 1944. *Newsweek*: 82, 84–85.
"United States Treasury Publishes Council Productions." 1943. *English Journal* 32 (October): 463.

6 Marion C. Sheridan: A Lifetime Commitment

Sharon Hamilton-Wieler, Indiana University–Purdue University at Indianapolis

Marion C. Sheridan
ca. 1900–1979

Marion C. Sheridan, president of the National Council of Teachers of English from 1949 to 1950, is best known for her work with the nonprofit group Teaching Film Custodians, but that is only a partial reason for her inclusion in this volume. That she pioneered the use of film in the English classroom; that she was ahead of her time in emphasizing writing processes, publishing student writing, and advocating writing across the curriculum; that she was an actively contributing member of NCTE for almost sixty years and of the New England Association of Teachers of English for more than sixty years, serving two separate terms as president of NEATE; and that she committed her professional life to working with colleagues to help students in English classes become active inquirers: these are the reasons why Sheridan is an important figure in English education. "A lifetime commitment" are the words used by Alfred H. Grommon, chair of the Commission on the History of the Council, to summarize his oral-history interview with Sheridan on 18 July 1977. What follows is one of many possible stories this "lifetime commitment" could have engendered.

As Faulkner, one of Sheridan's best-loved authors, dramatically illustrates in the structure of *Absalom! Absalom!*, to reconstruct the past is to challenge the hazards of imprecise memory, partial glimpses, preconceived expectations and biases, and real-world limitations of time and access to as much information as one would like. Sheridan herself, during her interview with Grommon, cautioned him, and any listeners, to "Be very careful when working from these vague remembrances." With this caution in mind, for this author and for the reader, Sheridan's life story is retold based on a combination of conversations with and letters from Sheridan's colleagues and contemporaries as well as articles she authored during the 1940s, 1950s, and 1960s. Out of these has emerged the following biographical sketch of Marion C. Sheridan.

Sheridan was born in New Haven, Connecticut; she acquired her B.S. degree at Columbia University, her M.A. at Yale in 1928, and her Ph.D., also at Yale, in 1934. She began her teaching career in 1913 at Connecticut High School and then moved in 1914 to James T. Hillhouse High School in Hew Haven, Connecticut, the same high school from which she had graduated four years earlier. Here she stayed, becoming head of the English Department in 1931, a position she held until her retirement in 1961. Her professional concerns, however, did not retire. Sheridan became a self-employed consultant in the teaching, speaking, and writing of English from 1961 until her death in 1979; she served as archivist for the New England School and College Conference on English in 1962; she served as chair of the World Heritage Film and Book Program, affiliated with the National Advisory Committee of Educators, also in 1962; she was a member of the Connecticut Service Council Steering Committee for WNAC-TV from 1963 to 1966 and served as a liaison between the American Association of University Women and WTNH-TV from 1966 until the mid-1970s; and in 1966 she participated in a panel at the International Federation of University Women in Paris. In her spare time she maintained work on a history of the teaching of reading in New Haven, Connecticut, a continuation of her dissertation: "The Teaching of Reading in the Public Schools of New Haven, 1638–1930."

In addition to Sheridan's nearly sixty-year affiliation with NCTE, during which she spent seventeen years as chair of the Committee on Film, working with the Teaching Film Custodians, she was also a member of the American Association of University Women, serving as president of the Connecticut division from 1954 to 1958 and as president of the New Haven branch from 1963 to 1965. She was also a member of the New York branch of the English Speaking Union of the United States and of the Connecticut Council of Teachers of English. She was affiliated with the New England Association of Teachers of English for longer than sixty years, serving as president in both 1935 and 1952, after which she was awarded a life membership. She was also awarded lifetime memberships to the New Haven Colony Historical Society and the Columbia Scholastic Press Association, where she served as a member of the Scholastic Advisory Board in 1942–43.

Sheridan's contribution to these committees was honored by more than life memberships. The New Haven branch of the American Association of University Women awards an annual scholarship in Marion C. Sheridan's name and honor. She was awarded the Gold Key to the Columbia Scholastic Press Association in 1949; she was given an NCTE citation for "Outstanding Contribution to the Teaching of English in Secondary Schools" in 1958, followed by a grant for her work in English classrooms in 1962-63; she received Yale University's Distinguished Teacher Award for "Outstanding Service in Secondary Schools" in 1962 and the Education Press of America Award in 1973.

All the above are touchstones, markers of the paths that Sheridan chose to tread throughout her professional career. They are silent testimonials to the directions of her continued dedication, but say little about the substance of that dedication. More substantive is the voice that speaks through her writing. Here we find Marion Sheridan the teacher, who faced classes of high school English students in her own community, day after day, year after year, and decade after decade for forty-eight years; here we find Marion Sheridan the colleague, who shared her insights and concerns with fellow educators as they sought ways together to improve the teaching of English; here we find Marion Sheridan the postwar president of NCTE, questioning traditional values, defending or assaulting them as the circumstances of a rapidly changing world deemed necessary. Several themes weave throughout her writing, but major among them are notions of creativity, the importance of literature, the role of film in the English classroom, the significance of writing in relation to learning, and the roles of teacher and student in their interactions with English and the language arts. Since Sheridan, in her interview with Grommon, singled out her attention to creativity as the dominant theme in her pedagogical interests, in this chapter her views on creativity will serve as the Faulknerian pebble that ripples into ever-widening areas of pedagogical concerns.

During the late 1920s, Hughes Mearns's *Creative Youth: How a School Environment Set Free the Creative Spirit* (1925) inspired Sheridan to experiment with creative projects in her classroom and influenced much of her subsequent thinking about creativity in the English curriculum. Her earliest pedagogical applications of creativity involved writing. She encouraged her students to publish what they had written, and pioneered high school literary publications at Hillhouse High School with the establishment of the still functioning *Literary Magazine*. Although the publication of student work is an integral part of today's English classrooms (at least in the rhetoric of current pedagogy), Sheridan stated that "these creative aspects were perceived as very novel at the time." One poignant memory that she drew upon when talking of her students' work in the *Literary Magazine* was a poem by Constance Baker Motley, currently a lawyer who has been influential in obtaining recognition for blacks within the legal system. Sheridan recited Motley's poem, "Lord, Listen to the Slums," published decades earlier, in a somewhat halting but nonetheless powerful voice (1977). Both the words and the pauses demonstrated Sheridan's caring for this student and for her ideas and concerns. Perhaps this memory was symbolic for a host of other memories of other students, other stories, and other poems.

Creativity was a focal point in Marion C. Sheridan's 1949 presidential address, titled "Beyond Fancy's Dream," wherein she called a noncreative, skills-oriented conception of English teaching "degrading. It reduces English to too low a level, to a sum of unrelated parts. It confines English to mechanics, to externals, to outward shells, to husks" (1950, 62). Later in the address, she drew upon Allison Davis's Inglis Lecture at Harvard, "Social-Class Influences upon Learning," when he spoke of "the absence of the creative in schools with middle-class emphasis on 'a rather narrow range of mental abilities and problems'" (quoted in Sheridan 1950, 62). Sheridan went on to say that "English to develop powers of individual students beyond fancy's dream must be directed to the human, creative side of a person whose dignity is respected" (62).

This theme of creativity was more fully developed a decade later in Sheridan's article celebrating the fiftieth anniversary of *English Journal*, "Creative Language Experiences in the High School." Early in her discussion, she wrote: "We cannot think of what our world calls for without realizing that today it is most important to stimulate the creative. That has not always been the aim of education. In some civilizations . . . the aim was to memorize, to follow the past, to insure conformity. In contrast in all aspects of education today, there is an urgent need for the creative" (1960, 563).

Sheridan would offer firm argument to those anachronistic educators who still think that the "creative" is for those students already competent in basic skills. She wrote about the importance of creative learning experiences for students in technical-vocational as well as university-bound classes, implying the hazards of classifying students into rigid categories and foreseeing the burgeoning flow of adult learners into tertiary education:

In pleading for the creative, I am well aware that people have been classified at least tentatively as creative, less creative, and noncreative. I have hope that there can be some shifts in these classifications. . . . The creative approach regards no one as hopeless. . . . For all students . . . the creative approach seems to be a wise one, discovering all that is potential in young people of varied backgrounds. This approach is appropriate for those who know they are going to college, for those who hope they are going, who may never go, and the increasing group of those who may go, not immediately after secondary school but at some later date. (563–65)

Sheridan did not directly define what she meant by "creativity," but implied a definition in her discussion of what she termed "the creative approach":

[The creative approach] is concerned with the practical, the concrete, the imaginative, the logical, and the abstract. The creative approach should jog the students out of passivity, out of mechanical ruts, *out of unthinking acceptance of what is* [emphasis added]. It should make familiar things strange and worthy of note, give new instruments for thought, and encourage daring combinations of the old. It is directed towards making students alert, curious, responsive, independent, original, and pioneering individuals. . . . Something wholesome, life-giving should happen as a result of day-to-day encouragement of curiosity or inquiry, illumination, imagination, and thinking. Students may then place value on flexibility and originality *with power to organize and perhaps, more important, to reorganize* [emphasis added]. (565–69)

It is tempting to take the words "power" and "reorganize" in that last sentence and to build with them an argument for Marion Sheridan's prescience of today's emphasis on empowering students through developing their ability to reenvision and thereby to re-create their world views and relationships within these world views. Such a connection would be tenuous at this point in the discussion, but the subsequent delineation of how Sheridan applied her notions of "the creative approach" to her classroom teaching and her professional presentations and articles should implicitly construct this connection.

Sheridan's "creative approach" embraced all aspects of the English curriculum that she developed for her own classroom and for the English Department at Hillhouse High School. Her 1952 article, "Teaching a Novel," directly demonstrated this relationship between her notions of "the creative approach" and the study and enjoyment of literature: "Faith in the value of teaching a novel may be based upon belief in the significance of the imaginative" (9). Themes and concerns that Sheridan expressed about creativity in general are evident in her discussions of literature. At a time when critically authorized judgment and closure were typical features of literary analysis, Sheridan was striving to "jog the students out of passivity ... out of unthinking acceptance of what is" (1960, 565) and into "alert, curious, responsive, original, and pioneering individuals" (569). As early as 1944, she was drawing upon the intertextual influences of literature in its many forms and genres to encourage her students to assess and reassess their views and attitudes: "Study of the essay often has revolutionized a student's attitude toward poetry and literature, making him discredit finality of judgment in favor of independent analysis and the use of touchstones" (1944b, 418).

Postwar pragmatism, however, posed a threat to the teaching of literature to all students, with the move toward early streaming of university-bound and vocational-bound students. This threat prompted Sheridan, in her status as incoming president of NCTE, to make public her concerns, both in talks given to teachers in New England and in a 1948 article, "Life without Literature," which condensed these talks. She stated her concern bluntly at the outset: "The question of life without literature is based upon realism in the teaching of English, for suggestions have been made that operate in the direction of its omission from school courses. . . . [For non-college-bound students] a trend is for the practical, with literature in competition with a wide variety of more or less practical courses" (1948a, 291). Her abhorrence for the move to eliminate literature from the course of studies for non-university-bound students is shown when she paraphrased the contending viewpoint. Her professional passion came close to being an almost vitriolic diatribe:

> [Some educators contend that] to study vocational material in a broad and in a narrow sense, to study budgeting, or safe driving, is more valuable than to study literature. Literature may be said to have little to offer, to be a frill: poetry should be for the poetical; novels for the elect; literature an elective or an omission. . . . Yes, literature is for you and for me, but not for these others. They are different, you know. They do not grasp ideas. They do not feel. They can use their hands. They must have the practical. Think of the individual students in public high schools, of their wide range of color, ability, religion, environment, background, receptiveness. Statistically and arbitrarily we say, "No literature," and we may go on: "No literature for I.Q. 95, 90, or below." Perhaps one of our next studies should be to determine statistically the exact mathematical point at which literature should be out. It may be, however, that literature should be in: since at least the time of the Bible and of Aesop a story has been an effective way of presenting an idea. (292, 294)

Sheridan's mistrust of positivistic, statistical approaches to language learning, implied above, was reiterated four years later when she wrote, "the outcomes of the study [of literature] . . . are not measurable" (1952, 14). She cautioned: "As we plan to teach novels—or literature—we may well keep in mind the complexity of the undertaking" (14). This concern for ensuring that educators appreciate the complexity of responding to literature echoed her 1948 article, wherein she quoted a colleague who was also upset about rigid and limited approaches to literary response, especially for those students who, in the years of postwar pragmatism, were at risk of having literature eliminated from their course of studies: "Well, I suppose we may have to blame our profession for giving so much meaningless material to average children or to less than average children" (1948a, 292).

In the 1952 article Sheridan warned about the potentially reductive hazards of definition, particularly teacher definition or literary critical definition, at a time when instruction by definition was an integral part of the teaching of literature: "A definition of a novel may grow out of the study of the novel. Attempts at definition should come from as many sources as possible, including a wide reading of novels . . . in preference to a reading of criticism. . . . Students should be as wary of definition as Mrs. Yeobright was" (1952, 13).

Long before Louise Rosenblatt's transactional view of responding to literature became part of English teachers' common pedagogical lore, Marion C. Sheridan's views of multifaceted roles of literature indicated her awareness of Rosenblatt's work. While "New Criticism" dominated the field of literary inquiry and literary studies in secondary English classrooms, Sheridan was envisioning much further reaching goals for the study of literature. Central to her view was the idea of literature as revelatory not only of the characters in the novel, but of humankind in general and, most interestingly, of the reader in particular: "Literature, one of the humanities, reveals man to himself and to others, reveals others to him, and it does so in a highly charged way, vividly, dramatically, memorably" (1948a, 295).

Her view of reading as transaction, implied in the above statement, was asserted more directly later in the article: " . . . the impact of literature is a continuing process: in the reader so much is dependent on what has gone before; so much is raised as question, held in abeyance, ready to emerge; so much has to be checked against life" (296). The primary transaction, according to Sheridan, engaged students in developing awareness of themselves and others in a world that was psychologically as well as technologically complex. In 1944 she wrote of her students who learned through the reading of literature that "only the unwary think the author always expresses his own views" (1944b, 418); that "men and women are not so simple as they seem" (quoting Real in 1944b, 419); and that "stereotypes are as dangerous as they are amusing" (420). Sheridan reiterated these ideas four years later when she wrote: "It may be that the more stodgy a student is, the more he needs literature—to stir his heart, to expand his world, to stimulate his imagination—if it be only to make him see his neighbor" (1948a, 293).

But Sheridan's views of the transactional nature of literary response went beyond the purely individual. In 1942 she spoke of wartime goals of English in general and of literature in particular:

> In April 1942, addressing the New York State Teachers Association, Marion Sheridan said that in early December the nation's emphasis had been on winning the peace after the war, but that later developments (the Allies were losing battle after battle) were showing that the most pressing need was "conversion, physical and mental, to the ways of war." What, she asked, does English offer toward winning the war? She answered: [English] "is a powerful subject, far more than drills or skills. It is a means of communication seldom if ever mastered; a means of stimulating emotion, of effecting success or failure, with the sorrow that failure brings.... a means of sharpening perceptions and understandings .... A democracy depends upon the use of words, upon the ability to understand and to discuss questions of freedom, liberty, labor; upon the ability to trace the course of thought and to detect specious argument.... Literature is a storehouse of the experiences of mankind.... Its peace and serenity may give balance and a sense of normalcy, and fortitude, when total war dominates the situation." (Hook 1979, 133)

She also stressed in her classes the public service that literature performs in its political task of criticizing the state (1948a, 296). In focusing on this political role of literature, Sheridan reinforced her view of teaching English as jogging students "out of unthinking acceptance of what is" in order to help them to become independent, thoughtful, and creative thinkers in their society.

Typical of Sheridan's writing is that she rarely remained long in the world of theoretical abstractions. She moved her ideas directly into the English classroom, not in simplistic "how-to" terms, but rather in terms which challenge teachers to determine how best to do "what must be done." In her wartime article, "Literature: Freighter, Fighter, and Star Steerer," she asserted that "first of all ... books must be taken out of ivory towers and made to compete with other forms of communication—radio, motion picture, and talk. Today, they must also compete with work, financially remunerative and volunteer. They must be neither remote nor forbidding, but human, part of thinking and living" (1944b, 415). Her attack on teachers who viewed the canon as unassailable and who treated students unfamiliar with classical literature as culturally deprived could position Marion Sheridan with timeless grace right into a modern classroom: "It is sentimental and foolish to defend the teaching of *The Idylls of the King* by telling questioning sophomores that all cultured people have read of Arthur and Lancelot" (415).

Sheridan implied the often-overlooked role of literature teachers as also reading teachers, who guide and assist their students' exploration and appreciation of literature. For example, she decried the traditional approach to reading complex and conceptually difficult books from cover to cover while at the same time appearing prescient of current emphasis on narratology and intertextuality in her discussion of how to approach Boswell's *Johnson*: "To begin with, students should dip into it to find human stories to retell" (416). She also alerted teachers to the necessity of emphasizing the need to develop, in themselves and in their students, a range of ways of reading and of responding to reading: "Readers, of course, must be flexible. They must make unconscious and rapid adjustments to the demands of different purposes, types, and eras. Needless to say, a serious logical essay, approached as if it were Milne's *When We Were Very Young*, will be disappointing" (417).

Sheridan discussed students' sensitivity when responding to nuances in the voices of their parents and their teachers and then spoke of the need to transfer that sensitivity to students' literary responses:

> Very likely a student is a canny interpreter of his father's mood, tone of voice, and gestures, possibly of his teacher's too. He recognizes firmness, teasing, scolding, persuading, commanding, humor, and sarcasm. Is he equally astute in apprehending the curtness of Caesar's reply to Decius' invitation: "The cause is in my will: I will not come." Sensitiveness to mood, tone, and gesture is revealed in oral reading. (418)

She developed this idea of oral reading within a collaborative framework four years later:

> Granted that the teacher is sensitive to the perplexity of students in a new reading situation, he can help students through the group reading of something students would not read without assistance. Group reading does not exclude extensive or independent reading; it should stimulate both.... Group reading and

discussion should avoid the hazy impressions that result when each student in an English class is always on his own. (1948b, 128)

This collaborative approach to reading and talking about literature was explored more thoroughly in Sheridan's 1952 article: "The study [of a novel] may be a socialized activity of a kind which has been growing in the teaching of music and art.... Through a sympathetic group there may be care for individual differences. Classmates who become enthusiastic may by contagion stimulate others" (9).

Her 1948 article titled "Out of Chaos" expressed yet another concern with the teaching of literature:

> Chaos—lack of order, lack of pattern, lack of sense—is what too many students find in new reading situations. To bring order, pattern, and meaning—intellectual and emotional—out of reading chaos is one of the problems of an English teacher.... First of all, to appreciate the chaos facing students in new reading situations, reflect upon the chaos facing adults confronted with new forms.... Students, too, may be impatient with what is new to them and possibly arrogant and hasty in their judgment. Perhaps something is gained if they are aroused even to impatience. Teaching students to respond to new situations often requires turning impatience into patience, bewilderment into ferment. (1948b, 126-27)

Her concern over the increasing prevalence of multiple-choice and fill-in-the-blank means of assessing reading was indicated in her warning: "reading that is vaguely checked results in the rattling off of titles and authors, a glib knowledge of the periphery, responses indicative of neither intellectual nor emotional responses" (128). Instead, to enable students to make "order out of chaos," Sheridan recommended the following: "Re-reading and reflection [should] be encouraged.... Discussion, re-reading, a broad context, a motive for reading—inseparable from ... broad experience with literature and as far as possible with life—should result in open-mindedness, patience, concentration, curiosity, willingness to make-believe. Order, pattern, and meaning should then emerge" (133).

Sheridan picked up her attack on both the literary canon and traditional methods of teaching it again in 1952, when she questioned the common six-week devotion to one particular literary work: "It has been urged that students of different abilities and interests should not be strait-jacketed by the reading of one book, confined in subject matter and time. It is all to the good that spending six weeks or so on *The Talisman, Quentin Durward,* or *A Tale of Two Cities* is questioned" (1952, 9). She offered a view of assessment of the teaching of literature that in its simplicity went far beyond what we currently measure: "A measure of the success of the teaching of literature is whether a student will take up a good book voluntarily, deliberately, and without self-consciousness; respond intellectually and emotionally to what is between the covers; talk of it, perhaps; and remember" (1944b, 420).

Marion Sheridan summarized her view of literature in the English classroom when she wrote words in 1948 which may reverberate well into the twenty-first century: "In spite of new forms of extending meaning to man—new forms of communication—literature is still unique. Life without literature in America today? It is inconceivable" (1948a, 297).

Not only was the teaching of literature at risk in Marion C. Sheridan's day; so was writing. In her 1951 article, "Can We Teach Our Students to Write?" Sheridan referred to the Wisconsin study, reported on by Robert C. Pooley in *The Teaching of English in Wisconsin* in 1948, wherein teachers estimated that 18-19 percent of total English time was devoted to written composition, "one theme in nine days, about one hundred twenty-five words per week" (Pooley 1948). Sheridan's suggestion that "at least three times as much writing should be done if students are to learn to express themselves on paper" (1951, 323) would be regarded today as gross understatement; yet it was offered long before the critical relationship between writing and learning had been widely acknowledged.

Even more prescient of current pedagogical emphases is Sheridan's desire to establish cooperative writing links across departments, in a version of writing across the curriculum that positions teachers of all subject areas as educators concerned with their students' use of written language: "Theoretically, in the teaching of writing we should get assistance from all the teachers of all our students. There is, however, still much for us to learn about co-operation with those of other departments. It is decidedly worth making an effort to increase the power of writing by teamwork" (321).

Sheridan categorized the nature of writing into three "powers" which have close parallels to the matrix developed twenty years later by James Britton. Writing to what Sheridan called "the first power" parallels Britton's transactional mode, in that it is writing "to fulfill an urgent need" (Sheridan) or "to get things done" (Britton). This kind of writing, she stated, is what is most frequently taught and done in schools. Writing to "the second power," wherein students move from the world of the practical to the world of ideas, engaging with concepts more in what Britton calls "the spectator role" than in "the participant role," is similar to Britton's poetic mode. This kind of writing, Sheridan suggested, is encouraged less frequently in schools, particularly for non-college-bound students. Writing "to the third power," she maintained, is rarely required or encouraged in schools, yet should be developed in all students. This power is most similar to Britton's expressive mode, wherein, to use Sheridan's words, a student writes in response to an "urgency to express himself." She went on to say that "we must aim to develop as much power as possible, aspiring, in general, to the third power for all students.... Many question teaching to what we are calling the third power" (1951, 321). Sheridan implied some interrelationship among the powers, though not with the same depth and intricacy as in Britton's matrix, in the following statement, which, at the same time, cautioned against a simplistic view of written text as message:

> Appreciation of writing to the third power should give us respect even for writing to the first power. On the way, there will be some drills, some explanations, but the so-called "mechanics" are not the end. The end—communication between human beings, communication of the trivial and of the vital—focuses on purpose and material. It focuses on getting across a request, an idea, an emotion. I should not dare say "message" or you would misunderstand, but there is a message. (324)

Marion C. Sheridan further cautioned English teachers about separating writing from other language arts and activities. At a time when language arts and English curricula categorized speaking, writing, reading, and listening as separate areas of the language arts, and long before the work of Douglas Barnes, James Britton, and Deborah Tannen emphasized the importance of student talk in language learning, Sheridan wrote: "Effective communication in writing is inseparable from communication by speaking, reading, and listening.... Chatting may stress the exceedingly important question of the order.... So much of writing in English is determined by order, and so little has been said of it" (322). As she stressed the importance of a "socialized" approach to the study of literature, Sheridan also developed an increasingly collaborative approach to writing. The following could as easily describe activities in a modern classroom as in her 1950s one: "The activity was largely student activity: students raised questions and answered each other; students asked for help from the class and in conferences. All stages of the undertaking were subject to group discussion. Discussion meant challenge" (1954, 87).

Sheridan drew upon the writing of others as a context for her views on teaching writing. She quoted from Alfred Haas's 1950 *English Quarterly* article "Keep Them Writing" to provide a focus for her concern with postwar writing instruction, a concern that, despite the work of many excellent English language arts educators in today's classrooms, is nonetheless still relevant. Haas stated that the need for much more writing to be done in English classes "should be of particular interest to those who share our dissatisfaction with the status quo in composition teaching, the red-pencil and drill-book technique" (quoted in Sheridan 1951, 323).

Sheridan's views of writing pedagogy also drew from what professional writers had said about writing. Emphasizing the complex process of writing, in contrast to the then-prevailing focus on written products, she quoted from Hemingway's discussion of the need to delay and mull over experiential response; to play with it verbally in different ways before setting it into a textual vision: "See that pelican? I don't know yet what his part is in the scheme of things" (quoted in Sheridan 1951, 324). She reiterated the idea that writing takes time—time for observation, for reflection, for vision, and for revision—with her reference to Joyce Carey's *The Way a Novel Gets Written*: "Writing takes time. Joyce Carey writes and rewrites" (323). Possibly her most interesting reference to writers' views of writing, and one that I would like to have read more about in her article, is the reference to Tennessee Williams, which almost parallels Roman Jacobson's notion of poetry as violence done to ordinary language: "To achieve power in writing, students must have respect for writing. Perhaps they should ponder on what Tennessee Williams meant when he wrote: 'But writing is actually a violent activity. It is actually more violent than any other profession that I can think of, including that of the professional writer'" (323).

As mentioned earlier, Marion C. Sheridan inevitably located her views in the actual classrooms of the teachers she was addressing, with advice not on "how to" but on "what must be done" or, as in the following instance, "what must not be overdone": "Communication does not result from a terrifying emphasis on usage or on grammar, even though pronouns should have antecedents and most participles should not dangle" (322). Sheridan's 1960 article, "Creative Language Experiences in the High School," offered advice even closer to the current emphasis on helping students to locate their personal life experiences in ongoing textual and intertextual written conversations: "We can help students to write what they will have to write. We can broaden the scope of what they will have to write about and wish to write about; we can give them an idea of how to do it. Students may write of what is on the streets, on the country roads, in books, in lectures, over the radio, in conversation" (566). Sheridan concluded a

1950 address to teachers in Milwaukee with words that are equally applicable to many of today's educators' feelings about current writing pedagogy: "My first impulse was not to call this paper 'Can We Teach Our Students to Write?' but to give it a new title of three words—'Writing, Writing, Writing'—with varied intonations: questioning, despairing, determined and hopeful" (1951, 324).

Although Marion C. Sheridan's practical wisdom in the teaching of literature and writing exemplifies her "creative approach" to the teaching of English, it is her work with film in the classroom that is most strongly associated with her pioneering spirit. The Teaching Film Custodians was a nonprofit, noncommercial corporation established in 1938 to "enrich education by making available film material from productions of theatrical motion picture producing companies" (Sheridan et al. 1965, ix). For seventeen years, Sheridan served as chair of the NCTE Committee on Film, which "worked closely with the Teaching Film Custodians in preparing excerpts from feature-length pictures as well as guides to accompany them" (ix).

She met monthly with the Teaching Film Custodians, usually in New York, to see films that might be used in the classroom. Years later, in her conversation with Alfred H. Grommon (Sheridan 1977), she recalled these meetings with much fondness, speaking of the wonderful camaraderie of the group, which often included the governor of New York. Sheridan was directly involved in selecting which excerpts would be appropriate and in writing study guides for the approved selections. Frequently she would arrange to have these excerpts, or in some cases the whole film, screened at NCTE conventions in order to glean the opinions of a wide range of English teachers. Out of this association of NCTE with the Teaching Film Custodians emerged the idea of producing a book to enable classroom teachers to be more effective in introducing and using film in their classrooms. In 1965, spurred on to do for film what Neil Postman had done for television in the school, NCTE sponsored a publication of *The Motion Picture and the Teaching of English*, under the shared authorship of Marion Sheridan, Harold H. Owen, Jr., Ken Macrorie, and Fred Marcus.

Although welcomed by classroom teachers, Sheridan's views on the use of film in the classroom were not universally acclaimed. Her work was devastatingly reviewed by Pauline Kael for its emphasis on the educational value of film, particularly as a means of further appreciating literature. According to Kael, film is an art form to be studied in its own right, not as a means to study literature. James Squire, caught in the midst of this imbroglio as executive secretary of NCTE, recalled being impressed with Sheridan's handling of the situation:

"She cried, then rallied, then reaffirmed her position. She didn't slash; she didn't attack. She went on about her business, with quiet strength" (March 1989).

One example of how Sheridan viewed the role of film in the classroom can be seen in the following reference to the work of her close friend and colleague, Dora V. Smith:

> In speaking, writing, listening, and reading, students need to be made sensitive. It may be to levels of usage, to tone, to gesture, to shades of meaning, and to shifts of meaning. There are many ways and new ways to do so. Dr. Dora Smith in *Educational Screen* last April, for example, showed how films might be made to help students grow in the capacity to use modifications and to sense relations between ideas expressed in proper subordination and co-ordination. (1949, 127–28)

At the same time, Sheridan was aware of potential pitfalls in becoming too dependent upon media technology. Sanford Radner's *Fifty Years of English Teaching* (1960) drew upon Sheridan's views of media in the classroom expressed during her presidential address:

> This recent enthusiasm [for instruction in the mass media] has called forth a tempting voice from other leaders who urged English teachers not to go overboard completely and expect the newer media to solve all of their teaching problems. President Marion Sheridan (1949), in particular, warned against the depersonalizing effect of mechanized communication. In using the machine, man must not abdicate his personal responsibility or critical awareness. "Man as a consumer of messages to millions becomes increasingly lethargic, passive, apathetic, unwilling to assume responsibility, unwilling or unable to make distinctions or to recognize beauty." (12)

Sheridan's career-long involvement with film is best summed up in *The Memory Book of the New England Association of Teachers of English*, which stated, "the period of the teens was a creative one. The impact of motion pictures was an issue in 1914; in the 40's and 50's, the Teaching Film Custodians, with the involvement and leadership of our own Marion Sheridan, was concerned with making what was best in motion pictures readily available to the classroom teacher" (Walen 1981, 11).

Marion Sheridan saw the classroom teacher as a crucial intermediary between students and curricula, not just in the use of film, but in all aspects of the teaching of English. In 1948 she wrote: "If the new curriculum offers ways [to become aware of different approaches to teaching] how will the changes be brought to students? I have faith in teachers that they can do it" (1948a, 292). She had already publicly referred to her faith in teachers in an article entitled "The Impact of War on the Teaching of English," which appeared in NEATE's *English Leaflet*:

> The solution to problems imposed by the impact of the war on the teaching of English is to be found in a broad view of life, of government, and of the entire secondary school population, as individuals and as a group. It is not to be found by thinking of courses of study or by prolonging the life of textbooks. It cannot be found in forgetting the past. . . . It will be found in part at least by groups of English teachers. . . . Standing on the brink of the future is all so different from writing history (quoted in Walen 1981, 136–37).

Sheridan put forth her ideas on the role of teachers in her address to the general session of the NCTE convention in 1948:

> As teachers and particularly as teachers of the language arts, of English, we play a prominent part in the equilibrium of our students. Environment, training, and ability influence the way our students dance on their tightropes, remain on a plateau, or climb mountains. And we become part of their environment and of their training, stultifying or stimulating toward the dynamic. Without vanity, we say that consciously and unconsciously we control actions, thought, emotion. We challenge and elicit responses. . . . We can stimulate to maturity, to growth in self-esteem and self-direction. Studies in England, for example, indicate that students wish to respond and to grow. We forget it in our busy days, but the power of teachers is staggering (1949, 126–27).

She went on to point out that what is taught and how to teach it are both curricular concerns that influence pedagogical decisions. Her discussion demonstrated a major move toward the realization that *how* we teach is indeed *what* we teach:

> It is not only what we decide to teach but how we go about it, a concern of the Curriculum Commission in the search for the development of units of instruction. Providing for equilibrium in a changing world, by considering life-adjustment and reaching the souls of students—as we can through English—is different from focusing on skills as an end, on forms, on classifications, on drills on isolated words, on covering a syllabus, or on utilizing a standardized test and then the score, perhaps unaware of what came between the first and the last page of the test. (127)

In her 1950 address to teachers at the NCTE Secondary Section meeting in Milwaukee, Sheridan expressed her concern that students' enthusiasm over changing technology was blinding them to dramatic changes in human living conditions:

> In discussing the text, *The Challenge of Ideas*, seniors could grasp the fact that ideas resulted in material things, in inventions, which are

> sometimes—in their opinion, always—rewarded by wealth. They were slow to apprehend that the most important ideas were not expressed in gadgets but in drastic changes in the conditions under which [people] live and die—the ideas written, for example, by political and religious leaders. (1951, 323)

These remarks are an indication of how far-reaching Marion Sheridan's conception of pedagogy, and of the roles of teachers in the classroom, extended. She saw the English language arts, in all their interdependent, interactive modes, as forces to enable students to learn about, to question, and to work toward the betterment of their society and their world. She perceived the role of teachers as taking on the tremendous and complex responsibility of organizing their learning environments to enable all this to happen. She concluded her address at the 1948 NCTE convention with a message intended to inspire teachers to meet the challenge:

> Where does all this leave us? It leaves us concerned about people, about individuals, human beings, who may too easily be passed over, who may be expected to be paragons. It leaves us concerned about the delicate nature of balance in group relationships. As teachers of English or the language arts, we work with human beings—as fellow teachers, as students, and as the subject or the author of writing. We work with the speech of human beings and the words written and heard with which they communicate. Students must gain certain automatisms for their tightrope dancing. But they must go beyond the mechanical and mechanics toward equilibrium—with variations. They must go on scaling mountains and reaching for the stars. (1949, 129–30)

Throughout this discussion of Marion C. Sheridan's views of pedagogy, her concern for students has been noticeably paramount. Her presidential address, "Beyond Fancy's Dream," encapsulated this concern at the 1949 NCTE annual convention, whose theme, "English for Every Student," was chosen by Sheridan and was set forth early in her address:

> for man and his essential dignity are often forgotten, even in the schools of today.... With a high opinion of people, of human beings and their possibilities, we desire English for every student, the theme of this 39th annual convention of NCTE. English has no monopoly of wisdom, but it can make a unique contribution ... [by] recognizing these wonders of mind and spirit. (1950, 57–58)

Sheridan went on to describe the scope of who was to be included in her notion of "English for every student," noting that this concept "assumes responsibility for every student in school, for every student entering college.... English for every student means English for the privileged and for the underprivileged, regardless of economic distinctions or class distinctions, which are increasingly appearing as an important factor in education" (58).

Sheridan's views on educational equality went far beyond the need for equality of access and exposure, in the belief that nothing is less equal than the equal treatment of unequals: "Dr. Bush in *Modern Arms and Free Men* points out our confusion of equality of educational exposure with actual equality of opportunity" (quoted in Sheridan 1950, 64). She expanded upon that idea by referring to Charles Eliot, then president emeritus of Harvard, who spoke in 1911 to NEATE about the inequality of the ability to seize opportunity. Sheridan used an anecdote from the political arena to force her point home: "Last week our Vice President was married. After the ceremony, Mrs. Barkly was quoted in the *New York Times* as saying, 'I hate to go out and face this mess.' Mr. Barkly's quick response was: 'That's no mess. That's the American public.' And it is the American public of all ages, sizes, shapes, abilities, stages of maturity, and social levels for whom we must plan" (64).

Today, it seems that justification for any proposed educational program or project must be phrased in practical terms, often with reference to future employment possibilities. Marion Sheridan's justification for her program included, but also transcended, pragmatic considerations:

> Even though English is our vernacular, the language of our country, a program of English for every student may need some justification. And the justification is not that it is needed for practical purposes: the world of business, of labor and of labor relations, of conferences and of work, important as communication is in those places. The justification is that English can help to develop [people] beyond fancy's dream and to help make clear that, though wonders are many, none is more wonderful than man .... Many forces beyond our control have tended to dwarf man and to dwarf the conception of his powers, to make him far from the lofty ideal in *Antigone* ["Wonders are many, and none is more wonderful than man; ... Cunning beyond fancy's dream is the fertile skill which brings him, now to evil, now to good."].... to Wordsworth's "Have I not reason to lament what man has made of man?" ... Man as a consumer of messages to millions becomes increasingly lethargic, passive, uncritical, apathetic, unwilling to assume responsibility, unwilling or unable to make distinctions or to recognize beauty. (1950, 59–60)

Sheridan's justification for a program of "English for every student" suggests that the English language arts have the power, when taught and learned appropriately and effectively, to forestall unthinking, uncritical passivity.

Almost as though in anticipation of the still-too-often-heard fear that open admissions leads to mediocrity, to the lowering of standards, Sheridan asserted: "English for every student does not mean leveling to mediocrity.... English teachers should resist every effort to level and seek every possible way to raise people to the highest plane attainable: in discrimination, in discernment, in abstractions, in resourcefulness, in inventiveness, in reasonableness, in responsibility, in ethical ideas" (62).

She confronted directly what this program of English for every student should accomplish and also of what it should consist:

> Of what is the program to consist? One who is skeptical asked: Will there be more foliage trips with Wordsworth or with Washington Irving—or another spreading chestnut tree? And often to avoid hackneyed choices and formal instruction there has been emphasis on the utilitarian, on English as a tool.
>
> English for every student assumes that English is a very useful tool, but it is as a tool, not as an end. The teaching of English is not a question of how many days should be spent on traditional exercises in workbooks, review books, or mimeographed sheets. The end of English is not glibness with grammatical forms; with the dates of authors or settings; the memorizing of the spot marked "climax" in the notes; the memorizing of a title and an appositive in a so-called "survey," usually of English literature; drill on a handbook illustrated by cartoons. It is not the spelling or the definition of a list of unrelated words. It is not a question-and-answer recitation in a schoolroom with stiff seats and awesome order; nor of answers to true-false tests, the giving back of items in a factual passage, the kind of thing stressed in some reading tests. It is not formal composition, oral or written, without consideration of its power to communicate. It is not a knowledge of arbitrary rulings on usage about which experts cannot agree. It is not identification: identification of the proper pronunciation of words, identification of what seems to be a simile because "like" or "as" has been used. It is not confusing as aesthetic experience with literature with the identification of an allusion or the identification of the author of a verse of poetry. It is neither "correctness" nor so many books required for outside reading—really a strange term. Such a conception of English is too complicated. (61–62)

Instead, returning to the theme that began this journey through her spoken and written views on the teaching of English, Sheridan concluded, "If English is to develop individuals divinely, there must be a unifying idea ... directed to the human, creative side of a person whose dignity is respected" (62).

Respect for the dignity of the individual while nurturing the growth of creative thinking in herself and in those she encountered, as teacher and as colleague, is the unifying idea that runs throughout all that Marion C. Sheridan has written and all that people who have known her recall about her. It is also evident in what she had to say about herself, as she looked back, during that oral-history interview with Alfred Grommon in 1977, over sixty-four years of service to the teaching of English. When Grommon asked her what she had found most compelling, most exciting about her year as president of NCTE, she recalled how wonderful it had been to have the privilege to travel all over the United States to meet and talk with classroom teachers, to share ideas, and to visit their classrooms. She spoke of always trying to arrive a day or two early to conferences and to Council meetings so that she could spend time in the schools of the community (Sheridan 1977).

When asked by Grommon to comment on the major issues, the major controversies, which she had encountered, both as president and throughout her career, Sheridan at first balked, with obvious dislike of conflict. But then, with urging, she began to speak of some of the uneasy confrontations with which she had been involved. She discussed having to refuse the selection of Baltimore to host an annual convention of NCTE because, despite its guarantee that it was "a very pleasant place for blacks to stay; they could eat with the whites" (Sheridan 1977), it did not conform to the Minneapolis Resolution, which stipulated that only cities which could guarantee full accommodation to all members attending the meeting would be considered as convention sites. She recalled the terrible tension during the 1941 annual convention in Atlanta, which had precipitated the Minneapolis Resolution. During the general session in Atlanta, blacks had not been allowed to sit with whites. In protest, several whites and blacks were noticeably absent at the next day's luncheon, during which the speaker, a Mr. Agar, considered a representative of the "aristocratic whites," spent the whole luncheon "worrying whether a shot would be heard." In ironic contrast, Sheridan recalled her appointed room in Atlanta, a large, exquisitely furnished room filled with flowers (Sheridan 1977).

Sheridan spoke also of "the *Reader's Digest* issue," which involved allegations of antidemocratic articles in the magazine that was used widely in the classroom. [See chapter five of this book, "Angela M. Broening: Implacable Defender," for a discussion of Broening's role in the dispute.] Sheridan was named to the new Committee on Magazine Study in 1944, which replaced the Committee on Newspapers and

Magazines after Broening refused to accept the latter committee's controversial report on the *Reader's Digest*. Sheridan and fellow committee members Thomas Pollock and E. A. Cross concluded that the report of the original magazine committee "falls short of the objective viewpoint necessary for sponsorship" by NCTE and recommended that the Council prepare a general report "on the choice and use of periodicals" in the classroom (quoted in Hook 1979, 143). Sheridan recalled her own involvement in the issue some thirty years later:

> I was on the committee as Secretary of Curriculum: English in Secondary Schools . . . I don't remember exactly what caused the ruckus but it was a serious one. I had a speech to give but was never called upon to do it . . . By attorney's ruling, no one could attend the meeting who was not an NCTE member . . . *Reader's Digest* threatened to sue NCTE unless the report were released . . . no meeting was held because the *Reader's Digest* people were not members and would not leave . . . Angela Broening ate lunch at the same local restaurant as the *Reader's Digest* people, so she was alleged to have been bribed or tainted by them. (Sheridan 1977)

While perusing her notes made during her year as president of the Council, Sheridan came across the notation "Waived rights to exclusive distribution of Frost's readings." This prompted the recollection of another confrontation. She told of a dinner meeting (possibly the Harvard Dinner in 1936 that is mentioned in Walen 1981, but with no reference to the controversy) after which Robert Frost was scheduled to give a poetry reading. Friends of a poet named J. Coffin, who was living in New England at that time though not "officially" a New England poet, requested that Sheridan also invite him to read. Not knowing of the severe animosity between Frost and Coffin, Sheridan complied. When Frost rose to speak and noticed Coffin, "he became so angry he left the podium for fresh air" (Sheridan 1977).

Sheridan laughed as she told this story, and it seemed to warm her up for more short anecdotes. She spoke of the "scandal" raised by Helene Hartley. Both she and her second husband, Floyd Altborn, held positions at Syracuse University, but since husband and wife were not allowed on the same faculty, she kept "Hartley" as her last name. One night her students saw her out dancing with Floyd Altborn, and "were all excited—she was out with 'another man' who, as it turned out, was really her husband." Sheridan also laughed when she recalled the installing of Albert H. Marckwardt as president of the Council in 1966–67, wherein "he styled himself as the 'first Ivy League President of NCTE.' I told everyone that I thought I was the first President with Ivy League connections," citing her connections with Yale University as an M.A. and Ph.D. student and then as a teacher when Yale still had an active graduate program in education, working in special programs for both disadvantaged and gifted students (Sheridan 1977).

In her interview Sheridan also spoke of one dreadful meeting in Minnesota, when a bad snowstorm was preventing people from getting to the opening session at a theater some distance from the hotel headquarters. Her friend Dora V. Smith, who was scheduled to speak, had sprained her ankle, so Sheridan was trying to find a way to get her to the meeting. Finally, one of Sheridan's students located a car, and they struggled through snow and wind to get to the theater. Scarcely anyone was there, and the sound of the wind howled throughout the almost-empty theater. She spoke with pride of how Smith addressed the scant crowd warmly and enthusiastically (Sheridan 1977).

This friendship with Dora V. Smith was long and close throughout their professional years. James Squire tells of how they would always room together and "look out for each other" at conferences and Council meetings. The last time he saw Smith and Sheridan together was at the opening of the new NCTE offices in Urbana, Illinois. At that time Smith was very weak physically and was losing her memory. Sheridan stayed close and covered for Smith's memory lapses, acting as her behind-the-scenes pillar of strength. This kind of behavior, said Squire, was typical of Marion Sheridan (Squire 1989).

The pebble which has rippled into these ever-widening circles of professional concern and involvement was Sheridan's focus on creativity. It seems therefore fitting to conclude this portrait of Marion C. Sheridan with words from her article "Creative Language Experiences in the High School": "We shall not directly motivate the building of incredible structures for the earth or air, but we have the privilege of working with those who have a part, proud or modest, in the achievements of the coming years" (1960, 563).

Works Cited

Hook, J. N. 1979. *A Long Way Together: A Personal View of NCTE's First Sixty-Seven Years.* Urbana, Ill.: National Council of Teachers of English.

Mearns, Hughes. 1925. *Creative Youth: How a School Environment Set Free the Creative Spirit.* Garden City, N.Y.: Doubleday, Page and Co.

Pooley, Robert C. 1948. *The Teaching of English in Wisconsin.* Madison: University of Wisconsin Press.

Radner, Sanford. 1960. *Fifty Years of English Teaching: A Historical Analysis of the Presidential Addresses of NCTE.* Champaign, Ill.: National Council of Teachers of English.

Sheridan, Marion C. 1934. "The Teaching of Reading in the Public Schools of New Haven, 1638-1930." Ph.D. diss., Yale University, New Haven, Conn.

———. 1944. "Literature: Freighter, Fighter, and Star-Steerer." *English Journal* 33 (October): 414-20.

———. 1948a. "Life without Literature." *English Journal* 37 (June): 291-97.

———. 1948b. "Out of Chaos." *English Journal* 37 (March): 126-33.

———. 1949. "Equilibrium with Variations." *English Journal* 38 (March): 125-30.

———. 1950. "'Beyond Fancy's Dream.'" *English Journal* 39 (February): 57-64.

———. 1951. "Can We Teach Our Students to Write?" *English Journal* 40 (June): 320-24.

———. 1952. "Teaching a Novel." *English Journal* 41 (January): 8-14.

———. 1954. "The Menace of Communism." *English Journal* 43 (February): 87-88.

———. 1960. "Creative Language Experiences in the High School." *English Journal* 49 (November): 563-69.

———. 18 July 1977. Interview with Alfred H. Grommon.

Sheridan, Marion C., with Harold H. Owen, Jr., Ken Macrorie, and Fred Marcus. 1965. *The Motion Picture and the Teaching of English.* New York: Appleton-Century-Crofts.

Squire, James. February and March 1989. Telephone interviews with author.

Walen, Harry L. 1981. *The Memory Book of the New England Association of Teachers of English.* Chicago, Ill.: Science Research Associates.

Part III:
Looking to the Future

7 Lou LaBrant:
A Challenge and a Charge

David A. England, Louisiana State University

B. Jane West, University of Georgia

Lou LaBrant
1888-1991*

Some lives are much fuller than others, and some lives are blessed with greater longevity. Very infrequently we come upon a person who, like Lou LaBrant, enriches individual lives and a whole profession with great productivity, a fullness of spirit, and an indelible impact born of high standards and insightful passion for teaching. To have had Lou LaBrant active in our profession for over eight decades leaves us with a full life and a wealth of writing to consider, and a depth of insight to capture in these few pages. Her longevity almost defies relegation to a particular period; LaBrant has been involved with the National Council of Teachers of English throughout most of its history, and active in English education through five decades (1930-70). But what a rich opportunity and challenge it is to reflect upon that life.

Beginning with her first interest in NCTE in the 1920s, LaBrant was a visible, outspoken, and active woman in what was a man's world professionally. To be a woman and to have impact, one had to excel— and be persistent. In those ways, LaBrant was much like the other NCTE leaders whose lives are told in this volume. The role and visibility of women in the Council would change during her lifetime, though LaBrant herself would remain much the same: passionately advocating what she believed in, intellectually active, unfailingly committed to the highest standards. Her pedagogy would remain constant, too, over five decades. What always mattered to Lou LaBrant

*As this book goes to press we are deeply saddened to learn of the passing of Lou LaBrant, at age 102, on February 25, 1991, in Lawrence, Kansas.

was what young people could do with and through language. She spent a lifetime exploring with teachers how young people could grow and express themselves as readers and writers and speakers. To say that for LaBrant the child should be the focus of the curriculum would only understate what she always took for granted.

This portrait of Lou LaBrant will begin with a brief biographical overview: dates and places; positions, honors, and roles; some of the important when's and where's in her life. Then our attention will turn to the woman—not just *who* she was and is, but *what* she was and is, both personally and professionally.

Our study of Lou LaBrant's life, our talks with her and with some who knew her well, and our reading of her work have led us to recognize several broad themes in her personal and professional life. We believe hers has been a remarkable life. We trust that what we say about her high standards, her respect for and belief in individuals, her independence and initiative, her understanding of language, her passion for literature, her lifelong learning, and her clear perspectives on the teacher's role and potential will help readers begin to understand and respect Lou LaBrant as we do.

For LaBrant, being a centenarian has been lively and also a little bit lonely. Even after she was a hundred years old, LaBrant would not give the impression of being a woman with whom one would want to trifle. She has her sense of humor, to be sure, and the eyes sparkle. But when her longtime friend and former student, Frank Jennings, described her as a teacher, we could definitely picture her in this role: "She was demanding, charming, winsome, tough, and no nonsense—all those things at once. She would cut your heart out if you were impudent, dishonest, or sloppy in your work or thinking" (1989).

This insight into LaBrant suggests potentially confusing paradoxes. On the one hand, she is exceptionally respectful of teachers' abilities to make their own decisions and to conduct learning wisely. Her works are similarly permeated with respect for students as individuals, and by her defense of students' rights to read, think, write, and speak independently. She could display passion for the oppressed, exhibit sensitivity to language and to the connections between language and our humanity, and show unrestrained love for books, for those who read them well, and for those who write books she feels are worth reading. Her sense of humor has lasted into her eleventh decade. (When we told her in the spring of 1989 that we were looking forward to seeing her in November at the 1989 NCTE Convention in Baltimore, she chuckled and said, "Don't worry about me. Just make sure you hold on long enough to make it.")

At the same time, LaBrant could apply that trenchant wit with a cutting edge, showing little respect for those she respected little. She could be outspokenly blunt and aggressive. One intimate suggested "abrasive" in describing LaBrant in committee work. She was bright, usually right, ahead of her time—and she knew it. LaBrant often showed little restraint in expressing exactly where she stood. Moreover, she would often let an audience know she believed the rest of the world should be standing right there with her.

Her niece and nearest living relative, Betty Fiehler, stated that LaBrant "really did not like women" (1989). We would soften that statement to indicate that LaBrant really did not like *most* women, nor was she sympathetic to women who settled for a back seat in the profession. She, after all, had made *her* own way. Yet, she did have close personal friends among professional women and was not so fond of males that she ever found one she wished to marry.... The paradoxes abound.

Lou LaBrant was born in 1888 in Hinckley, Illinois. She grew up, along with her brother and sister, in small midwestern communities. She began teaching in a "dusty" Kansas cattle town following her own high school graduation at age fifteen. She soon enrolled at Baker University, majoring in Latin with a "weak minor" in English. Because her father had recently died, she immediately resumed her teaching career in order to help support her mother and sister. Though having a job was a necessity, LaBrant was unwilling to compromise in order to get one. Upon learning that her initial contract would be for ten dollars a month less than that offered a man hired for the same position at that time, LaBrant refused the offer until it was changed to her satisfaction.

So it was that LaBrant's independence of spirit and sense of equity were obvious very early in her professional life. Upon her terms she was hired as a new teacher and was instructed by the principal to "get that school accredited." Doing "the English part of it," she said, "was easy. I was the only English teacher, and had a good sense of how things ought to go." But in this first job, Lou LaBrant, not yet twenty-five years old and not having majored in English or in education, had a whole school to get into shape, and that meant having the math and science teachers replaced. They were, she put it simply, "incompetent" (LaBrant 1989a).

In the early 1920s LaBrant continued her education at the University of Kansas, where she received her master's degree in 1925. She was awarded a doctorate by Northwestern University in 1932. The Ohio State University Laboratory School was then being developed, so LaBrant joined the staff and took part in its beginnings. The program was experimental in that teachers and professors could develop curriculum from the ground up. LaBrant was able to apply successfully her ideas of free and wide reading of literature and to challenge assumptions behind traditional English programs. It was during this time that her first book, *The Teaching of Literature in the Secondary School* (1931b) was published, a book she described as "radical at the time" in a 1977 interview with Alfred H. Grommon, chair of the Commission on the History of the Council. Partly as a result of LaBrant's contributions to the Laboratory School program, the students themselves also authored a book, *Were We Guinea Pigs?* (University High School 1938), which described their experiences in many experimental programs. During LaBrant's tenure at Ohio State she edited *Educational Method* for four years.

In 1942 LaBrant received an invitation to go to New York University. She was undaunted by the prospects of metropolitan life and of teaching in an urban setting despite her small-town upbringing. It was the stated practice of the university to hire new faculty members as associate professors and then, as the appropriate time arose, to offer full professorships. LaBrant discovered, however, that very often the appropriate time arose only for men, so she declined the offer. LaBrant was then hired by NYU at the rank of professor. Her first summers in the East were spent teaching at Harvard and the Breadloaf School, where she knew Robert Frost. LaBrant remained at NYU until her *first* retirement at age sixty-five.

Taking a rather dim view of retirement, LaBrant chose to continue teaching, and she moved to Atlanta University for two years as a visiting professor. During that time she served as president of the NCTE (1953–54). Following a short term at the University of Missouri, LaBrant, at age seventy, went to Dillard University in New Orleans, where she felt she might be able to offer some assistance in the educational preparation of black teachers. She did so—first as a professor of English and later as head of the Division of Humanities— for eleven years, with the exception of two or three years which she spent traveling in Europe. After her second retirement at age eighty, LaBrant remained ten more years in New Orleans before returning to her childhood home of Baldwin City, Kansas, where she resides at this writing (November 1989) remarkably on her own, at age 101. We will draw frequently from a long and pleasant interview with LaBrant in Baldwin City in April of 1989 in the following discussions of her life.

During her rich career, LaBrant was the recipient of many honors. She received an honorary doctorate from Baker University in 1941 and was named emeritus professor by New York University in 1953 and by Dillard University in 1969. NCTE's W. Wilbur Hatfield Award was bestowed upon her in 1962. In various years LaBrant was included in such listings as *Who's Who, Who's Who in Education, Who's Who in the East, Personalities of the South,* and *World's Who's Who among Women.*

At this writing LaBrant continues writing, publishing essays (as recently as the spring of 1989 at age 101) and corresponding with friends of many years. She is still an avid and wide reader. According to her niece, Betty Fiehler (1989), "There is a good bookstore in [nearby] Lawrence, Kansas, and she just calls them periodically and tells them to send her whatever she wants—and if they haven't got it, she tells them to find it." She still talks of traveling again—perhaps, as a longtime friend informs us, because she is bored with Baldwin City. Fiehler, too, reports that LaBrant "complains about the intellect" in her housing complex because "there isn't anybody interesting enough to talk to" (Fiehler 1989). With the exception of swollen knees that creak when she gets up and down, Fiehler asserts that LaBrant's good health still allows her to have eggs and bacon every morning for breakfast and to spend hours quietly reading during the day. She remains the independent woman she has always been. Today, though, LaBrant would disagree with Robert Browning's view that 101 is "the best." Given the former pace of her life, all that she had been and all that she had seen, LaBrant would admit that "101 is a bit lonely."

Frank Jennings was right in his assessment: Lou LaBrant *was* tough. Throughout her *English Journal* contributions, she extolled the profession, challenging teachers to be all that they could be and to be better than they were. Being better meant staying informed, resisting orthodoxy and tradition for their own sake, and being independent. LaBrant would tell teachers, "As a teacher of English, I am not willing to teach the polishing and adornment of unimportant writing," and enjoined the profession to resist "the dubious privilege of spending our best efforts to produce more conventionally stated futility" (1946a, 123).

There was a consistently demanding edge to LaBrant's many challenges to teachers: "I believe, then, that the teacher should know the agony of putting words on paper. We have some pretty careless talk about writing for fun" (1955, 245). Because she worked so hard at her own writing, as demonstrated by the clear, measured, and pointed precision of her own prose, Lou LaBrant knew full well that good writing was neither easy nor fun. She was impatient with teachers who did not think about that or know it from experience. For LaBrant, the only writing worth worrying over was writing which said something worth saying. That standard went for her students, as well as for those published authors whose writings she read.

LaBrant lived and wrote through a period of "soft pedagogies" frequently mistaken as appropriate applications of progressive education. Putting the child in the center of the curriculum could be misconstrued to mean that the child's needs to have fun and to play must be addressed in the English classroom. LaBrant saw it differently. To address a child's intellectual needs did not mean pandering to the child. Thus, telling boys and girls "writing is fun" just would not do. LaBrant wrote and worked hard at her writing and would consequently reason that only those who worked similarly hard could understand how growth through writing could be trivialized in the pursuit of "fun."

Not every teacher of English was equally intelligent or thoughtful in LaBrant's view, and she did little to keep her disdain for lazy teachers to herself. She would frequently suggest distinctions in teachers' qualities by appealing only to those who were both professionally inclined and intelligent. She believed such teachers naturally made choices—and that they had better be good ones. "Every intelligent teacher of English," she once wrote, "knows that his program is a selection" (1959, 295).

Lou LaBrant's views on professionalism were not from the top down, from the ivory tower to the classroom. Indeed, the title of her most enduring work is *We Teach English* (1951), and a major theme in that book is that "we" are part of a profession in which there are high expectations and great responsibilities. LaBrant challenged teachers to be models and to set the highest standards: "We need to display by our very living that we believe in the importance of language as man's highest achievement and in literature as a record of life" (1959, 303).

The assumption that the best teachers acted on knowledge—and the fervent belief that all teachers must learn to act on what was known about teaching and learning—was a common theme in LaBrant's frequent calling of teachers to a higher plane. In a 1939 publication with her Ohio State colleague, Frieda M. Heller, LaBrant wrote, "Understanding is fostered by the study of child development and psychology. It is not sufficient that the librarian know the listed studies of reading interests.... it is important also that she know about the physical, mental, and psychological development of children. *That the teacher of English should know this also would seem to go without saying*" (LaBrant and Heller 1939b, 81; emphasis added).

James Squire, executive secretary of NCTE from 1960 to 1967, greatly admires LaBrant and was always fascinated by her manner. He termed the following story "famous in its day." "At a late thirties NCTE conference, a teacher asked LaBrant how any teacher could ever read all those books to help students in their wide reading of literature." From the podium, LaBrant responded, "Well, if you haven't read the books, you ought to take a year off and go home and read them so you're fit to be an English teacher!" (Squire 1989).

LaBrant could be blunt and direct, wise and right, and maintained unfailingly high standards for her profession. Her teaching colleagues and students must have known this, though for some their tenure with her was brief. She once refused to allow two women to take one of her courses because, though they were "undoubtedly lovely people," her previous experience with them indicated that they were not suited to working with children. Nice ladies or not, if they did not measure up academically and intellectually, LaBrant simply would not have them in her classes. Frank Jennings echoed this in remarking that LaBrant would have nothing to do with poorly prepared or ill-equipped people entering the profession (1989).

Precisely because of these high expectations for students and teachers, Jennings was able to say that LaBrant "makes teachers better than anyone I've ever met. Her students are damn useful in the profession" (1989). Because of her, countless teachers in the profession would learn what their highest callings were time and time again for eighty years. The lessons were not always painless or easy to accept. LaBrant was demanding.

It would be too simple merely to balance the toughness LaBrant displayed by establishing that she also "respected the individual." She clearly believed in an individual's potential worth—but she believed just as strongly that to deserve respect, one must earn it by making the most of one's potential. LaBrant saw her role as an educator as helping learners earn self-respect and the respect of others through the power of language.

A reader of *We Teach English* quickly recognizes that LaBrant was never much interested in teaching "English" or any of the traditional aspects of it. That 1951 work captures the best of an innovator's vision first employed decades earlier at the Ohio State University Laboratory School. Like all LaBrant's works, this book suggests that LaBrant was devoted to nurturing the minds of students, increasing their critical capabilities, and helping them live in and understand a world she frequently would say was "at risk." Similarly, LaBrant spoke and wrote often about the "teaching" mind and potential of teachers. Thus, this strong theme of respect for individuals emerges from her work in two related ways: She respected the ability of students to learn, often largely on their own, and she respected the ability of thoughtful teachers to teach—again, often on their own. She believed that teachers *and* students could have too much of certain kinds of prescriptively spoon-fed help.

In her 1961 *English Journal* discussion of "The Rights and Responsibilities of the Teacher of English," LaBrant cast both teachers and students in the same light as she wrote, "A teacher or student without the urge to know more is doomed to fall behind" (381). She argued strongly that teachers freed from the constraints of conventionality could indeed get their jobs done and succeed in inspiring young minds to significant learning. She wrote, "Throughout our country today we have great pressure to improve our schools. By far, too much of that pressure leads toward a uniformity, a conformity, a lock-step which precludes the very excellence we claim to desire." Further, she argued, there is "little consideration of the teacher as a catalyst, a changing, growing personality" (383, 391).

Because she herself was the embodiment of the lifelong learner, LaBrant challenged teachers to think and act independently as they continued to grow and to learn. She firmly believed that thinking teachers would find their own best ways. Beyond the contemporary ring and appeal of LaBrant's early message on teachers' rights, contemporary readers of LaBrant's works will here again be reminded of her faith in and respect for teachers as individuals.

To deal with language and literature in significant ways, to enable learners to sense the liberating power of language, and to nurture growth in writing demanded the very best of the profession. LaBrant not only believed teachers could, but also that they *must*, work things out for themselves. But she believed just as adamantly that lazy or passive teachers, or teachers who allowed themselves to think or write without precision, would never meet the challenges she saw in teaching.

It was her beliefs about teaching literature that clearly demonstrated Lou LaBrant's trust in individuals to find their own way. Her own high school experience with a master teacher ("the best I *ever* had or knew") convinced LaBrant that teachers can "teach" too much. "He would come in and introduce us to a piece of significant literature," LaBrant recalled seventy-five years later, "but really not tell us much about it at all. He would set us to reading and discussing it, and come back some time later to see what we had made of the piece. We all seemed to learn a great deal that way and were about as 'typical' a group, I suspect, as one could get. I never quite got over it!"(1987b). Later, when she translated her own learning experiences into a pedagogy for teaching literature, she was decades ahead of those who would devote primary attention to readers' responses to literature.

LaBrant learned early that her own responses to literature could be trusted and reliable—as well as changed and stretched in dialogue with others. She learned in her own education that the teacher's role could go well beyond pouring out content and explicating the difficult passages worthwhile literature presented. Thoughtful readers could do that for themselves, given time, only a little guidance, and other thoughtful readers with whom to talk.

Such were the lessons from her youth—from her father, who had inculcated wide reading and discussion, and from her high school experience with that one unforgettable master teacher. Later she would find a kindred spirit in Louise Rosenblatt and would continue to grow herself, both as a teacher of literature and as a reader of many types of literature. LaBrant's passion for literature and how it ensured her lifelong learning will be considered in more detail later.

Imagine, though, reader response in a small Kansas high school in the early 1900s. Imagine LaBrant in that classroom. The teacher she would become over the next eight decades, a teacher who trusted and empowered readers, is then easier to understand. LaBrant was ahead of her time with her emerging literary pedagogies, but she had learned from someone even further ahead of his time.

Only a teacher who would respect individuals would write, "A teacher who finds the classroom dull must be talking too much. The authors we read," LaBrant would go on to argue, "must have been sufficiently proficient at saying what they wanted to say, or we would not be talking about their works so much" (1987b). Teachers, she contended, are not as necessary as they might think in explaining and interpreting literature to students who could read on their own and who were excited about learning. Her long-standing advocacy of free reading, and of reading freed from a pedant's regurgitation and interpretation, was born in a Kansas high school in the early 1900s.

Drawing from what students knew and building on what they could do on their own was fundamental to LaBrant. She also believed that boys and girls would *want* to learn on their own; she respected individuals too much to assume they would be disinterested in language and ideas. In an article on vocabulary development, she wrote: "We can encourage the use of what the student knows, deepen his understanding of the possibilities in a word (poetry is ideal for this), open his eyes to the simple ways for learning new words . . . and teach him to respect the words he speaks and writes. The drive to lift his vocabulary will then be his own" (1944, 480). In a later article on writing instruction, LaBrant expressed the same kind of faith in teachers to be self-directed when she wrote that "any imaginative teacher can work out a program with a class" once freed from the constraints of "practical writing," which she felt should be "dismissed with quickly" (1959, 296, 302).

LaBrant was frustrated by the two extremes between which she found herself, and her frustration forced her to become a reformer in writing instruction as well as in literature instruction. In both instances her respect for the individual was the key. To her right LaBrant saw those who advocated drill and skill and grammar and mechanics and correctness and surface structure. To her left were those who saw free self-expression (and "fun" in achieving it) as the goal of instruction. Certainly those poles are familiar to those who follow the course of writing instruction in our schools, both yesterday and today. LaBrant's refusal to trivialize writing with concerns for correctness only or with the merely expressive impulses of writers was founded in her belief that, properly challenged, young people *would* think significantly and *would* express themselves well in writing. She felt that focusing on mechanics was "incidental" and that pandering to undisciplined self-expression was "pointless." She would give in to neither.

For LaBrant, respecting individuals went beyond considering their capacity for growing through language and had implications for life and for issues outside the classroom. It was this same abiding respect for the quality of the individual mind that found LaBrant speaking out against implicit or explicit segregation long before doing so was popular. It was her belief that we must learn to teach individual students and believe in their ability to learn that made her a quiet, but increasingly persistent, advocate of human rights, respect, and responsibility.

Max Bogart, a former student, recalled that LaBrant had a great influence on minority students. Few blacks were in northern universities until after World War II, when they began to come from the South for summer sessions. According to Bogart, LaBrant would seek out minority students and teach them not only linguistics, but how to be self-respecting human beings. "She told them not to sit in the balcony, but to sit downstairs with the white people when they went to the theater—to sit at the front of the bus. They adored her as the rest of us did" (1989). In affirmation of her belief in quality education for minorities, James Squire stated that during her years of teaching in black universities in the South, she succeeded in "holding the teachers there to the same high standards she's always had" (1989).

In 1946 LaBrant's concern for equality surfaced clearly in an article on semantics entitled "The Words of My Mouth," in which she asserted, "Classifications which result in racial or cultural segregation, encouragement of small cliques, avoidance of crucial issues—all these may do evil in the English class" (1946b, 327). What is worse, she argued, English teachers might be contributors to needless, harmful classifications through grouping students on the basis of "test scores" or by referring to and thinking about students in groups. "Do the words we use influence how we view others?" she asked. Answering her own question with an emphatic "Of course!" she went on to explain how teachers might guard against their own prejudices and help students understand how words shaped how they thought about themselves and others. She concluded, "for what is the study of English but the search for meanings and the methods for expressing them?" (327).

Though she did spend over a decade teaching at Dillard, LaBrant was never known to talk or act or write as if she were a white messiah. However, given changes in demographics, social and economic needs, and teacher shortages in major cities, one might speculate about where LaBrant might be most active today: it is easy to imagine her preparing teachers for inner-city schools or teaching in an urban school herself.

As a teacher, as a professor, and as an NCTE president, Lou LaBrant retained a strong faith in individuals. In her 1953 NCTE presidential message she stated, "The reading, listening man learns today from the whole world; his own words affect the whole world." She challenged the Council to "the sincere, devoted, teaching of how to read, speak, write, and listen." Strength and progress in the Council would be measured, she said, "by the events in your own classrooms" (1954, 119).

The faith and belief she expressed both in teachers' minds and in their teaching *of* minds was predicated on freedom for students and for teachers alike. But freedom, LaBrant once wrote, "is something we rewin every day, as much a quality of ourselves as it is a concession of others" (1961, 391). It was through the teaching and learning of language that students and teachers were to find and to practice intellectual freedom and growth. Lou LaBrant was unwavering in her faith that both teacher and student had the responsibility to learn and had the capacity to succeed.

LaBrant was well known for being independent and quick to seize initiative. Because she believed "individuals must be challenged to achieve anything beyond mediocrity," she would challenge a profession to change just as she would challenge her own students. Though she certainly respected the individual, she would not let an individual's feelings stand in the way of her doing a job that needed to be done. She was an authority, and she was authoritative, once remarking that "an authority is someone who has an idea and speaks up for it."

LaBrant lacks neither ideas nor opinions, and she has frequently spoken up and spoken out. Her niece, Betty Fiehler, suggested that being opinionated "runs in the family. I don't argue with her; she would put me down in a minute! And when Lou does it, you know you have been put down" (1989). Given both vision and strong opinions, LaBrant consistently advocated interdisciplinary teaching, the importance to the world community of knowing foreign languages, allowing children free time after school rather than loading them with unnecessary homework, understanding the importance of ideas versus rote learning of information, and the importance of prior knowledge in reading.

Today, LaBrant expresses her failure to understand the current call for the "basics" in education. She explains that she "was taught the *basics.*" Had it "not been for my parents' teaching at home," she would have remained "uneducated" (1987b). In her autobiography she stressed the support for and practice of literacy in her early home life. What the schools did to teach her the basics could have "ruined me for learning" she said, even allowing for the occasional exceptional teacher under whom she had studied—such as the Kansas high school English teacher who had trusted her to learn. "I wonder," she wrote, "whether those who talk about 'back to basics' have any real experience with what was taught ninety years ago... or whether they just have a vague idea that once upon a time education was in some ideal state" (1987b).

The fact that LaBrant did not become president of NCTE until rather late in her career is significant. She was opinionated and outspoken. Her niece described LaBrant "as never being interested in winning any personality contests" (Fiehler 1989). Intimates might speculate on several reasons for her becoming president while in her late sixties, but there is a quick, if implicit, consensus that LaBrant did not seek the job. It would not be hard to argue that the NCTE presidency *came to her* so late in her career because of her independence—and her characteristically frequent bluntness. Those unfailingly high standards for all with whom she worked must be kept in mind, but, in fairness, so should LaBrant's candor—and what was considered by some to be her "arrogance."

Missing Chapters 153

At her best, though, LaBrant did operate with directness and independence, and these were not qualities she developed late in life. In fact, she suggested that her reasons for being drawn to NCTE initially were not necessarily related to the quality of what she thought the Council was achieving in the late 1920s. Instead, her impatience with the trivialization of teaching English may have led to her membership. She described a "silly" presentation on teaching Shakespeare which she endured at her first NCTE conference in 1929 and quickly determined that thoughtful English teachers should be receiving better from their national organization, in addition to offering more thoughtful ideas to it. For the next sixty years, Lou LaBrant would become one of the most active, enlightened, and consistently professional voices in NCTE—even if her ideas were not always the easiest to accept nor among the most popular.

One of her very earliest *English Journal* articles may have reflected the impatience LaBrant felt at early NCTE conferences. In a piece she entitled "Masquerading," she wrote, "To be, for a moment, coherent: I am disturbed by such practices . . . as using the carving of little toy boats and castles . . . as the *teaching of English literature*." Though she would not deny the potential from some student interest in such activity, she did add, "But it makes a difference whether the interest be such as to lead to more *reading* or more *carving*." LaBrant never fired a shot at another's practices without offering an alternative: "The remedy would seem to be in changing the reading material rather than turning the literature course into a class in handicraft" (1931a, 245).

She argued that if Shakespeare were all that inaccessible to boys and girls, or if teachers could not make Shakespeare accessible, then alternative literature should be sought. Knowing LaBrant makes one wonder if she might not have preferred substitutes for the *teachers*, not for the literature. In any event, those teachers who were having their "Shakespeare" students build elaborate models of the Globe Theater could not have been comfortable.

One does not get the impression from her work that LaBrant was overly concerned with making teachers or students comfortable, however. There were always standards to be considered and a respect for individuals' ability to think. Her response to and brief involvement with the NCTE Curriculum Commission and its report, *An Experience Curriculum in English*, tells even more about her sometimes-controversial disposition. Though LaBrant's name is listed as a contributor to the 1935 *Experience Curriculum*, her contributions were not acceptable to the committee and her work was not included. "I did not fit the mold," she said, "and the mold was clear for teachers and for contributors" (1989a). Such molds were not to her liking. She would not accept the *Experience Curriculum* because of its attempt to conceptualize English teaching, not because her work was unacceptable to its organizers.

In LaBrant's view the *Experience Curriculum* was too structured, with its complex listings of enabling objectives, strands of "experience," and increments of content. She felt that "too much had already been worked out for the teacher" (1989a) and that the experiences students would have were by and large experiences adults wanted them to have. She recognized the struggle to have this NCTE curriculum reflect John Dewey's views of the importance of a child's prior experience in learning. The *Experience Curriculum* organizers were, however, only espousing a progressive child-centeredness. What resulted was an approach to teaching English which necessitated a teacher's careful management, all in the name of students' "experiences." Consequently, LaBrant did not believe the *Experience Curriculum* "came close to accomplishing what it set out to accomplish, and claimed to have accomplished" (1989a).

Given her outspoken nature and strong independence, LaBrant was candid in her views of other Council publications and efforts as well. She was unabashed in saying she boxed her unread back issues of *English Journal* for a period of time and relegated them to her attic. When she felt the quality of thought "deteriorated," she simply "quit reading lest I would become somehow influenced by what others thought teachers ought to be doing" (1987b). Such views and outspokenness do not make for early or easy ascendancy to the NCTE presidency; they do, however, represent LaBrant's concern with being her own person and maintaining her own clear vision of how English ought to be taught.

LaBrant therefore developed a reputation as being somewhat of a maverick in NCTE, even as she was working with independent initiative in other aspects of her professional life. When a job needed to be done and could be done in a better way than tradition and bureaucracy would seemingly allow, LaBrant just took over and flailed away at red tape. Longtime friend Frank Jennings recounted one illustration: "In 1948 she called a dozen or so of her English Education students in and explained that, in New York, student teaching consisted of 90 hours in the classroom. She told the group that such an exercise would not do them any good, and that she had arranged for them to work in a junior high school on the lower East side. She told them they would work for a full academic year, 8:30–4:00, for twelve credits. They went, and she went as well as their supervisor, with no university grant, support, or sanction. Saturday mornings were for seminars. The students got their credit, and an education" (1989).

Even as she made waves, stood up for what she believed, and issued her challenges to orthodoxy and inferior teaching methods and ideas, LaBrant did not need or seek the limelight. To be so unassuming and low in profile in some situations and yet so much on the cutting edge suggests the complex nature of her professional postures. She was, for example, the only NCTE president not to make a presidential address at the annual conference, deferring instead to J. N. Hook, who had just been named Executive Secretary in NCTE's reorganization. When she did speak or write, her popularity and candor ensured her an audience, though it is unlikely the audiences were without their detractors.

To hammer away so persistently and for so long against restrictive curricula, to be so impatient with teachers who would not seize initiative for their own teaching, and to be so adamant in setting such high moral and intellectual standards for students took great energy, commitment, and resolve. To implement free-reading reforms and personally meaningful writing for students; thoughtful, reflective teaching for preservice teachers; and publications with her brand of integrity in the Council took considerable initiative and time. The initiative was always there. Being blessed with her longevity has given her much time to grow in her own wisdom and in her opportunities to share what she knew.

Professional honesty was important to LaBrant, as were responsible uses of language throughout society. For LaBrant, how language was used and taught in classrooms, in professional life, and in our social lives was anything but a casual affair. She had a deep interest in languages generally and a passion for the English language and its study in particular. Her concerns with language were both academic and moral. As Frank Jennings said, "You had to be as honest as she was" (1989).

Many of her professional writings, including her dissertation, pertained to language development and use. Her respect for the value of language was also reflected in her dealings with students. She demanded honesty and clarity. She did not waste words, nor was there any doubt as to her meaning. According to Jennings, "She has the kind of honesty that makes some people uncomfortable" (1989). Max Bogart, another of LaBrant's students, recalls that same quality: "She was always so clear and precise. She expected her students to be precise as well. You couldn't fake with her; you had to be careful about what you said and how you said it. Every word was looked at. You had to be as honest as she was. Her comments were always very thoughtful and appropriate. Through her teaching she helped me to gain insights into what language is all about" (1989).

LaBrant's unfailingly eloquent methods book (1951b) contains seven long, thoughtful chapters on English teaching, language instruction, and the English language. She commented once, "If teachers are to teach anything about a language to people *who already speak it*, they better know a great deal about what they are teaching and how to teach it" (1989a). The temptation to quote long and frequently from *We Teach English* is great. As James Squire indicated, "*We Teach English* is one of the best statements of pride in a profession that I have ever seen from anyone. It reminds us of the high calling of English more than any other document of that kind" (1989).

LaBrant began her methods book with some skepticism regarding the state of language instruction, but ended by issuing one of her many "high calls" to the profession: If shouting and superlatives had not dulled our thought and feeling, this book might begin with exclamations about the strange way with which educators in general, the public whom we have taught, and teachers of English themselves deal with the English language. Teaching a language spoken by a quarter of a billion people, a language using half a million word symbols, a language designed to deal with the minutiae of daily life and the affairs of the world, a language capable of describing the chemistry of a cell or our theories of the great Universe, a language not infrequently beamed to every country on the globe within a day, a language with potentialities for becoming the communication device for the world— teaching such a language, we have built courses around errors in usage and punctuation and the preservation of disappearing forms, and have argued the merits of a dozen minor pieces of writing as though *Ivanhoe* and *Silas Marner* were the mainstays of our culture. Faced with invasion and destruction, we have powdered our noses and arranged our skirts as sufficient devices for protection. Instead of lamenting our shortcomings, however, we may better spend our time in some examination of the instrument of the human mind, the English language, to the end that problems and materials and procedures may take place in a large scene (1951, 3-4).

And that she did, just as she had been doing for two decades previously and would continue to do for decades after. Lou LaBrant simply railed against textbook approaches to language study because of the insignificance of the textbooks' focus versus the significance of language in world and daily affairs. She wrote: "Language is a most important factor in general education because it is a vital, intimate way of behaving. It is not a textbook, a set of rules, or a list of books" (1940,

364). This was to become a theme she would repeat throughout her career.

During the war years and into the McCarthy era, LaBrant continued to speak passionately about the need for relevant, meaningful instruction in and about language. She said once that her "first request of every teacher of English is that he teach in his classroom the honest use of language and an *understanding of its relation to life.*" She disavowed the primary importance of memorized language rules time and time again and offered that "making neat diagrams of sentences which pervert the truth *is as wrong as participating in sabotage or obstructing the common defense*—more wrong because language deals with the most precious concepts we have" (1941, 206; emphasis added).

This is strong language indeed, but it is born of two impulses. First, Lou LaBrant was frustrated throughout her career by what was passing as language instruction in schools, particularly in light of what she felt the youth of America needed to be learning about language in order to function in—and perhaps to maintain—the democracy into which they were born. Secondly, Lou LaBrant felt passionately about the sanctity and the power of language in daily life. Her speeches and her writing stressed how language shaped and governed our affairs, who we were, and who we would become.

The best and most concentrated evidences of LaBrant's interests in language came about through work with NCTE. In 1949 she chaired the NCTE Committee on the Role of English in Common Learnings, which was charged with answering this question: "What are the English (language arts) contributions to common learnings courses, and under what conditions are they best made?" Her committee proceeded from the assumption that "the use of one's native language is of great importance, and desirable use cannot be learned by mere drill, by good will, nor by accident." Teaching language well would require well-trained teachers responsible for "studying, guiding, and promoting" language growth. Such a responsibility "is not light," as the distorted use of language "by totalitarian countries has recently emphasized" (LaBrant et al. 1951, 7). The committee advocated "a broad understanding of the role of English; and that changes in language habits and attitudes and knowledges be handled as developments" (23).

In one sense, what LaBrant and her committee, and often LaBrant alone, advocated was not revolutionary. Of course language was important to democracy, to tolerable race relations, to human understanding. Of course language was fluid and dynamic. Of course language instruction could be reduced to banal linguistic trivia. But few, if any, other educators of her day were as current with linguistic science, as firm in their understanding of semantics, as aware of a field of inquiry that would grow into semiotics, and as able to apply a growing body of research on language and language development. Only a few before or since her time have matched Lou LaBrant's success in translating a passion for language, a theoretical understanding of language, and research on language into methodologies that teachers could use. What she presented, discussed, and theorized about language in the first seven chapters of *We Teach English* was far ahead of its time in 1951. It remains well worth our time today.

There was a time in our profession's history when most of our outstanding English educators were generalists and able to divide their time and focus among the teaching of literature, the teaching of language, and the teaching of composition. LaBrant was such a generalist in the formative years of English education. More recently, however, many of our leading methodologists and researchers have specialized, devoting more time to a particular language art, or even specializing in a particular aspect of writing or reading instruction. LaBrant's seminal and still current methods text, *We Teach English*, indicates that she was the truest and perhaps deepest generalist of her day. The range of her interests and the depth of experience and insight she has into language, and writing, and literature suggest that even today she would be a widely productive generalist in English education.

She was as devoted to the study and teaching of literature as she was to the importance of responsible language study in schools. Her unpublished autobiography details more of her early upbringing. The importance of being brought up in a family of readers was particularly clear. LaBrant wrote at length about her father's passion for literature. As a result, "we read together," she remembered, "and we talked about what we read. Knowing what wisdom was found in books of all kinds was important to my father, and what was most important to my father became most important to my family" (1987b). As one gets to know LaBrant, it is impossible not to be impressed with how her own reading has continued to range far and wide.

When we last visited LaBrant in the spring of 1989, her apartment was neatly strewn with contemporary literature, including books on politics, the arts, and the sciences. Recent issues of *English Journal*, no longer relegated to attic boxes, were by her reading chair. At that time LaBrant had been recommending *Peristroika* to her reading friends.

With LaBrant, it was always one book or another that everyone ought to have read or should be reading. James Squire recalled

Missing Chapters

LaBrant's excitement over *Dr. Zhivago* in the mid-sixties and her insistence that "all English teachers should just stop what they are doing and read that book for its wisdom about the world today and where we are going in international relations" (1989). LaBrant was only in her eighties at that time. Long before and since that time, LaBrant has been an avid reader of periodicals with a range too broad to detail. However, the fact that LaBrant has subscribed to the *Bulletin of Atomic Scientists* for years should suggest something of her reading breadth.

The kind of literary pedagogy which would proceed from such a reader, true to her own values and experiences, should not be hard to imagine. One would expect wide reading. One would expect minimum interference from a teacher. One would expect the values and perceptions of the readers being taught to be of significant issue. One would expect an advocacy for teachers themselves to read and to read broadly. By now, one would expect LaBrant to remember the best of what she learned from that one masterful high school teacher of English—and she does.

LaBrant's career is perhaps most clearly marked by her consistent interest in broadening the reading base of high school students. She saw reading lists as dangerous and believed that teachers who used them were either intellectually lazy or not very well read themselves, or both. She began a 1949 *English Journal* article by saying, "In the first place, it is easier to follow a prepared list than to think." She went on to argue that assuming someone else's list and basing a literary curriculum on it avoided responsibility, precluded personal fitting of reading to readers, and enabled external control of the curriculum (1949a, 38).

Her earliest experiences of trying to teach an inappropriate literary canon to poorly prepared, midwestern youth gave rise to her career-long interest in promoting free reading. Accordingly, one of her most extensive and influential research studies was entitled *An Evaluation of Free Reading in Grades Seven through Twelve, Inclusive*. Today's researchers might learn much from considering the goals of LaBrant's 1939 collaboration with her Ohio State colleague, Frieda M. Heller. The two sought to determine (1) to what extent had reading proved to be a factor in the student's life pattern; (2) to what extent had reading interests of students been extended; (3) to what extent did reading vary according to needs, abilities, and interests; and (4) to what extent was there evidence that the reading reflected standards that *students* (emphasis added) had developed (LaBrant and Heller 1939a, 2, 3).

LaBrant worked with several classes for three years. There was no outlined or predetermined course in English for these experimental groups. The documentation, reporting, and analysis of what happened is as extensive as it is compelling to read. LaBrant wanted evidence for her convictions about the virtues of free reading. In seeking support for her convictions, she provided much information about what adolescents could and would do when freed from reading lists and able to select and read literature on their own. Space here will allow only the briefest report from the many conclusions.

LaBrant and Heller would argue that the present culture contains sufficient demand for reading to provide a powerful stimulation to adolescents who are freed from required reading; conversely, adolescents respond readily to the reading elements in their *own* culture pattern (78). What we have here is a paradox easily enough understood by those who would dig out this 1939 research. Some cynics would argue that generations of literature teachers have yet to understand fully or to apply what LaBrant and Heller were advocating.

As her own pedagogy was being transformed by research, LaBrant was therefore inclined to criticize NCTE's *Experience Curriculum* specifically for failing to include plans for teaching students to use the library and to select books they would enjoy (17, 295). LaBrant consequently called for new emphasis in literature study—first on contemporary reading available in and demanded by our culture, along with reading reflective of a youth's own culture. LaBrant and Heller found that for either emphasis to be translated into curricula, the adolescent reader must be, again, "freed to receive this stimulation" (1939a, 78).

Her interests in both how and why young people read involved her with a few other leaders of her day who, like LaBrant, were concerned with the art of reading texts in personally significant ways. LaBrant was a contemporary and colleague of Louise Rosenblatt's, who wrote *Literature as Exploration* and other progressive texts on the importance of reader response and subjective considerations in reading. Rosenblatt and LaBrant shared a belief in the value of the reader's response to literature. LaBrant's chapter in the NCTE-sponsored monograph *Reading in an Age of Mass Communication* provides a good explanation of why she believed understanding the experiences of the reader was so central to success in literature study. In this early piece focusing on reading processes, LaBrant recommended the following: an abundance of varied materials covering wide ranges of human endeavor, careful discussion of what actually happened in the readers' minds, an understanding of readers' "blind spots," and the readers' growing understanding of factors which make a writer's work more accessible. To justify her recommendations, she discussed personal factors which influence reading with very full and careful consideration of why individual readers differ (1949b, 39). Social circumstance, previous experience, maturity level, and so on were among the perhaps obvious considerations. But for its time and given the sophisticated, experience-based manner in which LaBrant made her points, this was important reading for teachers of the early 1940s.

LaBrant believed that, "In considering the role of reading . . . we must never forget that the act of reading always concerns an individual and a piece of material" (56). This was a simple enough premise, to be sure. However, LaBrant believed teachers' lack of reading, their use of reading lists, and their inability to trust readers reading on their own combined to misdirect literature programs in schools. She had, after all, learned to read and learned to love to read at home, without a "teacher," and the best school teacher of literature she had "ever had or known about" really did not tell her much about what she had just read. Lou LaBrant had been trusted and enabled to read and to understand on her own, largely according to her own needs and interests and abilities. She wanted no less for readers of literature in schools.

Knowing Lou LaBrant has led us to the following suspicion: if people are truly lifelong learners, they become impatient with those who are not. LaBrant is certainly a lifelong learner. At this writing, her "current" interests as reported by friends include frequent correspondence (her letters are still "feisty"), her writing (a publication as late as spring of 1989), contemporary affairs (she was outspoken on the Iran-Contra affair and is not a great admirer of all our national leaders), and, of course, avid reading—Umberto Eco and semiotics, genealogy, and on and on.

Longtime NCTE leader James Squire expressed a good sense of how LaBrant's capacity to learn influenced her teaching. "She is continuously alive intellectually," says Squire, "in ways that many professors of English and literature have never been. She is interested in a wide variety of ideas and manages to relate them all to language" (1989). It is this broad range of interests across fields as well as within the various possible divisions of English and the language arts which enabled LaBrant to be the renaissance equivalent of an English educator of her age. Whether she discussed promising developments in science and technology or in social theory, LaBrant was more than superficially aware and had what approached a specialist's understanding of the theater as well as of atomic science; of linguistics as well as of architecture.

LaBrant is well traveled, well read, and inquisitive. Her memory remains very sharp late in her life, and she is fully aware of her own intelligence, insight, and intellectual advantages. LaBrant was always a progressive reformer and always, it seemed, a step or two ahead of her time. Some thought she was out of step, if not out of line. But her knowledge of what was happening in the world of contemporary affairs and in diverse research fields made it impossible for her to abide orthodoxy in teaching—especially, as seemed to her so often the case, when the traditions flew in the face of new knowledge.

For example, in a seemingly standard article on vocabulary development and study, LaBrant's formulations were well grounded in her knowledge of contemporary research in language growth and development. Such clear and sound applications of research were rare in the *English Journal* of that day. By then, though, LaBrant's biting wit was not so rare. Readers of her work knew to expect such darts as the following, with which she concluded the vocabulary piece: "If the discussion preceding seems to offer no short cut to vocabulary growth, it is because there is no short cut" (1944, 480). Neither were there any shortcuts to a teacher's understanding as much about teaching as LaBrant understood.

To know as much, teachers would have had to read as much and read as well as LaBrant had read—and to be as perceptively aware as she was, as well. Teachers through seven decades have read LaBrant's NCTE publications, though they have not always read comfortably. LaBrant always provided an insightful, strongly opinionated, well-informed voice on the pages of *English Journal*. Teachers must have known that. Certainly LaBrant did.

Consider, for example, an article on new resources available to English teachers. LaBrant wrote, "Every age has had to remember the past, act in the present, and consider the future" (1953, 79). Keeping up with the present in order to act in it and preparing for the future compelled LaBrant to keep current. She advocated and demonstrated the virtues of understanding all that one could about child growth and development, about the role of language in world events, about emerging world literatures, about the mass media, and about the real-world lives of the boys and girls one encounters in classes. Lou LaBrant was not only able to do all of that and to reflect it in her own teaching and writing, she expected all teachers to follow suit. We must go back to the notion of standards. She did feel that *all* teachers really must read *Dr. Zhivago*. She reasoned that her reading of Pasternak's work had moved and informed and humanized her. Believing that all teachers should be as fully informed and as fully humanized as possible, LaBrant naturally wanted teachers to read not only *as* she read, but sometimes *what* she read.

In one of her most vital, impassioned, and widely discussed NCTE addresses, LaBrant outlined a view of curriculum which emerges when teachers continue to learn. Her 1952 NCTE presentation in Cincinnati was entitled "New Bottles for New Wine." LaBrant's eloquence, global perspective, passion for language, and sense of urgency are captured in these lines with which she concluded a long and sound appeal for curriculum progress and reform:

> Twenty centuries ago a teacher whose words were to change the history of the world spoke in a parable: "And no man putteth new wine into old bottles; else the new wine will burst the bottles and be spilled, and the bottles shall perish." It is time to examine the patched and worn bottles into which we have put this magnificent, live wine of language. If our pupils miss its glory, if they use it carelessly as a form, a manner of dress; if they cease to guard it as a means for honest exploration of truth, the tragedy of atomic warfare may be slight. (347)

The view of a fluid curriculum in a dynamic world increasingly informed by research and new knowledge is clear in the preface to *We Teach English*. "The book which follows," LaBrant began, "is an attempt to point out aspects of philosophy, psychology, and scholarship in the field of language which I found relevant to the program in English, and to indicate some of the implications." The tentative nature of her own formulations is clearly acknowledged, and therein readers must sense the need for a curriculum which evolves: "Obviously, such a statement [of practice] must be imperfect and tentative, since no one is master of the rich research available, new information appears daily, and our language and its uses change as society changes" (1951, 7). Having said once again what she had been saying and practicing for fifty years, LaBrant challenged all who teach English: "For many of us, fundamental revision of attitude is required if we are to accept what modern scholarship has discovered" (7). The only points of pedagogy upon which Lou LaBrant seemed disinclined to change *her* position were those which mindlessly maintained outworn practices.

Finally, it was LaBrant's understanding of teaching, of teachers' lives, and of boys and girls in English classrooms which combined to unify what she knew, what she shared, and what she ultimately represented to generations of teachers. LaBrant clearly understood teaching. Her talks, her courses, her writing illustrated that understanding. But James Squire recalled that in offering her consistently useful advice and focus, "Lou LaBrant reminded us always of the high calling of English teaching" (1989).

"High calling" or not, teaching as LaBrant performed it was not for prima donnas. While she did describe teaching as "one of life's great experiences," she worked hard and was frequently involved in duties which many would consider outside the realm of a teacher's responsibilities. She served punch at a school "housewarming," provided daily janitorial services for a small country school, supervised prefreshman summer students at Dillard University late into the night (doing so one summer with a broken ankle), and spent her Saturdays conducting seminars with student teachers.

Though LaBrant was willing to pitch in and do more than her part, she refused to allow anyone to take advantage of her. She recalled a small country schoolhouse in which she taught in the early 1900s. Her duties included arriving early each morning in order to have the building warmed by the time her students came. After a day's teaching, she would remain to clean floors, desks, and chalkboard and to prepare the fire for the next morning. On the day of a farmers' meeting to be held in her school (the first since her arrival in the community), she meticulously cleaned the schoolhouse and left the key under the mat so that the men could let themselves in for their meeting. When she entered the room the following morning, she found it in complete disarray. Once she and the children had cleaned up after the farmers, she announced to her students that there would no longer be a rule against spitting on the floor. "Obviously," she proclaimed, "your fathers see nothing offensive in the habit!" From then on, the farmers left the schoolroom as tidy as they found it. LaBrant had demonstrated that being a teacher did not make her a "doormat" (1987a, 21). Teaching, then, was many things for Lou LaBrant—whether it was necessary custodial work, social activity, or extra hours and weekends of investment in the academic futures of students unaccustomed to such concern by a professor.

Even more importantly, LaBrant understood teaching well enough to know that to teach meant to change. The fact that the world was changing and that teachers must change with it was an important theme in her writing. LaBrant believed that given new knowledge and new experience in a new world, teachers must change both how they taught and what they thought. Such beliefs are characteristic of curriculum reformers, and Lou LaBrant was a curriculum reformer.

Her trust in individuals and her instincts about teachers and teaching helped her to realize two important facts about the generations of English teachers she tried to inform and to inspire. First, she realized that thoughtful teachers needed as much of her own background, conviction, and courage to change as she was able to instill in them. Secondly, Lou LaBrant realized the importance of forever encouraging teachers to their highest potentials while challenging them with the honor and responsibility of being a teacher of English.

Much that she felt about teaching high school boys and girls would be paralleled in her teaching of teachers. For example, she wrote, "I do not happen to adhere to the theory that students should look upon me as one of the class." She acknowledged that as the teacher she had read more, thought more, and lived more than her students. At the same time, however, she encouraged teachers to "respect the judgments they [the students] make in terms of what they have had time to discover" (1953, 84).

Lou LaBrant devoted her life to helping students—and their teachers—discover more about their world, their language, and their own potential as readers and writers. Tough as she was, her impatience with the profession and with teachers she found most difficult to reach was tempered by her awareness of teachers' knowledge in light of her own. As she taught teachers at conferences, in her classes, and through her publications, LaBrant talked and wrote as if she did, indeed, respect *their* judgments "in terms of what they have had time to discover."

Few people have read as much about teaching and learning and children. Fewer still have Lou LaBrant's range of experience. She was unique in her capacity to apply thoughtfully and then to express to others what she had learned from her own teaching and reading. But it was in her continuous attempts to challenge teachers and to instill in them a sense of professionalism that LaBrant achieved her greatest eloquence. Nothing she wrote better expressed how she saw English teaching than the short, concluding chapter of *We Teach English*:

> No one can teach English with completeness. It requires more knowledge, wisdom, and sympathy than any one man or woman can possess. It requires more reading, more writing, more study than the hours of the day allow. It results, as does all teaching, in defeats, in regrets, and in disappointments. But it results also in achievement, and adds to the very knowledge, wisdom, and sympathy it requires. It deals with the intimate matters of the mind, and so terrifies the thoughtful and sensitive teacher. There are a thousand reasons why you should not begin to teach English, and if you have begun, why you should leave for other fields; there are a thousand reasons, but there are a thousand and one why you should begin and why those of us who have begun would not stop—why, despite all that we know, we could not leave. We Teach English. (1951, 312)

Works Cited

Bogart, Max. 26 April 1989. Telephone interview with B. Jane West. Concord, Mass.

Class of 1938, University High School, Ohio State University. 1938. *Were We Guinea Pigs?* New York: Henry Holt.

Fiehler, Betty. 26 October 1989. Telephone interview with B. Jane West. Kansas City, Mo.

Jennings, Frank. 19 April 1989. Telephone interview with B. Jane West. New York, N.Y.

LaBrant, Lou L. 1931a. "Masquerading." *English Journal* 20: 244–46.

———. 1931b. *The Teaching of Literature in the Secondary School.* New York: Harcourt, Brace, and World.

———. 1940. "The Place of English in General Education." *English Journal* 29: 356–65.

———. 1941. "English in the American Scene." *English Journal* 30: 203–209.

———. 1944. "The Words They Know." *English Journal* 33: 475–80.

———. 1946a. "Teaching High-School Students to Write." *English Journal* 35: 123–28.

———. 1946b. "The Words of My Mouth." *English Journal* 35: 323–27.

———. 1949a. "A Little List." *English Journal* 38: 37–40.

———. 1949b. "Personal Factors Influencing Reading." In *Reading in an Age of Mass Communication,* edited by W. S. Gray, 39–57. New York: Appleton-Century-Crofts.

———. 1951. *We Teach English.* New York: Harcourt, Brace and World.

———. 1952. "New Bottles for New Wine." *English Journal* 41: 341–47.

———. 1953. "How Can We Make the Newer Resources Available?" *English Journal* 42: 79–84.

———. 1954. "The National Council Steps Forward." *English Journal* 43: 119.

———. 1955. "Inducing Students to Write." *English Journal* 44: 70–74.

———. 1959. "As of Now." *English Journal* 48: 295–303.

———. 1961. "The Rights and Responsibilities of the Teacher of English." *English Journal* 50: 379–83, 391.

———. 27 July 1977. Interview with Alfred H. Grommon. New Orleans, La.

———. 1987a. "Long, Long Ago." *Teaching Education* 1: 19–21.

———. 1987b. Unpublished autobiography. Museum of Education, University of South Carolina, Columbia. Unpaged.

———. 1989a. (23 April 1989). Interview with David England. Baldwin City, Kansas.

———. 1989b. "Why Did They Write?" *Teaching Education* 2: 12–15.

LaBrant, Lou L., et al. 1951. *English in Common Learnings.* Chicago: National Council of Teachers of English.

LaBrant, Lou L., and Frieda M. Heller. 1939a. *An Evaluation of Free Reading in Grades Seven through Twelve, Inclusive.* Columbus: Ohio State University Press.

———. 1939b. *The Librarian and the Teacher of English.* Chicago: American Library Association.

Squire, James. 10 May 1989. Telephone interview with B. Jane West. Marlborough, N.H.

8 Luella B. Cook: A Teacher's Teacher

Betty L. Powell Hart, Mt. Vernon High School

Luella B. Cook
1890-1976

Frequently, famous individuals will name their English teachers among those who have influenced them most. It is not surprising. English teachers, for their subject matter, are in a likely position to bring such positive impact upon young minds. Luella B. Cook, no doubt named by many as influential upon their adult values, was one such teacher who dedicated herself to passing on love and appreciation for life to her students. Looking back over forty-four years of classroom teaching and administrative service in the field of English education, Cook expressed her appreciation for the "special privilege" of being an English teacher (1959). In referring to "the hidden reservoir" of a pupil's unconscious thoughts and feelings, she said, "To help pupils become aware of this deeper self and then to explore this inner part of their being is one of the special privileges of the teacher of English. It takes patience and skill and insight to help them learn both to recognize and to trust those deeper layers of self that lie beneath the surface of their conforming selves" (250-51). Later in the article she advised that it was equally important for students to get beyond their private worlds and to become engaged in the world outside of themselves. She saw a threefold responsibility for language arts teachers toward helping students

> cultivate their appreciation and use of language, first for self-revelation and the development of each inner self; second, for social and public performance, so that they may live happily and effectively among their fellows; and third, for the sake of that larger vision of life in which they may share, no matter how

humbly, by listening and paying heed to the voices that call out
from above the street where they live. (252-53)

Tapping the resources of a student's hidden reserve became a theme of Cook's teaching philosophy. In that respect she felt that teachers were critically charged with teaching students not what to think but how to think, and thus teaching critical thinking skills—or as she called them, "original thinking skills"—was the primary aim of English studies. Further, she insisted that the best way to approach the teaching of these skills was to emphasize the instructional value of a lesson over the immediate and obvious practical value. This approach would provide the motivation and discipline necessary to engage students cooperatively in their lessons. Luella B. Cook devoted herself to developing and advocating these ideas during all of her long career in public education.

Her teaching career began in 1915 at a small school in Redfield, South Dakota. Her next three years were spent teaching at South High School in Minneapolis. Luella Cook followed up those beginning years with twenty-four years at Minneapolis Central High School (1920-44) As a classroom teacher, Cook was an example of an effective teacher for teachers throughout the state of Minnesota. Her classroom was a model of how one should coordinate educational objectives with available classroom materials and environment. As a result, her classes at Central High were constantly visited by other educators who sought her leadership and example. She always generously complied with visitors in her willingness to demonstrate teaching procedures. The success of her teaching approaches gained the attention of the administrators for the Minneapolis school district, and she subsequently crystallized her ideas and teaching philosophy in her editorship of two important bulletins published by the Minneapolis Public Schools for district teachers: *The Guide Book for Common Practices in School Work* and *The Guide for Teaching Communication*. Cook's work was well received in the state, and she was later asked to serve as a consultant to the Minnesota Curriculum Committee in Language Arts.

Her service as an educator was not limited to the classroom. Cook belonged to a number of professional and civic organizations, including the Minneapolis Citizen's Committee on Public Education, the Minnesota Education Association, the Minnesota State Federation of Teachers (for which she served as president in 1939), the National Education Association, and the National Council of Teachers of English (for which she served as president from 1956 to 1957). Though in later years she was active in her professional organizations on the national level, she was especially loyal to the Minnesota Education Association. Despite her demanding publication and speaking schedule and her job responsibilities on the national level, she was a perennial program participant for the annual spring conference of the Minnesota Education Association's English teachers.

Luella Cook's association with a wide variety of people and experiences made her a remarkable woman among her peers. Following the shock of the First World War, as the American vision focused more on events outside the United States, the idea developed that teachers would become better teachers by becoming more involved in the world and life itself. English educator Ruth Mary Weeks, in her 1930 presidential address to the NCTE convention in Cleveland, called for teachers to teach and *live* the "art of living." That call was a creed for Luella B. Cook, who took to heart Weeks's demand that teachers become "masters of that art." Cook took the idea a step further in the classroom. She believed that viewing one's world as a country, separate and independent of all other nations, was giving way to a view of the world as a more global society in which all cultures made active and valuable contributions to the good of humanity.

Cook's appointment as a full-time consultant in curriculum development in the Minneapolis Public Schools came after twenty-eight years of classroom teaching. She served as a curriculum consultant from 1944 to 1955. In that capacity she dedicated herself to exposing the potential and possibilities of knowledge to young minds by expounding a teaching philosophy that was based on the universality of all experience of all people as it shaped the world and values of those growing, learning young minds. She earnestly believed that the capacity for acquiring the values and experiences—the factual data of knowledge—was within the reach of all learners. She felt, however, that until the teacher empowered the student with the cognitive skills for conceptualizing and then expressing those values and experiences, students would yield only little application of that knowledge. Frequently in her articles for *English Journal*, Cook railed against teachers who traded the hard tasks of teaching and learning in the classroom for convenience and gimmicks. Neither unsympathetic nor unfamiliar with the paperload plight of English teachers, she proposed that teachers substitute a concern for the qualitative value of learning for its quantitative value. In other words, the value and meaning of a particular learning task need not be justified by a teacher-evaluated written assignment. Cook saw the problem as one of making students aware of the educative value of such assignments or of the relationship of their industry to their achievement: "A simplification of the correcting problem depends in large measure upon a careful distinction between quality and quantity of student effort; between faithfulness in practice of writing-skills, and the intrinsic merit of final performance" (1932a, 367). She proposed the use of peer evaluation, sampling, and keeping a daily check of student work and participation as alternatives to the meticulous red-marking of student papers. Less emphasis on mechanical error would lead to more attention to acquiring the skills needed to express oneself better.

Her concern for the human potential and limitations of both students and teachers was characteristic of her sensitivity to people and circumstances at all levels. Maintaining this perspective throughout her career, Luella B. Cook practiced unbiased acceptance and appreciation of people from all walks of life, traveled extensively to experience other cultures all over the world, and promoted the teaching of multiethnic literature both in the requirements of district curriculum for the Minneapolis Public Schools and in the content of her published literary anthologies.

Even though Luella Bussey Cook enjoyed a wealthy lifestyle as an adult, she began life in poverty, often doing without and only dreaming of opportunities for improving her family's circumstances. What little is known of her personal life is discretely shared by her longtime friend and coauthor, Walter Loban. She was born on 19 March 1890 in Chicago, Illinois, to a family that was barely able to eke out enough to sustain food and housing necessities. She had one sister, Marian, and later it was her daughter, Dorothy or "Dottie," who became Luella's favorite. Despite the odds against her, Luella was an energetic and bright child who loved school and saw education as a means to realize those better opportunities. After high school graduation, she enrolled at the University of Minnesota, receiving her B.A. in 1913 and her M.A. in 1914 while on a graduate assistantship.

As an undergraduate, Luella Bussey fell in love with her professor, Edward Cook, and married him. After their marriage Edward left his teaching job at the University of Minnesota to collaborate on the publication of a left-wing liberal newspaper which failed and left him jobless. Luella had begun her teaching career in the Minneapolis public school system. Soon her early publications with Harcourt achieved success and assured the couple's financial security. They built a home in nearby Wayzata, Minnesota, about twenty-five miles from Minneapolis, and there Edward guided and advised Luella's publishing career until his death in the late 1930s. Though Edward preferred her to write books alone, she collaborated frequently with coauthors and coeditors.

Luella B. Cook never forgot her fortunate rise from poverty to prestige and wealth, but few who knew her as an adult could appreciate her sympathy for and identification with poor people. Her own experiences as a poor person and as a wealthy person led her to a knowledge and acceptance of many kinds of people and lifestyles, each valid and valuable in the pool of humanity. She advocated a curriculum that would expose young minds to the varieties of experiences in life. Her concern was for developing a teaching method that democratically took into account the impacts of various cultural orientations upon the values and perceptions of a child's world. Later she would charge teachers with their critical responsibility to promote the teaching of literature toward that end. Teachers, Cook observed, had the power and tools to change and even to construct for all of their learners a positive self-view and world view.

At a time when most women were settling into marriage and child rearing, with teaching being one of a few liberating possibilities, Luella B. Cook was quietly amassing a comfortable fortune, traveling extensively all over the world—Europe, the United States, Mexico, South America, and the West Indies—and establishing an impeccable professional reputation as a writer and an educator. Her independence from a scripted lifestyle left her free to pursue the fullest benefits of personal and professional relationships. Cook made a point of knowing and enjoying a wide variety of people and lifestyles. Her personal associations included a wide circle of endeared friends—both male and female, young and old, rich and poor. Likewise, her professional relations attracted a variety of intellectual and social groups. Longtime friend and professional associate Walter Loban commented in a personal remembrance:

> Luella B. Cook was free of the restraints so often found in women in other parts of the world. She took seriously Jefferson's idea that if people do not use power wisely, the answer was not to take it from them but to educate them, to inform them. She abhorred racism or injustice toward any minority group; always she treated other people as ends in themselves, not as means to her purposes. (Loban n.d.)

Of her many achievements, perhaps Cook will be most remembered for her editorship of a number of composition texts and literature anthologies published by Harcourt from 1934 to 1958. These highly acclaimed texts were used all over the country in secondary literature courses. Her first publication, *A Project Book in Business English*, was published by Henry Holt in 1920 and revised in 1928. Cook began her long-term career with Harcourt in 1927 with *Experiments in Writing*, a high school composition textbook for junior and senior English classes. In 1932 she wrote the second volume to Lucy H. Chapman's *Using English* as part of Harcourt's Growth in Using English series. In 1939 Cook's English text, *Developing Language Power*, appeared, followed by *Using Language Power*, a rhetoric and grammar text, in 1940. All of her Harcourt composition texts were exceptionally successful, selling widely throughout the United States.

Cook's first published anthology was a three-volume set, *Hidden Treasures in Literature*, written in collaboration with George Norvell and William McCall in 1934. A resource for speakers and readers, the text was a collection of literary abstracts and selections from American and British authors. Norvell and McCall also worked with Cook on writing a workbook, *Experiments in Reading*, a three-volume set of exercises, diagrams, forms, and study questions to accompany *Hidden Treasures*.

Cook began work on her most successful anthology series, Adventures in Appreciation, in 1934. This began as a preliminary project for Harcourt, to be collaboratively edited by Luella Cook with a man named Schweikart from St. Louis. When Schweikart died unexpectedly in the spring of 1933, Cook was asked by Harcourt to name a replacement, preferably a young, but experienced, male teacher. She had been introduced at the annual Minnesota Education Association convention to a young man named Walter Loban, then a student of Dora V. Smith's at the University of Minnesota, who seemed to fit the bill. Loban later revealed that Cook, sometimes given to an ironic sense of justice, submitted his name—a young and unknown male teacher—to Harcourt senior editor Jim Reid simply in defiance to his specification that her co-editor be male. Loban suggested that Harcourt at that time did not wish for its female authors to be too independent in their power or in their profits from their successes with the company. Nonetheless, in the autumn of 1934 at the NCTE annual convention, Loban accepted Harcourt's contract to become Cook's co-editor. Also working with her were McCall, Norvell, and Harry A. Miller. Three Challenge titles in the series appeared in 1941: *Challenge to Explore* (1941a), *Challenge to Grow* (1941b), and *Challenge to Understand* (1941c). The Adventures in Appreciation series, a complete six-year program for grades seven through twelve, went through seven subsequent revised editions from 1941 to 1958, with a number of different coauthors.

Cook's Adventures series was followed by another successful series of anthologies, the Living Literature series, part of Harcourt's larger literary series, the Pageant of Living. As chief editor, Cook collaborated with Walter Loban, Ruth Stauffer, George Salt, Egbert Nieman,

Tremaine MacDowell, and Oscar J. Campbell on the four-volume set: *America through Literature* (1948a), *People in Literature* (1948b; revised in 1957), *Pleasure in Literature* (1948c), and *The World through Literature* (1949).

Cook's basic philosophy was simple. Her most important emphasis in any of her texts was always the same: that the primary goal of literature studies was the teaching of human values. In the preface to the 1949 edition of her Adventures in Appreciation series, Cook appealed to teachers to sensitize "the student to basic human issues and problems of today." The publication date is significant. This book was the first revision of her original 1944 edition to appear after the Second World War. Acutely aware of the recent social and moral changes in the postwar world, Cook commented in her introduction that the editors of the text

> recognize that the impact of the war years has emphasized several trends in secondary education that had begun prior to the war. The first of these is the recognition of the serious social problems facing the world and the realization that education has a vital role to play in helping to meet them. Second is the increasing realization that secondary education must provide for the intellectual and spiritual needs, not of the favored few, but of all kinds of people in a democratic society; the teacher then can expect to find in her class students from all social and economic levels, the children of the lawyer and elevator operator, plant foreman and stenographer, housewife and aviator—those planning to attend college and those for whom the high-school years represent the end of formal education—all future citizens in our increasingly interdependent society mingled even now in the classroom.

Her foresight was extremely accurate. Her adherence to the idea of a global society was evident in her selection of literary content for this volume. Her own travels had taught her that the entire world was engaged in a struggle to adapt to recent changes in how its inhabitants regarded relationships and differences among themselves. As her selection of literary works attests, Cook sought to dissolve the boundaries between races, nationalities, and economic groups. The authors of the selections represented a variety of races, creeds, and nationalities. In addition to stories, poems, and narratives from Third World writers, Cook included literature of American blacks and other American ethnic groups.

In the context of the usual thematic topics found in literary anthologies for young readers—maturation, discovery, and personal relationships and values—Luella B. Cook directed her subjects toward the learning of basic human values by young readers as they encountered the fundamental conditions and problems of human life.

Her section titles indicate her abstracted purpose: "The Will to Understand," "Wanderlust," "Imaginative Insight," "There Are No Distant Lands," and "Of Heroic Mold." Her aim clearly was to subordinate the teaching of literary form to the teaching of human values. She proposed that

> in a given work of literature the form is what it is because of the values the author is communicating.... When taught properly the appreciation of form enables the student to perceive better the total values of the work of art. Consequently, the main emphasis in these sections on form is directed toward a better understanding of the selections as significant comments on life which are to be interpreted and evaluated by the student. (iv)

Cook challenged her students to approach literature as she would have them approach life. It was her idea that meaning and form contend to shape a literary work, and while the students are not wholly engaged in an exercise of the New Criticism or formalism, they are using the rubric of that critical theory to get at the meaning of a literary work and to appreciate its structure as it contributes thematically to the author's commentary on life. But essential to those applications was the teacher's responsibility to give students the necessary means for getting at the significance of literary experiences. Cook saw the problem of teaching literature to be "one of widening the range of response to literature, of guiding reading experiences" so that students' reactions to books would be "vivid, sharp, compelling, provocative.... We cannot really teach interpretation until we are willing to explore student reaction to literature as we find it" (1936).

Cook's emphasis on the pragmatic application of literary meanings to the lives of her students was new for its time. In her emphasis upon the literary treatment of basic human values and problems, she allowed her students to discover value and meaning in reading that could transfer as personal attitudes and outlooks on their own lives. This was a vitally important approach to the contemporary matters of anxiety and change, not only to adults who had to contend with a wartorn and weary world, but to students as well, who needed some context in which to conceptualize the traumatic historical, political, and social changes of their present world and the uncertainties of a future based on an unfamiliar order of technology and global military powers.

In an address entitled "Fundamentals in the Teaching of Composition," given before a Texas Teacher's Association's regional conference in March 1940, Luella Cook described her method for teaching the value of language to her nontraditional "Y" students. This "Y" group represented students who scored between 77 and 110 on standardized IQ tests, with a median score of 98; this was a group with whom Cook sympathized, for they looked "as though they vaguely sensed the fact that they were considered 'dumb' and that no one would take time—now that they had been sorted and labeled—to do much of anything with them or for them, except to keep them rather aimlessly busy doing the things which they can already do." Her first insight was that these children were poor writers and spellers because, being passed over in traditional methods and materials, they had been given little "opportunity to write about the things they [knew] (it being assumed that they didn't know much) and the connection between the words and things had never been thoroughly established in their minds." Cook argued against mere rote learning and what she considered the more permanent learning that takes place through inductive teaching. And so she set her goal to get her students "to translate their own experience into words as accurately as might legitimately be expected" (1941, 360-67).

Luella Cook came to teach this particular group of students as a consequence of her angering the Minneapolis public school board with her leadership of the Minnesota Federation of Teachers, an organized labor union. Her "punishment," according to Walter Loban's undated personal account of the incident, was to be given an unruly, all-male group of poor learners in a windowless classroom located among the boilers and pipes of the school basement. Loban described Cook's rise to the challenge:

> Intrigued as always by a challenge, Luella was fascinated with her class and the situation in which they were plunged. Fearful that the authorities might learn how happy she was over the "punishment" they had given her, she would, from time to time, go to the principal's office to complain about the matter, thus persuading them to let her remain with her interesting challenge. She could be very insightful about how to cope with people and situations! (Loban n.d.)

The incident illustrates Cook's insistence upon the value of each student's ability and the obligation of every teacher to use that ability.

Cook criticized those teachers who concentrated on correct form, mechanics, and the red-marking of numerous errors in composition. Along with other leading, foresighted educators from her profession, educators such as Dora V. Smith and Rewey Belle Inglis, Luella B. Cook believed and endorsed the powerful, revolutionary ideas of Mina P. Shaughnessy, who also saw that a student's errors often grow from his or her lack of competency rather than lack of ability to perform. During her address to the Texas teachers, Cook advised, "On the level of mechanics—correct endorsement, legibility, spacing—this can be accomplished almost immediately by the simple process of rejecting, not 'failing,' papers that fall short of the standards set" (1941).

Cook's approach to the teaching of grammar was a combination of both the functional and logical approaches. Believing that students needed experience with language before rules about language, she contended that the grammatical analysis and study of language could come as late as the last year of high school, when pupils most likely would have the cognitive skills for conceptualizing their linguistic experiences in grammatical contexts. The point of teaching language skills at any level was "specific, conscious improvement . . . the foundation for a definite technical skill" that would facilitate a student's understanding and use of language (1945a, 123). Her method for teaching grammar was based on her beliefs that the place "of grammar in the English curriculum should be determined by need and appropriateness"; that grammatical concepts should be introduced inductively; that these concepts should be taught in different ways and at all levels as organic to a student's language use and development; and that the methods used to teach language should be derived, "not from the detection and correction of errors but on a study of the resources of language." These beliefs supported her major directive to teachers to know "that the problem of good workmanship *within the field of what a pupil knows but fails to apply* calls for techniques quite different in kind from those useful in teaching language concepts and that concern for one must not be allowed to interfere with the other" (1946, 188).

Instructional methods based upon these beliefs would bring about many positive benefits to language arts teaching. Such a method would lead to an increased emphasis in the early grades on writing and speaking, a decrease in attention to red-marking errors, an increase in understanding what grammatical errors mean in terms of specific needs for instruction, and, finally, a better focus and organization of effort and time in the classroom.

By lessening the emphasis on grammatical correctness in favor of inductive discovery of the grammatical structure of language, Cook did not advocate ignoring the mechanical and syntactical errors of a paper in deference to the global concerns of development of ideas. She saw an organic relation of units of ideas to the whole, from students' choices of words and order to their conceptualizing of a complete idea. According to Cook, everything proceeded organically toward the expression of that complete idea: "The sentence is a unit of thought and can only move on to new goals in conjunction with a corresponding improvement in thought" (1941).

Her concern with errors was with "what lies behind them and how one may forestall them in future writing" (1941). Her pedagogical idea of what possibly lay behind those errors had much to do with how a teacher perceived a student's educative process. Cook saw the responsibility for improving a student's writing to be "primarily a teaching responsibility," for a successful instructor would already have the teaching skills that would provide the appropriate methods for reaching a particular student on effective levels and by effective means. She said that "the teaching of composition as a tool of thought carries with it the responsibility of helping students on any level not only to discover more meanings but to sharpen and refine them" (1941). Her idea was that students had to have an internalized context for making meaning before they could generate and express those meanings in written form, or any form for that matter, and as she acknowledged that "intellectual growth is based on an ever widening appreciation of meaning" (1941), she urged other English educators to concentrate on providing those contexts for their students, both in terms of familiar environments, new and different environments, and people to be discovered and appreciated. Teaching the student, not the lesson, was her credo, and she was quick to admit that "teaching often degenerates to just such well-intentioned but futile shoutings of definitions of things we know to those who don't know, with no real understanding of the learning process. We have ourselves traveled far along a rambling path but have forgotten, if we ever knew, how we came" (1941).

Cook's point of view was always in sympathy with the student's perception of instruction, and as such, her teaching method was based on a recognition that the primary motivation for learning is knowing: being able to abstract meaning from and express oneself in a world which emphasizes the infallibility of facts. She complained that teachers were perhaps too riveted to product rather than the creative faculties behind it. Thus she invited teachers to concentrate on "toning up the whole mechanism" (1935, 382) by which students observe and perceive meaning, significance, resemblance, and relationship. She saw the teaching of form for which a student can interpret experience more important than the emphasis on process and product: "you cannot teach a person to react with his senses, or respond with his imagination to experience. All you can do is teach him how to react more vividly and to respond more significantly" (381).

Addressing the 1948 NCTE convention in San Francisco, Luella B. Cook said that basic to the teaching of form was a recognition of three things about form: that good form is a convenience, that good form is a courtesy, and that "it is a challenge in itself exerting a special kind of power," for form becomes "the vehicle for thought" (1948a, 222). Before then, she was to declare that "experience *with* language must precede and accompany instruction *about* language before instruction about language can mean anything at all" (1943, 139).

Cook's contention was that teachers must "train students to observe facts rather than to write words, and to use words solely for the purpose of discovering and communicating accurate meaning" (139). Earlier still she warned teachers that there were no easy means for teaching organic development. She admitted that "language improvement is a matter of slow growth. It is much more than mechanical change; it is organic development" (1939a, 632). She saw the hesitancy of a teacher to demystify the power of original thinking as one of the basic causes of a teacher's failure to educate. She defined the problem in a 1943 article as a need to "find a way to balance instruction *about language* with experience *in using it,* so that the two operate as a functioning whole" (1943, 142).

She felt the teacher's aim was to help students to draw conclusions from facts by pointing out the relationships between those facts which confronted them in their daily lives. In an address delivered before the Arkansas Education Association on 8 November 1946, Cook proposed "An Inductive Approach to the Teaching of Language," in which students would experience a "positive learning that builds respect for language and gives pupils insight into the power which words may exert over reader or listener" (1948b, 20).

Luella Cook knew that the incentive for language learning was not artificially motivated. She also knew that in formal education situations, language was taught unnaturally, going from concept to cognition rather than from observation to rule. She criticized her contemporaries for methods emphasizing mastery and memorization of rules for language instead of intuitively perceiving relationships between the word and the idea. She pointed out that teachers need not be so concerned with the final product—preferably an error-free, neatly written paper—as with the student's creative effort in arriving at the product: "Correctness, it should be understood, in reality, grows out of a respect for one's craft and pride in the object of creation. Inaccuracy is not so often a sign of ignorance as of indifference. A smudgy, careless paper is no more an indictment of a student than it is a vivid reminder to a teacher of the failure of the assignment" (1932a, 370). She further commented, "I would start with *experience in using language* rather than with *rules about language* because that is the pattern of learning already set by the years that have preceded schooling. Long before we could define sentences, we were using them" (1948b, 16–17).

Cook's educational philosophy and theory were the frequent subjects of her numerous journal publications and public addresses. Her foresight toward modern educational theory is apparent as early as her first *English Journal* article, "Old Wine in New Bottles" (1924). Not content to teach composition in the traditional format of rules, drill, and practice, Cook called for a new regard for the teaching of composition in the whole curriculum. As today's advocates of writing across the curriculum and whole language would agree, Cook said that composition could not be considered isolated from other subjects in the curriculum, that "it is rather synthesizing and correlating the knowledge students are acquiring elsewhere" (1924, 556).

A few years later she continued her campaign for the integrative function of language courses, noting that the tendency to separate knowledge into autonomous units called subjects was detrimental to "that synthesizing of knowledge which is education itself" (1929). She felt that the composition classroom, which should be least regimented, could unify the curriculum by allowing students the opportunities for giving intelligent form to the bulk of knowledge gathered in their other studies.

Critical to that ability to synthesize the bulk of knowledge into intelligent form was the student's ability to think. Luella Cook felt that not enough teachers knew how to appeal to the active intelligence of their students. Noting that "ideation precedes composition" (1929, 39), she would frequently propose a course in thinking for a progressive curriculum. She made the aim for such a course in "intellectual agronomy" more specific in 1945: "of its aim, I feel more certain: that of increasing a student's conscious control over his mind, of improving his critical awareness of his own thought processes. Such an aim surely does not run counter to the creative function" (1945b, 197).

In her article "A Technique for Training in Thinking" (1927b), Cook proposed how to teach the method of thinking, using specific and realistic problems as the means. It was important that the problems be specific, for Cook emphatically believed that writing situations should assimilate the real-life conditions and needs that stimulate communication. She was later to observe that students often retreated to the safety of vague, general thinking as opposed to specific mindedness. She suggested that teachers always give exact significance to their assignments, that they have students make specific criticisms in response to the tasks, that students analyze their own specific problems and ask specific questions to resolve those problems, and, finally, that teachers design their assignments to present specific tasks involving specific intellectual skills (1930, 37).

Her point was to divorce teachers from the mystical notion that pattern thinking and instinctive intelligence were superior to creative intelligence. In her article "Is the Whole the Sum of Its Parts?" Cook pointed out that teachers often equate proficiency as instinctive when actually such skill is "frequently the reward of a deliberate effort" (1933, 548). The effort, Cook noted in 1931, went against "the mind's natural reluctance to be specific." To encourage individual thinking power in students, she suggested that teachers arouse students to appreciate the unusual, use firsthand classroom experience, and require students to solve problems inductively (1931, 199).

In November 1956 Luella B. Cook gave her presidential address at the annual convention of the National Council of Teachers of English in St. Louis, Missouri. Her subject was the convention theme that she had selected: "Man's Reach Should Exceed His Grasp." In her remarks Cook once again emphasized the need for educators to determine whether the significance of the content of their instruction was appropriate for the needs of students as potential citizens of life. She spoke of the "philosophic dilemma" which educators of all times have faced—"a dilemma not new or peculiar to this age, but perennial and continuous in the life of man, who must ever adjust himself, not only to the physical facts of the universe but also to those mysterious psychological needs deep within himself: his need to hope, to dream, to aspire, to believe, and to understand—as well as he can." Thus she charged her fellow English educators with the greatest task of our profession: the job of "educating the human spirit to live happily in the new world created by science" (1957b, 73-78).

Speaking of a new world, a postwar world that saw absolute faith in scientific fact, Luella Cook noted in her 1956 address that "There must be not only a sound interpretation of what the facts mean and a practical idea of how to meet them; there must be in addition a set of values against which to view them and measure their worth and significance" (1957b, 75). She further charged her audience to teach students through literature and language skills "some appreciation of the values that have been preserved for us in the literature of the ages, and for developing language skills prerequisite to an assimilation of our spiritual heritage" (75).

Luella B. Cook was devoted not only to teaching the use and appreciation of language to her students, but also to helping them discover the more important purpose of language—its content of cultural and personal values for living in a world of traumatic changes. Her own life was a constant adjustment to the requirements of a new world, a world in which she felt perfectly at ease. She cared about all people and living things, and she loved life and her professional colleagues and friends most ardently. The changing world was a challenge to her energetic mind and physical strength. She traveled all over the world and wrote of the many exotic peoples, climates, and cultures she encountered. More than anything, she wanted American education to prepare our children for dealing with the increasingly multiethnic world and its rapid but certain changes.

Among the many profound changes that Cook was to witness was the changing role of women. She recognized the role of women in shaping the new attitudes and values of the postwar world. She and other female educators like herself were already unique in that they were fully able to pursue careers and to become outstanding in their professions without the usual and expected domestic encumbrances. Upon being recognized by the University of Minnesota as one of its outstanding alumni, she commented in the alumni newsletter of 1960: "What is needed is a national program that will provide continuing educational opportunities for women, while raising a family, and a more flexible employment schedule to fit her needs. That will help the woman of America not only to realize her complete self but to contribute significantly to the solving of the increasingly complex problems that lie outside the home" (*Alumni News*, 13).

Luella Cook felt it most important that we as teachers show our students "the possibilities for growth, the goals worth reaching for, and then accept with charity, their fumbling grasp" (1957b, 78). She concluded her presidential address by referring characteristically to our personal goal as teachers: "To believe in the goal, the ideal, yet still be compassionate toward those—even ourselves—who miss the mark; to respect excellence, even glory in it, but at the same time to respect also struggle and growth—even failure, if it be toward noble ends—this is the precarious inner balance required of members of the teaching profession" (78).

Her speech before the NCTE convention was an eloquent summation of her forty-four years of teaching students and teachers the appreciation of human values. In her last *English Journal* article, "The Search for Standards," Cook assessed the successes and failures in American English classrooms over the historic preceding four decades. She commented that despite teachers' failure to set realistic expectations for learners and a tendency to look for mastery over growth, they still had the same basic objective for teaching young minds. Teachers must teach them, she said, "to hold on to a belief in themselves, regardless of their failures in accomplishment, while they build their ideals or explore the vast world outside themselves." Luella Cook believed that the key to achieving that aim had been and always would remain true to two basic attitudes within teachers and their students: "a respect for excellence and a respect for the task to be done—a thing in itself" (1960, 334).

Luella B. Cook was a person who took language to heart. She was a brilliant classroom teacher, an inspiration to teachers through her practical demonstration and analysis of classroom procedures, a penetrating thinker and incisive speaker and writer, the author of universally used textbooks in composition and literature. Through service in local, state, and national organizations, she worked ardently and intelligently for the improvement of classroom teaching and curriculum in the field of English. Her services to NCTE as president and member of numerous committees was summarized in her "Counciletter" of 1957. Among the many accomplishments achieved during her administration and membership on the Council's Executive Committee were setting up the Commission on the Status of the Profession, establishing permanent headquarters in Urbana, Illinois, and studying the need and structure of Council committees. She also saw growth in the membership and financial status of the Council. In 1957 she described the Council as the "world's largest and strongest organization of English teachers (1957, 225). She valued her experiences and contributions to the Council as a true personal satisfaction: "Indeed, it is a rarity, and it is a sheer joy to give oneself over freely and wholly to the job at hand. I have never experienced a truer professional satisfaction than in working with and for the Council" (1958, 372).

Luella B. Cook was much more than a listing of her professional achievements and contributions could ever indicate. She was a forger of young minds, a leader to discovery and knowledge—Luella B. Cook was a teacher. In 1976, at the age of eighty-six, Cook died of cancer. She had long since retired from her demanding professional schedule and contented herself with keeping house, entertaining friends, and traveling, which she loved most of all. She loved to collect and care for plants and pets. She was concerned, as always, with the value of life in all living creatures.

That the entire history of this remarkable and dedicated educator is not known is largely the justification for examining what we do know of her life. Women such as Cook, who made monumental contributions to the profession of English education, have gone virtually unnoticed, uncelebrated for the invaluable basic pedagogical groundwork which they conceived and promoted in curriculum and methods for classroom instruction.

Luella B. Cook was part of a network of talented women educators. They all knew each other, they all encouraged each other, and they all shared in their pedagogical perspectives. They were the founders of modern teaching philosophy and practice. They were women who began their teaching careers in classrooms, gained their basic ideas and skills as teachers in those classrooms, served as local department chairs, earned advanced degrees, published extensively, and worked their way up through the networks of professional organizations.

Luella B. Cook advanced the teaching of writing and literature far into the future. Her contributions to classroom teaching and the pedagogical ideology of her profession are inestimable and will certainly extend further into forthcoming developments in the field of English education. Walter Loban described Luella Cook as "one of that group of fascinating women—unusual for their time. They were examples of what the American Dream should be" (n.d.).

During her closing remarks as outgoing president at the 1957 NCTE convention in St. Louis, Luella B. Cook spoke on the need and nature of humankind to rise to greatness. She quoted a poem, "We Never Know How High," by one of her favorite poets, Emily Dickinson:

> We never know how high we are
> Till we are called to rise;
> And then, if we are true to plan,
> Our statures touch the skies.

Works Cited

Alumni News. 1960. Vol. 59(5): 13. University of Minnesota, Minneapolis-St. Paul.

Cook, Luella B. 1920. *A Project Book in Business English.* New York: Henry Holt.

———. 1924. "Old Wine in New Bottles." *English Journal* 13: 549–59.

———. 1927a. *Experiments in Writing.* New York: Harcourt.

———. 1927b. "A Technique for Training in Thinking." *English Journal* 16: 588–98.

———. 1929. "Individualism in Our Composition Classes." *English Journal* 18: 31–39.

———. 1930. "Specific-Mindedness." *English Journal* 19: 36–39.

———. 1931. "Creative Writing in the Classroom." *English Journal* 20: 195–202.

———. 1932a. "Reducing the Paper-Load." *English Journal* 21: 364–70.

———. 1932b. *Using English, Book II.* Growth in Using English Series. New York: Harcourt.

———. 1933. "Is the Whole the Sum of Its Parts?" *English Journal* 22: 542–51.
———. 1935. "An Experiment in Observation." *English Journal* 24: 381–87.
———. 1936. "Reading for Experience." *English Journal* 25: 274–81.
———. 1939. *Developing Language Power.* New York: Harcourt.
———. 1940. *Using Language Power.* New York: Harcourt.
———. 1941. "Fundamentals in the Teaching of Composition." *English Journal* 30: 360–70.
———. 1943. "What Kind of Lesson Plan Is Best Suited to Language Development?" *English Journal* 32: 138–42.
———. 1945a. "A Dual Approach to Grammar Study." *English Journal* 34: 122–27.
———. 1945b. "Writing in Terms of the Individual." *English Journal* 34: 194–99.
———. 1946. "Teaching Grammar and Usage in Relation to Speech and Writing." *English Journal* 35: 188–94.
———. 1948a. "Form in Its Relation to Thought." *English Journal* 37: 221–29.
———. 1948b. "An Inductive Approach to the Teaching of Language." *English Journal* 37: 15–21.
———. 1957a. "Counciletter." *English Journal* 46: 219, 225.
———. 1957b. "Man's Reach Should Exceed His Grasp." *English Journal* 46: 73–78.
———. 1958. "Reminiscences of the Senior Past President." *College English* 19: 371–72.
———. 1959. "Writing as Self-Revelation." *English Journal* 48: 247–53.
———. 1960. "The Search for Standards." *English Journal* 49: 321–28, 333–35.
Cook, Luella B., et al., eds. 1948a. *America through Literature.* Living Literature Series. New York: Harcourt.
———. 1948b. *People in Literature.* Living Literature Series. New York: Harcourt.
———. 1948c. *Pleasure in Literature.* Living Literature Series. New York: Harcourt.
———. 1949. *The World through Literature.* Living Literature Series. New York: Harcourt.
Cook, Luella B., William McCall, George Norvell, Harry A. Miller, and Walter Loban, eds. 1941a. *Challenge to Explore.* Adventures in Appreciation Series. New York: Harcourt.
———. 1941b. *Challenge to Grow.* Adventures in Appreciation Series. New York: Harcourt.
———. 1941c. *Challenge to Understand.* Adventures in Appreciation Series. New York: Harcourt.
Cook, Luella B., George Norvell, and William McCall, eds. 1934a. *Experiments in Reading.* 3 vols. (Workbook set to accompany *Hidden Treasures in Reading.*) New York: Harcourt.
———. 1934b. *Hidden Treasures in Reading.* 3 vols. New York: Harcourt.
Loban, Walter. N.d. Personal correspondence.

9 Helen K. Mackintosh: Expanding the Concept of Our World

Lisa J. McClure, Southern Illinois University at Carbondale

> The world stands out on either side
> No wider than the heart is wide;
> Above the world is stretched the sky—
> No higher than the soul is high.
> The heart can push the sea and land
> Farther away on either hand.
>
> Edna St. Vincent Millay, "Renascence"

Helen K. Mackintosh
1897-1980

President Helen K. Mackintosh chose these lines of poetry as the theme for the 1957 convention of the National Council of Teachers of English. It was an especially appropriate theme for 1957: the Soviet Union launched Sputnik, the first earth satellite, into orbit that year, and the world grew wider. In her presidential address Mackintosh reminded her audience of the power of the individual to expand his or her own world through language: "So much depends upon the individual as a person, whether he be teacher or student. Can he through his own efforts expand the concept of his world beyond the classroom, the local community, the state, and the nation to include all countries and all peoples?" (1958b, 152). Mackintosh's own life, both professional and personal, was one of expanding the concept of her world as well as the worlds of the children who were always the focus of her attention.

Born in Hopkinton, Iowa, in 1897, Helen Katherine Mackintosh attended high school locally before entering the State University of Iowa in Iowa City in 1916. Taking courses in English, French, and education, she initially prepared to teach high school. During her senior year Mackintosh, reportedly one of the finest students ever trained at Iowa, received many honors, including Pi Lambda Theta, an honorary education fraternity for women; Mortar Board; Phi Beta Kappa; and Representative Woman. After receiving her A.B. in English in 1920, she taught English and French for one year in a high school in Tipton, Iowa. Although these moves to Iowa City and Tipton kept Mackintosh within a sixty-mile radius of her hometown, they mark the initial steps of a career that ultimately would span more than half a century, take her around the world, and chronicle many educational developments.

Over the next ten years Mackintosh mixed the roles of student and teacher—always learning, always growing, always expanding her world. Returning to the university in 1921 after only one year of teaching, she began her graduate studies, shifting her emphasis to elementary education, an interest which, combined with language arts, would remain the focus of her career. For the next three years she attended the university and taught fifth grade in the University Elementary School. Her demonstration teaching and her scholarship earned her the praise of her teachers and peers. Again she was recognized as one of Iowa's most distinguished students. In 1924 she received her A.M., majoring in education and minoring in English. From 1924 to 1926 Mackintosh held a position as assistant professor of elementary education in the School of Education at the University of Pittsburgh. Taking a year's leave of absence in 1926 to 1927 from the university, she began her doctoral work in Iowa. She returned to Pittsburgh to teach one more year before accepting a position during the 1927-28 school year as supervisor of later elementary grades and open-window rooms for the Grand Rapids, Michigan, Public Schools, a position she held for the next six years. During the summers Mackintosh continued her graduate work at the University of Iowa, receiving her Ph.D. in 1931, with a major in education and minors in English and psychology.

The most important development during this formative period of Mackintosh's career was her research in children's interests in poetry. Concerned with the apparent lack of interest in poetry among elementary school children, she theorized "that the fault is not with the children, but with the poems which are presented to them. The time has come when the factor of interest is recognized as stimulating children to a much greater appreciation not only of poetry but of literature in general" (1924, 85). Beginning with research for her master's thesis, "A Study of Children's Choices in Poetry," Mackintosh ultimately tested this "factor of interest" through a series of experimental studies in elementary schools in Iowa City; St. Paul and Duluth, Minnesota; Green Bay, Wisconsin; and Detroit and Grand Rapids, Michigan. The culmination of this research appeared in her dissertation, *A Critical Study of Children's Choices in Poetry* (1932). While the studies themselves varied in design, grade level, and location, the outcomes were generally the same. "Children," explained Mackintosh, "tend to choose poems which are characterized by action, child experience, humor, dialect and repetition." Although children in her studies did choose poems of literary merit and were "highly consistent [as a group] in their ratings of poems," they often disagreed with teachers in their ratings (1931, 19–20); i.e., children's and teachers' selections revealed markedly different interests in poetry. Thus, she argued, poems chosen from prepared lists based on assessments which reflect only teacher evaluations and interests may have little or no appeal to children. Instead of relying solely on the canon of literary texts, she suggested that such lists should include numerous poems containing the largest number of interest elements (such as humor, story, dialect, surprise, excitement, fairies, boys and girls, and animals) from which teachers might select poems based on the interests of grade groups and individuals (1927, 297). Furthermore, she argued that the way poems were presented was crucial: "children get more real enjoyment and remember more poetry when they are not required to dissect or memorize the selections read" (1932, 39).

This early research gave Helen Mackintosh exposure to the world as author and speaker: her master's thesis was the basis for her first published article in *The Elementary English Review* in May of 1924, and an article based on the dissertation research, "Recent Data on Children's Interests in Poetry" (1931), was the basis of her first NCTE presentation in 1930. Although her ever-increasing supervisory and administrative work took her away from direct research in this area, she did return to it periodically throughout her career. More importantly, the understandings established by this early research became the cornerstones of her theories about teaching and about the language arts. Paramount among these cornerstones was her belief that children themselves should have a hand in their education, exemplified here in her recognition that children's attitudes affect their learning.

After she completed her academic training, Mackintosh, already entrenched in the profession, became increasingly active professionally. During the latter summers of her tenure in Grand Rapids, she lectured at the University of Michigan and the University of Nebraska, a practice she continued for many years, ultimately teaching in such schools as her alma mater, the State University of Iowa, the University of Maine, George Washington University, Syracuse University, and Howard University. She also began to serve on state and national committees, including the *Seventh Yearbook* Committee for the Department of Supervisors and Directors of Instruction, Detroit, 1934; the Survey Staff, United States Office of Education, Survey of Cincinnati Public Schools, 1935; and the literature subcommittee of the NCTE Curriculum Commission, 1935. This committee work foreshadowed her later involvement in both the Office of Education and NCTE.

Mackintosh's career as classroom teacher and university professor virtually ended, however, with her next position as associate professor and head of the English Department in the Elementary Division of the School of Education at Miami University in Oxford, Ohio. Not long after she accepted the position in September of 1936, the United States Office of Education (USOE) offered her an appointment as elementary education specialist. It was not until April of 1938 that Miami University could make arrangements to replace her and that Mackintosh moved to Washington, D.C., beginning a new phase of an already distinguished career. Although she continued the practice of lecturing at various universities during the summers, she did little actual classroom teaching after accepting the USOE position.

To her new job Helen K. Mackintosh brought eighteen years of teaching and supervisory experience. Her knowledge and experience in teaching English, French, science, and social studies at various levels, her doctoral training in psychology, education, and English, her participation in regional and national conferences and workshops, and her teaching in the education programs of several major universities prepared her well for the tasks that she would be assigned over the next several years. She remained in the Office of Education until her retirement, serving as Chief of the Elementary Schools Section from 1955 to 1963.

Established by the Department of Education Act of 1867, the USOE was primarily charged with collecting and disseminating information. As an arm of the federal government, the USOE could not interfere with the rights of the individual states to determine and maintain education programs. It was designed to report trends, not to make them; it was to provide assistance *when asked* in the form of expert consultants, books and materials, and supervisory assistance. Mackintosh and other Office of Education specialists participated in conferences and workshops, compiled bibliographies, and contributed to numerous USOE publications. Mackintosh played this facilitative role well. Naturally unassuming and unwilling to speak unless she had evidence with which to back her assertions, she was willing, on the other hand, to share her experiences and understandings, to listen to the views and advice of others, to give specific experiential examples in response to most questions, and to assimilate great amounts of information and report it to others.

Most importantly, this position gave her access to the children of the nation and of the world. It gave her a larger audience with whom she could share her knowledge and understanding of children. Through her publications and her participation in workshops and conferences, she had an opportunity to influence the education of children. In the more than one hundred manuscripts to which she contributed, she repeatedly expressed her views of education, views which she had developed through her early research and honed through her early teaching and supervisory experiences: the need to focus education on the whole child; the responsibility of learners for their own education; respect for children's interests, views, and needs; the experienced-based, integrated curriculum, with language arts at the core.

Painting word pictures with specific examples gleaned from her own and others' teaching experiences, often contrasting a negative and a positive view, Mackintosh helped readers visualize children and teachers at work, learning together:

> A group of older children are given lists of words either duplicated or written in columns on the board, or use a list from a spelling textbook, to be arranged in alphabetical order. The job is done and the work checked for accuracy within the limits of one work period. On the other hand, a comparable group of children discuss under the guidance of the teacher how they may collect the new words they are adding to vocabularies as they study a unit of experience on "How People Earn a Living in the United States." They decide that they will make a card file index on 3×5 cards of all new words they become acquainted with. They quote the sentence in which each word occurs and organize the cards in alphabetical order. Further examples may be added to each card. In the course of the unit children may collect two or three hundred words. These may be the basis for a game, a test, or individual projects of a wide variety so that the learnings may be functional. (1959, 397)

This classroom sketch, which appeared in her 1958 NCTE presidential address, was typical of the manner in which Mackintosh presented her ideas. She also occasionally used analogies or stories to illustrate her views:

> A LEGEND TELLS US that once there existed in the world two clans or tribes of people. One believed that life is like a wheel, going round and round, never changing except in speed of

movement. The other group believed that life is like a tree growing, changing, expanding, adjusting itself to different conditions. Those who would have the elementary school be merely a duplicate of the school they themselves attended are thinking of child life and experience as a turning wheel whose spokes mark off the boundaries of arithmetic, spelling, reading, geography and other subject fields. But those who believe that an elementary school program is capable of change, conceive of living for the child as well as for the adult as consisting of some of the old, but many new and different experiences adapted to the changing times. (1941, 154)

Instead of bombarding her readers with her views, Mackintosh constructed such "extended illustrations," as she called them, through which the reader would be convinced of her point before she ever stated it. No wonder she became a valued speaker and consultant.

She was so much in demand, her contributions so highly valued, that it became necessary to schedule her appearances six months to a year in advance, especially after she became chief of the Elementary Schools Section of the Office of Education. In a letter to J. N. Hook dated 17 June 1957, Mackintosh noted the following schedule:

During the next six weeks I shall be at the University of Oklahoma as a consultant to the Third Annual Association for Childhood Education Conference. On July 3rd I go to Philadelphia for one day of the NEA Convention. July 8th I fly to the University of Michigan for one day. July 18th I leave for ten days in Oregon returning on Sunday the 28th. That same week I go to the Kent State University ... for two days and am then leaving on a 10 day vacation. (1957e)

Apparently Helen Mackintosh maintained this kind of schedule throughout her tenure as section chief. She often spent government holidays and rainy Sunday afternoons in her office, straightening out her files or tending to correspondence that she could not get to during regular working hours. She wrote letters and speeches in airplanes and hotel rooms as she traveled about the country. Her NCTE correspondence alludes to this active schedule and gives us a sense of the self-confidence and grace with which she accepted this active role in the education of the nation's children. Many of her letters addressed to Hook, Executive Secretary of NCTE at the time, itemized concerns, gave brief responses to questions which he had obviously posed, included handwritten notes or addenda apparently tacked on just prior to mailing, and were often concluded with "These are the things I have on my mind at the present time" (1957c) or "These seem to be all the items that I have on hand today" (1957e) and signed "Hastily, Helen." Somehow she found time to fulfill most requests for information and appearances, often exhibiting a sense of humor and frankness about the demands on her time. In a letter to Hook dated 14 January 1957, the year of her NCTE presidency, she wrote: "The day you were here I think that I agreed to set up some alternatives for 'something'. What that is I have forgotten. Can you help me" (1957b). In a letter addressed to Marie Bryan, professor of English at the University of Minnesota, she explained, "Since I cannot find a copy of a letter sent to you since the meeting of the American Council on Education, I assume that I thought about writing several times, but did not actually get off a letter to you" (1957b). She must have enjoyed the fervor though. When she was no longer NCTE president and her correspondence with Hook lessened, she remarked, "I miss writing to you, but I know that Brice Harris [her successor as NCTE president] is no doubt keeping you busy" (1958a).

Despite the fact that as chief of the Elementary Schools Section of the Office of Education, Mackintosh was responsible for elementary education across the curriculum, her personal interests lay with English and the language arts. Some colleagues even accused her of being territorial. In fact, when as section chief she hired specialists for all other areas of the curriculum, she reserved the role of language arts specialist for herself. Foreshadowing the whole language movement of the 1980s, Mackintosh argued that the skills of reading, writing, speaking, and listening were integral to the whole curriculum, that communication skills were necessary in all phases of learning—whether it be collecting and sharing information in a science class, reading the history of our nation, presenting a report on one's hobby, producing a school newspaper, or writing a letter to a friend in a foreign land. It was through language, for example, that she found ways of expanding the worlds of children at home and abroad. In such articles as "Pen and Ink Friendships for the Americas" (1941b) and "Building World Friendships through School Correspondences" (1944), Mackintosh suggested that communication skills could "easily bridge the distance between the Americas" (1941b, 297). It was also through language that hobbies, camping and outdoor activities, and school newspapers became integral parts of the curriculum; Mackintosh believed that participating in such activities required students to use the skills of reading, writing, speaking, and listening in learning that is "real and vital":

> Discussions that were in no way artificial, reading that was guided by a purpose, need for following directions, recognition of value in waste materials, use of creative ability in adapting materials and ideas to the principle of use, recording the results, planning a

social occasion for their mothers at which they told about the project and displayed the resulting products were all phases of the experience. To look at the program from a purely subject-matter point of view, boys and girls had experience with oral and written expression, with reading, with arithmetic, spelling, writing, science, and crafts especially. For all of this learning they had a definite purpose, and that purpose fitted [sic] into actual living. (1939, 276)

For Mackintosh, language arts was both the common carrier of education and the key to the survival of humankind:

Without the balance of the humanities, of the arts, and especially the use of all forms of communication in ways that contribute to the common good, the products of the scientist may defeat the very ends they are designed to further. . . .
Through literature with its emphasis upon human relations, the individual can connect past, present, and future. Writers can interpret the current scene realistically, so that people in other lands may understand us better through our mutual human experiences. (1958b, 151–52)

This was an especially strong statement to deliver in 1957, considering that most educators had responded to the U.S.S.R.'s launchings of Sputniks I and II with an almost maniacal transference of interest to math and science. The United States reacted with the National Defense Education Act's lopsided emphasis on math and science, an act which initially ignored the role of language arts in the curriculum—not to mention the role language plays in the acquisition of math and science skills. (An expanded version of the National Defense Education Act was passed in 1962, largely due to the efforts of NCTE, and included a provision for curriculum study centers in English.) Mackintosh calmly argued, though, that to avoid the predictions of Orwell's *1984*, "the acquisition of skills [and we can assume she meant language arts skills as well as skills in math and science] is not enough. They must relate to situations in which the individual needs to listen, speak, read and write" (154).

It was this interest in the role language plays in education that had initially brought Helen K. Mackintosh to NCTE. Although she presented her first paper at the NCTE convention in 1930, published that paper as an article in *The Elementary English Review* in 1931, and participated intermittently in various NCTE capacities, including serving on several committees, Mackintosh dated her active participation in Council activities with her appointment to the Commission on the English Curriculum in 1945. When elected to the office of second vice-president in 1951, Mackintosh was unaware that this identified her as a future president of NCTE, but she accepted this role with the same confidence and grace with which she had accepted most other developments in her life, and she set out to do the job well. As a matter of course, she served on the Executive Committee from 1956 to 1958. Serving as president in 1957, she was considered the first president to fully represent the Elementary Section; although Dora V. Smith was the first person from the Elementary Section to become president, Smith had always taught at the high school and college levels. According to J. N. Hook, Mackintosh's presidency also marked the initiation of "the principle of annual rotation of the presidency"—so that all three sections, Elementary, Secondary, and College, would receive equal representation (1979, 164).

Mackintosh's membership on the Commission on the English Curriculum undoubtedly is also what brought her to the attention of others in the Council and marked her potential for later membership on the Executive Committee and for her ultimate rise to the presidency. The commission, chaired by Dora V. Smith, was responsible for the publication of five volumes in the Curriculum Series. Appropriately, Mackintosh was appointed cochair of the Production Committee for the second volume in the series, *Language Arts for Today's Children*. This volume, a guide to the development and evaluation of a comprehensive language arts program, placed the language arts program in the context of children's needs, interests, and abilities.

Published in 1954, the volume is still of interest today. It established the goals for language arts: "to think clearly and honestly, to read thoughtfully, to communicate effectively, and to listen intelligently" (Commission on the English Curriculum 1954, 431). Inherently, these have always been the goals of language arts; the task of each generation is "[to interpret] these goals in the light of the conditions of living that it finds" (Mackintosh 1957a, 368). Perhaps more significant today, the volume stands as a tribute to the direct and indirect results of such collaborative efforts as its production. Mackintosh and her codirector, Elizabeth Guilfoile, noted in their preface:

> The committee which produced *Language Arts for Today's Children* found stimulation and gained added insight through cooperative endeavor and face-to-face discussions out of which grew a common point of view. It commends the method to all those concerned with building, improving, or appraising language arts programs in the elementary school. Teachers, principals, supervisors, parents, and if possible, children themselves, all should have a significant part in planning if the program is to be a dynamic one. The importance today of effective listening, speaking, reading, and writing justifies this total involvement of all concerned (Commission on the English Curriculum 1954, vi).

Collaboration was a common practice in both NCTE and the Office of Education at this time; in fact, one reason a complete listing of Mackintosh's publications cannot be documented is because so many of the USOE publications are attributed to "The Elementary Staff." Ironically, only recently has the value of collaboration in both learning and teaching been fully recognized.

Helen Mackintosh's expertise in the language skills which she had developed as teacher, supervisor, and education specialist obviously contributed to her role as committee member and leader. Most notable among her qualities, however, was a distinctive quietness that some attributed to an inherent shyness. Whether or not she was actually shy, it is apparent that Mackintosh felt most comfortable responding to the issues of elementary school language arts. According to fellow committee workers, she had little to say *except* when the conversation turned to elementary language arts. At such times she illustrated her considerable knowledge of and experience with elementary school curricula and instruction as well as her concern for children. Through succinct and poignant comments, often using specific examples, as she did in her writings, and understated humor as a subtle way of getting her point across, Mackintosh never hesitated to express her views on the teaching of language arts to children. Hook recalled an incident during an Executive Committee meeting in which Mackintosh called for the abolition of basal readers:

> Helen spoke up strongly against basal readers that ... were far too repetitious as well as dull. Helen said that such books failed to enrich children's minds and might impair their use of language. "Maybe even their teacher's," Helen said. "There's an anecdote that I half believe. A second grade teacher looked out the window of her classroom at her car, parked in the school lot. 'Oh, look! Look!' the teacher said, more to herself than to the class. 'See my car! See my car! It has a flat tire! It has a flat tire! Damn! Damn!' A little boy, sitting near enough to hear her, piped up: 'Oh! Oh! Look! Look! See teacher's car! See teacher's car! It's got a flat tire! It's got a flat tire! Damn! Damn!'" (1989)

Perhaps it was shyness that caused Mackintosh to defer to others whom she felt were more knowledgeable than she. Perhaps she was simply unwilling to offer opinions when she was not fully knowledgeable about the issues. Or perhaps she realized that if she spoke seldom, but with confidence, she would be heard. Perhaps subtlety was a key to her getting things done. Certainly a woman administrator—still an oddity in the early part of this century—had to find less direct ways of dealing with people and issues. And there *was* a distinct subtlety to her manner, both in her publications and in her interactions with people. The issue of gender, for example, was seldom dealt with directly in her publications or correspondence. Yet in her published articles she frequently substituted "she" for the conventional generic "he," a practice which is not evident in many of her colleagues' publications. Sometimes, though, a stronger stance was needed, and Mackintosh was not hesitant to take such as stance; for example, she worked openly to secure a female speaker to balance the otherwise "completely masculine" lineup for the 1957 NCTE convention (1957f). After efforts to get Pearl Buck and several other outstanding women in education failed, she wrote, "Unless I can find an outstanding woman, I'll leave the spot vacant" (1957g). This mixture of subtlety and directness along with her unwillingness to respond to issues without careful consideration and understanding made her an excellent leader and administrator.

Mackintosh's expertise as moderator was frequently called upon in both her roles as chief of the elementary section of the Office of Education and as president of NCTE. One example stands out. During the year of her presidency, the Resolutions Committee chose to address the issue of whether the Council should support the recent Supreme Court's ruling on desegregation. James Squire, chair of the committee, recalled that it was

> an incredible day of frank, blunt, but friendly discussion—which culminated in our asking Helen as president for 20 minutes for each side to argue whether it was appropriate for NCTE to even vote on a resolution of support (which had been drafted). Helen presided beautifully over the lengthy discussion and deliberation session (about two hours in length) and even though the Council decided by *one* vote not to take up the resolution, both sides had had an airing and were satisfied. (1989)

The fact that her term of office in NCTE paralleled her tenure as chief of the elementary section of USOE placed Mackintosh in a pivotal position for both organizations. As section chief of the USOE, she had access to the most current information about education throughout the country and the world; as president of NCTE, she had the concern, power, and influence of a special-interest group, a group which shared her beliefs about language arts. This dual role, whether she was officially representing the USOE or NCTE, often put her in a position to represent the other group unofficially and to use her combined experience and access to information. It also made her a primary resource of information for both organizations: for example, through her government travels she discovered that many elementary school teachers knew nothing of NCTE, and she quickly brought that fact to the attention of the Council; she made sure that NCTE publications were made available in the USOE's textbook laboratory and elsewhere; when NCTE executives questioned the feasibility of sending listings of publications to the Soviet Union or wondered who would be the best liaison person in other national organizations, they consulted Mackintosh. If Mackintosh herself could not answer the questions, she had access to others who could.

The dual role, however, was not without conflict. Often because of her USOE schedule, Mackintosh was unable to represent the Council at various meetings. More crucially, the structure of the USOE did not allow her to "involve the office in controversial or propaganda activities" (1957d), which often meant she could not sign her name with her USOE position on NCTE documents. She was constantly having to evaluate her actions so that she would not jeopardize her position in the Office of Education. Nevertheless, Mackintosh handled the dual role with directness and diplomacy.

Although Mackintosh retired in 1963 (or close to this date—NCTE and USOE records are not available to document the date), she continued to contribute to the profession and to participate in USOE and NCTE activities. In 1964 she served as editorial chairman for *Children and Oral Language*, a statement by a joint committee of the Association for Childhood Education International, the Association for Supervision and Curriculum Development, the International Reading Association, and NCTE. She also collaborated with longtime USOE colleague Elizabeth Guilfoile in the revision of an earlier USOE bulletin entitled *How Children Learn to Read* (Mackintosh and Guilfoile 1964). In 1965 she worked with Lillian Gore and Gertrude M. Lewis to produce a series of USOE bulletins which dealt with the issues concerning the education of disadvantaged children. She accompanied teachers on the 1967 NCTE Elementary Tour to the British Isles and contributed an article to *Elementary English* describing the highlights of that tour (1968).

In the early 1970s, nearly fifty years after her initial research, Helen Mackintosh returned to her first interest, poetry. Her last publications represent perhaps the culmination of her life's work; yet they present the same themes. In her 1971 article entitled "Catching Color and Rhythm in Poetry with Nine-Year-Olds," she modeled a procedure for gently introducing poetry to children. In 1973 she collaborated with Bernard J. Lonsdale on the textbook *Children Experience Literature*. The title alone indicates the view of the book, a view Mackintosh never lost sight of throughout her career:

literature experiences can make a significant contribution to personality development and the enrichment of children's lives. Through literature children can come to sense their roles in the life of the family, the school, the community, and the world. It is possible for them to grow in understanding the behavior of people and the many relationships people have with their social and physical environments. Through meaningful experiences in literature children begin to become acquainted with the principles underlying democratic living. (Lonsdale and Mackintosh 1973, v)

Before and after her retirement, when she was not speaking, writing, or traveling about the world, Mackintosh was content to work in the walled garden of her Alexandria, Virginia, home. The house, in the heart of Alexandria's historic district, is listed in the historic register. While she lived there "the house was furnished mainly with antiques ... and ... souvenirs of [her] frequent travels" (Hook 1989). In an article written a year before Mackintosh's retirement, Elizabeth Guilfoile, citing Mackintosh as an outstanding educator, noted, "In the midst of her busy professional life, Dr. Mackintosh maintains a home in Alexandria, Virginia, works in her walled garden, and entertains her friends frequently, all as serenely as if she had nothing else to do" (1962, 250). Among her visitors were current members of NCTE's Executive Committee, whom she often chided when she discovered that they had recently been in the Washington area and had not allowed her the opportunity to entertain them in her home. She continued to entertain her friends long after her retirement.

Reviewing Helen K. Mackintosh's career is tantamount to reviewing the history of elementary education in America during the greater part of the twentieth century. In her college days she was involved in the then-popular demonstration schools which appeared on many university campuses. In Pittsburgh she was involved in the Extra-Mural Centers or Platoon Schools; designed to "bring about a varied education," these schools used staggered schedules to make maximum use of few facilities. In Grand Rapids she urged that activities previously considered extracurricular, such as newspapers and nature studies, be considered as cocurricular activities, as integral aspects of the curriculum. Through the Office of Education she became involved in the widespread interest in nutrition programs in the 1940s. During the war years she contributed to the plans for extended school days. Because of her position in the Office of Education she served as an educational consultant in Austria in 1947 and in Cambodia in 1954; in 1958 she was among the first mission of American educators to visit and observe schools in the Soviet Union. She contributed equally to the history of language arts education in America. Through NCTE she participated in the Experience Curriculum and served on the Council's first Commission on the English Curriculum; she helped increase the participation of elementary teachers in NCTE and drew in educators from all over the world. She was a representative to the Basic Issues Conference of 1958, a conference sponsored by the Ford Foundation "to investigate, clarify, and define basic issues and problems in the teaching of English in American schools and colleges, and to suggest means for possible improvements" ("Important Study Launched," 162). Mackintosh's activities and publications continued throughout the late 1960s and early 1970s. She contributed to research in the education of disadvantaged children in the late 1960s and may even have had a hand in the early planning of Head Start and "Sesame Street." Her textbook on children's literature for teachers and parents appeared in the early 1970s. No matter what the latest theory or current trend, however, Mackintosh's philosophy remained the same. Each new idea was tested against her long-held beliefs—if the idea fit into the student-centered, experience-based, integrated curriculum, she embraced it; if not, she argued against it.

It seems especially fitting that Helen Mackintosh—a woman who had devoted her life to the teaching of elementary language arts, who was a section chief of the major government agency dealing with education, and who had served as president of the nation's major organization in the field of English teaching—would be asked by NCTE to review the history of the elementary school language arts curriculum for the fiftieth anniversary of the Council. For approximately forty of those years Mackintosh had been an active participant in that history. Her address, "Language Arts Curriculum: Fifty-Year Highlights of the Elementary Program" (1963), chronicled the major influences on and developments of the ever-growing and changing curriculum. More importantly, perhaps, she used the address to argue once again for the experience curriculum and to empower the role of teachers.

Mackintosh "has [indeed] taken a long step toward widening an individual world" (Mackintosh 1958b, 154). From her small hometown of Hopkinton, Iowa, she moved across the country expanding not only the horizons of her physical world to other states and countries, but also the "breadth of her vision and experience" in the teaching of elementary children, in the development of experienced-based curricula, and in the recognition of the powerful role that the skills of communication play in helping us all adjust to an ever-changing world (Mackintosh 1963, 5). Who is to say how many children's lives she directly and indirectly influenced?

Helen K. Mackintosh's world was wide. Fortunately her heart was wide enough to encompass that world. Her understanding of people and of individual needs enlightened her work. Her own skills in listening, speaking, reading, and writing enabled her to contribute extensively to the education of young children, who were always at the focus of her attention. Her love of children made her a trusted friend and teacher among children and adults alike. J. N. Hook recalled firsthand her love for children. When he and his family visited Mackintosh in her Virginia home, "Helen spent much more time talking with our little boy than with us. She obviously liked children, and Jay took to her immediately, walking around the living room and dining area with her and listening with interest—sometimes wide-eyed—to what she told him about some of the pieces that adorned the room" (1989). In her 1956 convention address Mackintosh noted, "If educators were to set one focal point in the total school program today, it would be the child himself.... Children are always learning, both in school and outside the school day" (1957a, 367). Certainly children had remained her "focal point."

When Helen Mackintosh died in 1980, J. N. Hook, along with many others, felt that "we had lost a wonderful friend and that the profession had lost a hard-working, dedicated teacher and guide of teachers" (1989). Though we feel a loss, Mackintosh's own words come back to us: "Teachers are always teaching, whether consciously or by attitudes and behavior toward children or acceptance or rejection of them" (1957a, 367). Through her work Helen K. Mackintosh is still teaching today.

Works Cited

Commission on the English Curriculum. 1954. *Language Arts for Today's Children.* New York: Appleton-Century-Crofts.
Guilfoile, Elizabeth. 1962. "Leaders in Education, XLVIII." *Education* 83 (December): 250.
Hook, J. N. 1979. *A Long Way Together: A Personal View of NCTE's First Sixty-Seven Years.* Urbana, Ill.: National Council of Teachers of English.
———. 20 February 1989. Letter to author.
"Important Study Launched." 1958. *English Journal* 47 (March): 162.
Lonsdale, Bernard J., and Helen K. Mackintosh. 1973. *Children Experience Literature.* New York: Random House.
Mackintosh, Helen K. 1924. "A Study of Children's Choices in Poetry." *Elementary English Review* 1 (May): 85–89.
———. 1927. "Removing Drudgery from the Memorization of Poetry." *Elementary*

English Review 4 (December): 297–300.

———. 1931. "Recent Data on Children's Interests in Poetry." *Elementary English Review* 8 (January): 18–20.

———. 1932. *A Critical Study of Children's Choices in Poetry*. Ph.D. diss., State University of Iowa, Iowa City.

———. 1939. "How Hobbies Educate." *School Life* 24 (June): 260, 276.

———. 1941a. "Pen and Ink Friendships for the Americas." *School Life* 26 (July): 297–98.

———. 1941b. "What Do We Mean by an Adequate Elementary School Program?" *Childhood Education* 18 (December): 154–57.

———. 1944. "Building World Friendship through School Correspondence." *Education for Victory* 3 (December): 18, 23.

———. 1957a. "Elementary Schools Set Their Goals for Language Arts." *Elementary English* 34 (October): 367–70.

———. 1957b. (14 January 1957). Letter to J. N. Hook.

———. 1957c. (26 February 1957). Letter to J. N. Hook.

———. 1957d. (22 April 1957). Letter to J. N. Hook.

———. 1957e. (17 June 1957). Letter to J. N. Hook.

———. 1957f. (7 September 1957). Letter to J. N. Hook.

———. 1957g. (8 October 1957). Letter to J. N. Hook.

———. 1957h. (31 October 1957). Letter to Marie Bryan.

———. 1958a. (2 January 1958). Letter to J. N. Hook.

———. 1958b. "The 1957 World of the English Teacher." *Elementary English* 35 (March): 150–56.

———. 1959. "Respect for the R's." *Elementary English* 36 (October): 395–98.

———. 1963. "Language Arts Curriculum: Fifty-Year Highlights of the Elementary Program." *Elementary English* 40 (January): 5–14, 55.

———. 1968. "So You Are Taking the NCTE Elementary Study Tour." *Elementary English* 45 (January): 29–31.

———. 1971. "Catching Color and Rhythm in Poetry With Nine-Year-Olds." *Elementary English* 48 (January): 81–85.

Mackintosh, Helen K., and Elizabeth Guilfoile. 1964. *How Children Learn to Read*. Washington, D.C.: U.S. Government Printing Office.

Squire, James. 27 February 1989. Letter to author.

10 Ruth G. Strickland: Looking Back, Looking Forward

Tracey J. Johnson, West Virginia University

Ruth G. Strickland
1898–1987

The first strand is the past. It weaves, twists, coils upon itself, carrying with it prior experiences, a cultural history. The complex fibers themselves illustrate the plurality of history, conveying both the triumphs and mistakes of all eras past. Although each minutia of that history may not be evident, each is there, twisting, influencing the bits of history that one can see.

The second strand is the present. It also weaves and twists, coils upon coils, but it carries in its fibers the immediacy of the present. The moment lives within those coils, the actions of those in power influencing the actions of those around them, both intentionally and unintentionally.

The final strand is the future. This strand is an enigma in that there is not so much a concern for prognostication, but preparation. Its coils carry the discoveries and hypotheses of a culture, in hopes that the mistakes of the past will not replicate themselves in future generations.

Together, these three strands form a braid. Plaited together, these three create a highly complex view of history. The three strands work together, both independently and interdependently. Complexities of the past impinge on the future, while the present works its way around and through all three, interconnecting them all. When woven together with other braids, a single braid becomes a work of art, a tapestry. This tapestry represents the colorful history of a culture, bringing together all the individual elements into a unified whole.

And, singly, each braid can represent an individual. If a teacher were to be one of these braids, she would show a concern for the past—in this case, a child's past history and what a child brings to the learning environment. Her work in the present would involve teaching, researching, theorizing. She would emphasize pedagogy, theory, and research in her work and would strive to help those around her see the importance of this tripartite approach to her work. Finally, she would always be looking to the future, working toward making that future easily accessible to all of her charges, investing in them the desire to work independently and providing them with the skills to do so, but remaining ever-mindful of how the past and present influence that future.

These three strands represent the life concerns of Ruth Gertrude Strickland, research professor of education at Indiana University; president, National Council of Teachers of English; recipient, David H. Russell Award for Distinguished Research in the Teaching of English; recipient, Distinguished Service Award, National Council of Teachers of English. Her braid is but one in the vast tapestry of English education, but her history, interwoven with the history of a profession and of a nation, creates a brightly colored cord. Her never-ending concern for a child's past experiences, her pedagogical and research excellence, and her concern for the future worked together to lead Strickland to some of the most important discoveries of her era. However, in order to weave her braid, one must begin with her past.

Born in Duluth, Minnesota, on 1 October 1898, Ruth G. Strickland found herself living in an era with little opportunity for women. When she was sixteen her father passed away, and with his passing, the opportunity to attend a major university vanished. Since there was no money for a university education, Strickland "fell into" teaching by attending State Teachers College of Duluth, graduating in 1918 and receiving a certificate as a kindergarten teacher. At that time, Strickland believed that "I will teach kindergarten, but I will never teach in the grades" (1977)—an interesting statement from a woman who would eventually teach all elementary grades and who would later be named research professor of education at Indiana University.

One year, after working with a particular group of kindergartners, Strickland requested to stay with the same group of children through first grade and second grade. This was a form of experimental teaching in the 1920s, and through this experiment Strickland developed an interest in early language development while nurturing her immature students. As she worked with the first graders, her interests zeroed in on children's reading development. Rather than use the reading preprimers supplied by the district, Strickland had children develop their own stories. Students in Strickland's first-grade classes were writing and illustrating their own books, as well as participating in an individualized reading program. Students chose their own books to read, and they progressed at their own pace. As these children progressed, Strickland kept careful records of the vocabulary students learned, as well as any individual reading problems, so she could provide remediation early. As a result, none of Strickland's charges needed remediation in the later grades (Strickland 1977).

After teaching K-2, and teaching grades 3-4 part-time, Strickland returned to college. In the 1923 academic year she served as a training teacher for grades 1-2 at the Training School in the State Teachers College at Winona, Minnesota. Through extension courses and a subsequent residency, Strickland completed her B.S. degree at the Teachers College of Columbia University in 1925. She then began working as a training teacher in first and second grades for the State Normal School at Geneseo, New York, and the State Normal School at Bellingham, Washington. The summers from 1925 to 1932 found Strickland participating in summer demonstration teaching at the Teachers College, Wellesley College, Bellingham, and Ohio State University.

Strickland completed her M.A. degree at the Teachers College in 1932 and spent the years 1932-37 at Temple University, teaching grades 3-4 part-time and teaching at the Teachers College. Her last two years in Philadelphia were spent teaching undergraduate and graduate courses exclusively. In the fall of 1937, Strickland accepted the position of assistant director of elementary education at Kansas State Teachers College. By 1938 Strickland had completed her doctorate in the Department of Philosophy at Columbia University. Her dissertation, *A Study of the Possibilities of Graphs as a Means of Instruction in the First Four Grades of Elementary School* (1938), reflected the increased interest in scientific data prevalent in 1930s society.

The dissertation addressed the absence of graphs as an instructional tool in the schools, focusing on the early primary grades. (Interestingly, in her statement of the problem, Strickland discussed how "educators have often been slow to make use of new teaching tools" [1938, 1]. At that time the new tools were radio and moving pictures, the antecedents of our personal computers and satellite communications.) Print media were inundating the reading public with graphs and charts as a means "to clarify the text or to carry data not included in the printed text" (1). The schools were faced with a dual mission—to teach pupils how to read graphs and to use graphs in the classroom in order to teach. In the 1930s curricula, graphs were not introduced until fourth grade, and usually they were used in social studies classes. Strickland, relying on her background in the early grades, asserted:

> the curriculum of the primary grades in the modern school provides rich material in the social studies and many opportunities for concrete experience and activity of various sorts. All this involves a vast amount of quantitative thinking in estimating, weighing, contrasting, and evaluating, long before a child has any very definite concepts of abstract numbers. It is, therefore, quite possible that certain of the values that accrue from the study of graphs on higher levels of maturity may also be obtainable at lower levels and may be found of sufficient worth to warrant the inclusion of graphs in the list of teaching tools for these levels. (4-5)

By analyzing (1) what types of graphs were intelligible to children in the lower elementary grades, (2) what types of graphs could be understood at the mental levels represented in these same grades, and (3) what necessary minimum instruction teachers had to provide to make graphs intelligible, Strickland embarked on an "exploration in a relatively uncharted field in elementary education" (113).

The results of Strickland's exploratory study may not be groundbreaking—in fact, based on today's stringent research standards, her results may be considered mundane. Using six types of graphs (unit pictograph, developmental picture chart, circle graph, line graph, bars and figures, and bars on a grid), Strickland charted students' interpretive skills. Students in grade one responded best to the pictograph and developmental picture chart. Grade-two students used all six types fluently, with the picture chart and circle graph garnering the highest scores. In grade three, students scored lowest on the picture graph. Grade-four students used all types of graphs with relative ease (115–17). However, these results dovetail with a more important confirmation in Strickland's research. In poststudy interviews with students, as well as in comments provided by examiners, teachers, and parents, Strickland discovered that "the children of the grades studied in this experiment were interested in graphs presenting subject matter which was in line with interests current in their classrooms ... [this] serves to vindicate the philosophy stated earlier, that anything which adds to or enriches a genuine interest in which children are engaged is in itself of interest to them" (118). For Strickland, one of the most important duties a teacher had was to find a child's interests and build on them (1977). Strickland believed that the children's high scores were not a result of instruction. In fact, their instruction was limited to "a period of ten to thirty minutes" (1938, 118). Instead, Strickland found reinforcement in her belief that teachers must work with a student's prior knowledge and interests to provide a positive instructional environment. "Interest," stated Strickland, "in all learning situations, adds greatly to the ease of learning" (118).

Strickland's dissertation provided new insights into the use of graphs in the elementary schools. Her results indicated that graphs could be introduced as teaching tools at a much earlier grade level than previously believed. Most importantly, those graphs had to incorporate content in which children held an interest. Only by relying on a child's prior knowledge, and incorporating that knowledge with content, could teachers educate successfully. Prior experience was the key to unlocking a child's mind, a belief echoed by John Dewey in *Experience and Education* and, over thirty years after Strickland's study, by James Britton in *Language and Learning* (1970). Britton stated "that talking-and-doing must be given major stress throughout Primary School. Language must continue to grow roots in first-hand experience" (137). Begin with what the child knows, what that child experiences, and use that as the foundation for that child's education.

Strickland placed strong value on a child's experiences, both in and out of the classroom. She emphasized the importance of environment in a child's growth, often pointing to the impact of technology, changing cultural standards, and international political issues on the nation's youth. Oftentimes teachers seem to forget that their charges might be affected by massive social forces outside the school. Each child undoubtedly responds differently to any changes in his or her society, and Strickland knew that to reach all children, a teacher must resonate with those changes. However, the upcoming decades threw American society as a whole into chaos, creating new challenges for teachers in all content areas.

American society, and education in particular, faced upheaval after upheaval during the 1940s and 1950s. The involvement of American armed forces after the bombing of Pearl Harbor created a new educational environment, since a third of all teachers left the classroom and engaged in military service or other activities in support of the war effort. The government placed emphasis on the war effort, giving high educational priority to content areas that could further the cause. Consequently, the emphasis on the sciences in the 1940s left little room for English education, along with the fine arts and Latin (Hook 1979, 131). In the public's eye, such subjects had little use in the preservation of democracy and protection of American ideals. In a flurry of writing activity, various committees and commissions published several pamphlets delineating the importance of English instruction in the schools. This placement of English education in a political spotlight, coupled with the restructuring of Japan's educational system after World War II, created a new role for Ruth Strickland.

Prior to World War II Japan took as its educational guide the Imperial Rescript on Education, established in 1890 and later modified by the "Reform of Teaching" established by the Educational Investigation Council in 1937. This "Reform" called for students to follow the "Imperial Way"—a way that called for total discipline. Primary schools became "national schools," and education became tainted with extreme nationalism and militaristic doctrine (Japanese Education Reform Council 1950, 2). History credits this mentality with Japan's involvement in World War II.

Postwar restructuring called for a realignment of schools, and American military forces planned to have a strong hand in that restructuring. In order to prevent another "serious blunder in the spiritual and social realm" (2), the occupation forces, under General MacArthur, created the Civil Information and Education Section. This group, along with the Japanese Education Reform Council, set about redeveloping the philosophy of Japanese education. The council sought "to aim at the full development of personality, striving for the rearing of the people, sound in mind and body, who shall love truth and justice, esteem individual values, respect labor, have a deep sense of responsibility, and be imbued with an independent spirit, as builders of a peaceful society and state" (Fundamental Law of Education, Article 1). The American occupation forces sent consultants to Japan to assist the council in its restructuring, analyzing curricula, school physical plants, teacher education, and all other facets of education. One of those consultants, who had already been working with the government in the war effort, was Ruth Strickland.

Strickland was no newcomer to the war effort. Before her enlistment as consultant to the occupation forces, she served as senior specialist in extended school service for the U.S. Office of Education (*Indiana Daily Student* 1948b). In this position Strickland oversaw the disbursement of monies from the Lanham Act Fund in Wisconsin, Illinois, and Indiana. This fund, a direct outgrowth of the changing labor force in America during World War II, provided child-care funds for working women. As reported by the *Indiana Daily Student*, "nursery schools, kindergarten, and after school activities were organized to enable more women to enter the industrial field" (1948b). It seems ironic that Strickland, whose only career choice thirty-five years earlier was to attend a normal school and become a teacher, would come to administer a fund that made it possible for thousands of other women to enter a work force previously dominated by men. Her administration of the Lanham Act Fund dovetailed with her concern for the welfare of children during the war.

Strickland continued to work with children after the war, except with a change of venue as she switched her focus to Japan. During three months in the spring of 1948, Strickland served as a special consultant in the Civil Information and Education Office of the American Military Government (*Indiana Daily Student* 1948a). She worked with the Japanese Ministry of Education on the improvement of that nation's elementary school system and with a special program to simplify the method of teaching the Japanese language as well as the language itself (1948a, 1948b).

In a series of public lectures after her return from Japan, Ruth Strickland outlined the learning conditions she witnessed and what changes the American Military Government proposed. The Chapel Colloquy at Indiana University, the Indiana University Alumni Association, the State Teachers' Association, and various chapters of the Future Teachers of America in Indiana heard Strickland's accounts of Japanese culture and education. For the Japanese, she reported, "toughening of children seem[ed] to be the accepted way . . . to raise their youth" (*Indiana Daily Student* 1949). Barefooted children attended unheated schools in midwinter. Those children who repeatedly violated customs found themselves ostracized by their fathers. In short, Japanese education and culture prior to the occupation created a dismal environment for school youth. The new philosophy, as introduced by the occupation forces, emphasized "the worth of the individual" (Supreme Commander, 1952, 1:6). Therefore, the school's physical environment changed along with changes in the treatment of students. Parents concerned with preservation of the old culture worked with teachers on how to incorporate that culture with the "new education" (7). As a result, in modern Japanese education the ideology of total discipline as espoused in the 1937 doctrine manifests itself in the dedication and hard work Japanese students characteristically exhibit in their studies. However, individualism, a philosophy held by Strickland, coexisted with the discipline of contemporary students.

In her lectures Strickland spoke of the inability of Japanese youth to understand democratic thinking, especially as espoused by the American government. The prior nationalistic philosophy of Shinto demanded that children do what was expected of them, thus leading to the "serious blunder" of the war. Instead, American consultants proposed an atmosphere in which students could think for themselves. As a result, Strickland reported that "the Americans have taken centralization out of the Japanese school system; tried to build up a coeducational school system; sought to broaden educational privileges, and tried to improve the routine of the school year." Rather than isolate the privileged classes from the masses via two totally different curricula, Strickland and her colleagues sought quality education for all students. By broadening their experiences beyond mere development of reading and writing skills, Japanese students in the lower classes could also "learn, understand, and appreciate the culture of the rest of the world" (*Indiana Daily Student* 1948a). Thus Japanese students today now enjoy both their own culture and the strong capitalistic influences of American culture.

Strickland did not limit her professional experiences to lectures. In 1939 she joined the faculty at Indiana University, beginning a thirty-year tenure in the School of Education. She joined the National Council of Teachers of English this same year. The 1940s saw her academic and professional growth. She attended the 1947 NCTE conference in San Francisco as the representative of the Elementary Section on the Board of Directors and also represented NCTE at the Conference on the Role of Colleges and Universities in International Understanding, serving as chair of the editorial committee. By 1949 Strickland was a member of the NCTE Executive Committee, chair of the Elementary Section, and chair of the Committee on Intercultural Understanding.

Perhaps one of the more significant of Strickland's early accolades came from Indiana University's school newspaper. In the fall semester of 1948, the *Indiana Daily Student* began a series entitled "Women in the Headlines," "a series of articles on outstanding women faculty members." On 19 November 1948 the paper featured Strickland as the first woman to be showcased. Entitled "Educator; [sic] Professor Combines Travel and Teaching," the article outlined Strickland's accomplishments as teacher, researcher, and consultant. Thus, by fall of 1949, Strickland's accomplishments garnered her the recognition of her school. By the end of the next decade, her work would lead her to the presidency of what would become one of the largest professional teaching organizations in the world.

Strickland's path to the presidency of NCTE was undoubtedly paved by her ideas. The early inklings of her child-centered philosophy, as indicated in her dissertation, came to full fruition in "A Good Start in School" (1943), in which Strickland explained the work of the Indiana State Committee on Primary Education. As chair of that committee, Strickland synthesized the group's work into a unified handbook bearing the same title as her essay. Her concern for children as the focus of the curriculum shone through:

> It is the responsibility of the schools through their curriculum program to raise all children to the highest possible level of thinking, feeling, and acting and to prevent the development of those traits which are detrimental to the welfare of a democracy. Opportunity for each child to become the best, noblest, finest person he can become is the very essency [sic] of democracy. (Strickland 1943, 242)

Strickland also explained the purpose of language arts in the early grades, with an emphasis on spontaneous language: "Spontaneous discussion is important because it is the respect paid to the child's response that builds his confidence in his thoughts and their expression. Respect for his response also deepens his awareness of the response of others and his consideration for their thinking" (244).

This "spontaneous discussion" parallels Jean Piaget's concept of egocentric thought. According to Piaget, this egocentrism remains until some time between ages seven and eight (1959, 40), the exact age group that Strickland was discussing in the 1943 report. By respecting this egocentricity, then, the teacher can help students grow as individuals and, in turn, become respectful, productive members of their microcosmic society, the school, and later their macrocosmic society, the community.

Strickland explained, on behalf of the committee, that the concern was not for what a child would create with the oral or written word, but that "the value lies mainly in the growth of the child, his confidence in his ideas and his awareness of his power," and the teacher must not superimpose ideas onto a child's meaning making, but "weave them into the fabric of a child's response so that they spring spontaneously" from the child (1943, 244). The concern for children's language expressed here was the first inkling of Strickland's study on children's language, an inkling that reached full fruition in 1962.

In "The Development of Vocabulary" (1945) Strickland picked up again on the complexity of children's language, integrating this idea with her concerns about basal readers. Children, she purported, must be encouraged to develop extensive vocabularies, and one way to do so was through reading. But children seemed to lose interest in reading at a young age:

> The meager content of early readers may also be a problem. Children learning to read are thrilled with their progress in skill but frequently are thoroughly bored with the content of reader

stories and substance must be added from other sources than the readers if they are to grow in interest in reading. Is it possible that lack of interest in the content of early books may account in part for the number of boys who find their way into our remedial reading groups? Might they attain greater success if story content provided more intellectual stimulation? (10)

Once again Strickland expressed deep concern for children's personal interests when developing a curriculum, and she had detected a culprit in the schools that contributed to children's lackadaisical reading performance—substandard content in basal readers. Strickland now found the connections she needed to begin working toward her magnum opus, which analyzed children's language in detail and compared it to the language of basal readers. But there was other work to be completed before she could move forward on this major study, and one of the items on her agenda was serving as president of NCTE.

Strickland's professional growth in the 1950s followed a dual path. One path led Strickland to the lecture podium, where she spoke to teachers' institutes, workshops, and summer sessions. One of Strickland's greatest ventures as a professional was as director of the Indiana University Conference on Language Arts, which two hundred elementary teachers attended in the summer of 1957.

The other path led Strickland to Champaign-Urbana, Illinois. While participating in and directing conferences at Indiana University, she also began her ascent in the NCTE hierarchy. Several years after becoming involved in the Council, Strickland assumed the chair of the Elementary Section when the chair resigned. After successfully completing this term, Strickland served her own term as section chair, and remained deeply involved in NCTE (Strickland 1977). She was elected second vice-president of the Council in 1950; and in 1958 Strickland was elected first vice-president, thus leading to her presidency in 1960.

English education saw major changes in the 1960s. The NCTE Commission on the English Curriculum, begun in 1945 under Dora V. Smith, published a series of five reports on English curriculum development. These reports, which influenced the work of teachers in the 1960s, critiqued global educational concerns and placed them in an English education context, analyzed the different forces shaping students, and evaluated the place of literature in student development (Applebee 1974, 166–68). NCTE itself experienced major changes. After being burned out of its Chicago headquarters in 1953, the Council moved to its new home in Champaign in 1954. J. N. Hook, executive secretary and originator of such phrases as "Fifty by Sixty" (referring to the goal of reaching a membership of fifty thousand by 1960) and

"Each one reach one" (encouraging each member to recruit an additional member), retired from his post and was replaced by James Squire in 1960 during the presidential term of Ruth G. Strickland.

The year 1960 proved to be a banner one for Strickland, and it looked like it would be a great decade for her as well. She was now research professor of education at Indiana University, working with the state's elementary and language arts teachers to improve education via myriad workshops, conferences, and speaking engagements. She was the new president of NCTE, an organization then boasting a membership over 61,000, and in such an influential position Strickland found a means to voice her concerns about children's language and the need for better, more tightly controlled research. Her close work with James Squire, Walter Loban, and others would lead her to a major project, one on a far grander scale than her work with children's language—a project that could alter the course of English education. However, this large project would never materialize, and by the end of the decade, Ruth Strickland would retire completely to California.

Strickland's election as president continued the system, begun during Helen K. Mackintosh's term, of rotating the presidency every three years among the Elementary, Secondary, and College sections. In prior years the Elementary Section was always the least represented. According to Strickland, Dora V. Smith, who was said to represent the Elementary Section, had always taught at the high school or college level, so she should not be considered a true representative of the elementary teachers. Strickland regarded Mackintosh, president in 1957, as the first true elementary president (1977). The Elementary Section needed strong voices in leadership positions in the Council, and Strickland proved to be one of them.

As president of NCTE during its fiftieth anniversary year, Strickland enjoyed a special limelight. Squire referred to her as the "Golden Anniversary Girl," the Council's shining star during its celebratory year. Strickland used her position to make known her concerns for children, especially young children:

> A Golden anniversary is a time for glancing back at the path that is receding behind us. It is a time for looking intently at the road under our feet to see whether we are where we want to be, to find firm footing and avoid obstructions over which we might trip or ruts and pitfalls into which we might stumble. It is a time for looking ahead as far as our insight and foresight can take us along the broad highway of the future. (1961, 71)

With these words, delivered on 24 November 1960, Ruth Strickland opened the fiftieth annual meeting of the National Council of Teachers of English. She selected for the convention theme that year "All our past acclaims our future," a quote from Algernon Charles Swinburne. For the title of her presidential address, Strickland chose "What thou lovest well remains," a line borrowed from Ezra Pound's "Libretto." By carefully selecting these key quotations, and by integrating them with her concern for English education in general and for children in particular, Strickland set the tone for the 1960 NCTE convention. J. B. Priestley, keynote speaker at the first general session, spoke on "Literature, Life, and the Classroom." A session on linguistics heard two prominent scholars in the field, with W. Wilbur Hatfield asking, "Shall We Scrap Traditional Grammar?" and C. C. Fries showing how "Linguistics Moves Ahead." Alvina Treut Burrows lectured on children's writing; David H. Russell spoke on "Evaluating and Using Research in the English Language Arts." Special sessions addressed reading in the atomic age, critical thinking, trends in testing, interpreting the teaching of English to the public, and new directions in curriculum design and in teaching grammar, the humanities, poetry, and a host of other concerns. The new decade called for a fresh start, with a new emphasis on teaching and especially on the student. As Strickland completed her term as president, she helped send the membership home with new ideas and increased enthusiasm.

Ruth Strickland's presidential year had proved to be among the most eventful in NCTE's history. One interesting venture undertaken by the Council that year was a series of whistle-stop tours throughout the country. Strickland's tour began in Grand Forks, North Dakota, carried her next to Denver, Las Vegas, and northern California, and concluded in San Diego. Her talks encompassed the accomplishments and the ongoing projects of the Council and trends in education of the time. However, Strickland's main concern remained the unity of language arts in elementary education. These skills, according to Strickland, were to be taught in a content that had value for children, not in isolation.

Perhaps the most significant contribution made by the Council in 1960 to the future of English education was the establishment of the NCTE Research Foundation, which began making awards in 1963. Two early recipients were Ruth Strickland and Walter Loban, who were awarded monies to fund a conference on analysis of children's language (Hook 1979, 213). In her report as president, Strickland emphasized the importance of this foundation, stating, "the Foundation will make possible badly needed research looking toward the improvement of the teaching of English" (1960, A-1). This concern for research, one of Strickland's recognized fortes, led to the development of *Research in the Teaching of English*, a journal that has guided and influenced research and teaching methods in English education since its first publication in 1967. The establishment of both the Research Foundation and *Research in the Teaching of English* demonstrate the increased role that research was playing in the Council, and both continue to hold prominent places in English education today.

In 1963 the Council established the Distinguished Research Award. Renamed the David H. Russell Award for Distinguished Research in the Teaching of English to honor an outstanding researcher and past president of NCTE, the award reflected Russell's vision, which was described by NCTE President Richard Corbin:

> More than most of us, David had that fine, far-ranging perspective, that scholar's eye that, savoring the past, saw it always as a prelude to future action. His interest in research, especially research in that uncertain area we know as the teaching of English was no peripheral matter; he saw it as both instrument and tool essential to the extension and refinement of our craft. (Corbin 1965)

Russell exemplified the convention theme that he selected for his presidential year, "Re-renewal." In 1965 it was Ruth Strickland who was selected by the Council as the member who best exemplified that spirit. Through her research on children's language, Strickland illustrated how we as teachers can "savor the past" and work with it as a "prelude to future action." Her response upon receiving the award from Albert Marckwardt illustrated her love of and concern for research:

> As I realize that students make a teacher and that the many cooperative and at times self-sacrificing colleagues and professional co-workers make a researcher, I am mindful of some who might be standing with me here tonight—Eldonna Evertts, Evelyn Francis, Robert Ruddell [three of Strickland's doctoral students] who are here at the convention tonight, and many others. They are the people I look to pridefully, realizing the debt the research owes to them and that all of us together owe to research.
>
> I am happy that scholars and educators are recognizing the need for turning attention to the foundation of the pyramid, since what we do in teaching English even in our graduate classes is dependent upon what was achieved far earlier. The growth of interest in this area is evident in the independent studies of Kellogg Hunt in Florida, Mildred Riling in Oklahoma, and the monumental work of Walter Loban in California as well as in ours. It is humbling and gratifying to see the ripples spread from the pebble we at Indiana University threw into the pond.

Since I have always looked to David Russell's leadership with admiration for him as a scholar and affection for him as a person, it is with humility and gratitude that I accept this award named for him. (Strickland 1965b)

Strickland's research study, *The Language of Elementary School Children: Its Relationship to the Language of Reading Textbooks and the Quality of Reading of Selected Children* (1962b), which was supported by the U.S. Office of Education, analyzed the spontaneous language of young children. In a conference conducted prior to the study and supported by the Cooperative Research Program of the Office of Education, Strickland, along with Walter Loban, W. Nelson Francis, David Reed, Fred Householder, Harold Whitehall, Virginia Mini, and Eldonna Evertts, developed a scheme for analyzing children's language based on the work of Mansur Ekhtiar. This scheme discarded the accepted definitions for a sentence, opting instead for smaller divisions called phonological units. Utilizing this scheme, Strickland and her research team at Indiana University analyzed one of the largest bodies of children's spontaneous language for linguistic complexity and oral language nuances. The monumental study corroborated earlier beliefs held by Strickland and shed some much-needed light on children's language and reading textbooks.

Strickland and her project team tape-recorded the spontaneous talk of 575 elementary school children, ranging in age from six years to fourteen years/eleven months, in grades 1–6. Before taping their language, the research team collected demographic data on the children's parents, such as the occupational status and educational levels for both fathers and mothers. The children were tested for total intelligence quotients, verbal intelligence, nonverbal intelligence, and mental age. Through linguistic analysis, the researchers tabulated sentence structures as well as types, time, place, and cause in sentence usage.

The bulk of the study centered on child talk. Collecting language samples ranging from fifteen to thirty minutes for each child, the researchers worked to create as informal and unstructured an atmosphere as the constraints permitted. Three children were led to a room set for data collection. In the room were the recording devices, a unidirectional microphone, and several storybook figures for use as conversational prompts. Since all data collection occurred in the children's school environments, Strickland and her team did not make use of an observational room with two-way mirrors. Instead, the researchers sat with the children and served as prompters for discussion. Their only purpose during this data-collection phase was to keep the talk flowing.

After recording, the tapes were transcribed by each interviewer and noted for phonological units, with special consideration given to juncture, intonation, and meaning. A trained linguist worked with the research team members as a check for reliability. After each sample was coded, twenty-five consecutive sentences from each sample were analyzed and coded for patterns of stationary and movable elements. The final analysis yielded the following generalizations:

1. Children at all grade levels use a wide range of language patterns.
2. Certain patterns which children use with great frequency [such as subject/verb/object] appear to be basic building blocks of their language.
3. These basic patterns were combined in phonological units with other patterns in a wide variety of ways.
4. Children at all grade levels could expand and elaborate their sentences through the use of movables [elements] and elements of subordination.
5. The fillers [stops, pauses, and empty words and phrases] employed by children ... varied considerably, though there were few outstanding differences in the fillers used by children of different ages. (Strickland 1962b, 102)

Strickland also reported a relationship between the types of sentence structures used by children and variables of intelligence, mental age, and occupational and educational status of the children's parents. Those children having higher intelligence scores generally came from families in which the parents had a higher occupational and educational status. These children used more complex sentence structures more frequently and adapted to complex reading material more easily than their less fortunate peers.

Strickland and her research team also looked at child talk and four series of reading texts then in use in the schools. After analysis, Strickland discovered the evidence corroborating the concerns she had voiced in "The Development of Vocabulary" (1945) some twenty years earlier—children's talk, as compared to basal readers, was far more complex and much more mature than previously considered. Analysis of the texts revealed sentence structures far simpler than those the children instinctively used, and showed that the introduction of more complex structures followed no logical progression in complexity. In her conclusions, Strickland raised several new questions:

>These findings lead to other questions which badly need to be answered. Does the sentence structure in children's books influence the ease or difficulty of learning to read? To what extent? Can a scheme of order of difficulty of language patterns be devised which can be utilized in textbook writing? Can patterns of structure be introduced systematically and repeated until children read them with ease? (104)

Although her research discussed children's language and home environment, Strickland also felt that teachers were responsible for a child's language growth. In her *Guide for Teaching Language in Grades 1 and 2* (originally published under the title *English Is Our Language* in 1950), she charged teachers with the task of "find[ing] where each child stands in his development of the means of communication so that his program of learning can be based upon his needs" (1962a, 4). Concern for the individual, the background that individual brought to the classroom, and how that individual could best interact with the learning environment were Strickland's values in teaching, as well as antecedents to today's whole language approach to education. Her study of children's language brought all of these together and further honed her research interests.

Strickland's success with this research venture led to a multitude of speaking engagements and journal articles. However, her focus shifted to a much larger, more global project. One of her concerns about English education was the continued splintering of the profession into content and pedagogy, with divisive camps establishing territory in all areas of English education. (Squire [1989] spoke of a split between reading and language arts as content areas at Strickland's own Indiana University, a split she opposed.) This concern was shared with the leadership of the Modern Language Association, which at that time had an interest in reforming language education (Squire 1989). In 1962 Strickland began work on a project with James Squire and John Fisher, then executive secretary of the Modern Language Association. According to Squire (1989), Strickland envisioned a national clearinghouse of information, accessible to all involved with English education, that would bring together the best that NCTE and MLA had to offer, while at the same time converging with the MLA's interest in reforming language education. Strickland would serve as director of this Curriculum Center, which would be housed at Indiana University. By fusing together the elementary education specialists with the subject specialists, the Curriculum Center could ultimately revolutionize language arts education.

This project required huge sums of start-up money, and Strickland sought funding with great zeal. In a series of correspondence between Strickland and Squire, the money hunt went from one private foundation to another. Finally they chose to seek funds from the U.S. Office of Education, the same agency that had funded Strickland's prior study. Evidently, the group sought funds in excess of $500,000, which was a vast amount of money in the mid-1960s. Strickland rearranged her teaching load so she could be free to direct this clearinghouse, with Squire and Fisher both serving in administrative positions. Then, in January 1965, with a sabbatical arranged and release time provided by Indiana University, Strickland received the message from Squire—the USOE turned down the proposal. The project which meant so much to her, and for which she spent over two years in preparation, came to an abrupt end. In a handwritten letter to Squire dated 13 January 1965, Strickland expressed her disappointment:

> Thank you for calling me to tell me that my research proposal was turned down by USOE. As a person who has earned his own way since the age of fourteen, I am accustomed to blows but I can remember none that hit as hard as this. I wanted so badly to make this contribution....
>
> There are plenty of people in the profession ready at any time to criticize the work of the elementary schools, but few, apparently, who care enough to go beyond that. Money cannot be the entire problem because it has been poured into Secondary English [sic]. Witness the amount of it given to the University of Illinois. I keep remembering that I might possibly have money to go on working if I had not been drawn into the big project John Fisher envisioned, then dropped. Perhaps I am wrong. At any rate, unless you see more light ahead in Washington than I can see, perhaps I should give up research. These last two years of work and frustration seem to have been completely wasted. Yet everyone who has read the project and mentioned it has thought it very important. Some have been convinced, as I am, that a program of improvement should start at the foundation, not halfway up the educational ladder. But we are in the minority.
>
> If you learn any reasons for the discarding of the project it would help me to know them.
>
> I do greatly appreciate the interest you have always shown, Jim, and shall rely on you to help if I revive sufficiently to go on working. (1965a)

In his response, dated 29 January 1965, Squire suggested to Strickland that she rewrite the proposal, or a portion of it, and resubmit it as a research study, or that she perhaps approach one or more foundations in soliciting funds. Strickland did neither, and the project on which she worked so hard came to an end.

In the final years of the 1960s, Strickland continued to speak at various civic and professional functions. She wrote, but not as prolifically as before. And in 1969, four years after her proposal was turned down, Strickland retired from teaching and relocated to Pomona, California. She returned to only one NCTE convention, this one in 1984. In that year the Council honored her with the Distinguished Service Award. A press release from Indiana University about the award summarized Strickland's career:

> Strickland's 50-year career in education began as an elementary school teacher. She has served as vice-president of NCTE, chaired its elementary school section, and been a trustee of the NCTE Research Foundation. In 1965 she received NCTE's David H. Russell Award for distinguished research in the teaching of English.
>
> Strickland was cited for her contribution in the fields of linguistics and language arts as well as for her efforts to improve the teaching of English. She is the author of a widely-used textbook, "The Language Arts in the Elementary School." In the book she observed: "Classrooms should not be made into factories for pouring knowledge and skills into children as into empty cups. Classrooms should be made into workshops and studies where children seek creatively and cooperatively for experience and learning."

Ruth Gertrude Strickland passed away in Pomona, California, in January 1987. She left behind a legacy of research and teaching that affects all English educators today. Her drive to contribute to the profession, especially the corpus of work in elementary education, has left behind one of the largest bodies of research in the field. The collection of children's talk, taped in the early 1960s, remains as one of the largest bodies of children's recorded talk available today. Her concern for the past, both a child's linguistic roots and our collective histories as teachers, weaves its way throughout her works. Whenever she had an opportunity, she spoke of the need to respect a child's language and work with that language. As Strickland stated to NCTE historian Alfred H. Grommon, "as teachers, we must learn to accept and understand what children bring. Keep talk coming, or we can't improve talk. Then, we must find a child's interests and build on them. Make the child comfortable and make him feel that what he has to say is worthy of saying" (1977).

Her concern about children's language and subsequently her research in the 1960s translate into the current movements surrounding students' rights to their own languages and the work of Lucy Calkins, Donald Graves, Nancie Atwell, Myra Barrs, and the whole language movement. Twenty years after Strickland's study of the language of elementary school children, NCTE approved the establishment of a Whole Language Assembly and empowered the Elementary Section of the Council to organize a Whole Language Conference in spring 1990.

Strickland was not only concerned with children's language, but she also expressed concern with how a child's classroom experiences resonated with his or her life experiences. Note how the introductions to the two later editions of her 1951 text, *The Language Arts in the Elementary School*, reflect the times in which they were written. First, the 1957 introduction:

> The twentieth century has seen the daily life of most of the world modified by modern methods of communication. Telephone calls between Prime Minister Churchill in London and President Roosevelt in the White House shaped much of the strategy of World War II. A misinterpreted answer to an ultimatum to Japan is credited with responsibility for the bombs dropped on Hiroshima and Nagasaki. . . . Modern means of communication influence home life as well. . . . On this same day [Christmas], in some of America's least prosperous homes, a television set is the family gift. The children and their parents have agreed to do without individual gifts so that the family can have the television set for everyone to enjoy. One finds television aerials over the smallest and poorest of homes in many rural and urban areas. (1957, 3-4)

Second, the 1969 introduction:

> The lives of people in the United States are more and more closely tied up with the lives and destinies of people all around the globe. There are few places in the world where there are not Americans who have come under the auspices of government, business and industry, or religious, social welfare or other American or world organizations. The Peace Corps is a recent example. Many boys and girls now in our elementary and secondary school will, in the course of their lifetimes, be called on to go to parts of the world where people speak languages not taught in our schools. The success with which they meet their responsibilities and utilize their opportunities will depend in large measure on the speed and ease with which they acquire the language of the people among whom they must live and work. (1969, 1-2)

These introductions all but predict the economic and political upheavals in this world that we now refer to as the "global village." The children rallying around the Christmas television set of 1957 now spend family time playing video games on the high-resolution, cable-ready color television that is capable of receiving 120 channels. That television is a major influence on today's youth is not just a theory, but a given; in fact, the 1984 meeting of the International Federation for the

Teaching of English sponsored a study group on Language and the New Media, analyzing how best to incorporate television, film, and computers into the classroom and ultimately calling for teacher training in media literacy (England 1985). Strickland's comments in her 1969 text illustrate the importance of language skills—not just in one's native language, but in other languages as well. The growing interconnectedness of countries' economies, especially between the United States and Japan, illustrates the need for global communication and understanding. Our world is much smaller than Strickland's, thanks to such innovations as the microchip and such threats as nuclear warheads.

However, in this smaller world we have unique situations that Ruth Strickland could not have forecast, or possibly understood. In her 1962 study on children's talk, of the 575 children studied, none came from a single-parent household. Strickland apparently encountered few latchkey children and possibly no homeless children. However, she did recognize the influence a child's home environment exerts on his or her language development and emphasized the teacher's role in providing a positive, nurturing environment at school. In her *Guide for Teaching Language in Grades 1 and 2*, Strickland warned: "It is unwise to assume that all children who enter school linguistically handicapped are children of low intelligence. A bright child may be handicapped by the meagerness of his own preschool experience. Such a child will grow rapidly in linguistic attainment when he is given a rich program of experience" (1962a, 5). But could Strickland have foreseen that today a rich program of experience might be thwarted at every step by a child's caregivers? In "Arthur: A Tale of Disempowerment," LaVergne Rosow outlined her efforts to help a well-to-do nine-year-old boy achieve literacy. His family, however, had a different agenda: "Beneath the surface of this seemingly advantaged environment lurked a network of people who enable an illiterate minority to exist and to pass on its special system of values from one generation to the next. Arthur was surrounded by a cordon of significant others bent on disempowering him" (1989, 194). This child had no language skills and read on a first-grade level. With no support from the home and with the social stigma of being in the "special reading group" attached to this child by his peers, how can a teacher help Arthur? Or all the other Arthurs in our schools? Indeed, today's teachers face obstacles of a different nature than those of the 1950s and 1960s. In her writings Strickland may have told us that a teacher is responsible for providing a model environment, but she also told us more. She gave us an impetus to study our students and to research their abilities in depth.

Strickland's dedication to research led many of her colleagues, our teachers and professors, into more diverse areas of study. This dedication to improvement in English education is best reflected in the growth of the journal *Research in the Teaching of English*. Richard Braddock, director of the Rhetoric Program at the University of Iowa, served as the first editor of the journal in 1967, with Nathan S. Blount of the Research and Development Center for Cognitive Learning at the University of Wisconsin–Madison serving as associate editor. The first issue, publishing articles on sentence structure and prose quality, writing frequency, correction techniques in composition, and the profile of the poor writer, seemed to reach out for an identity of sorts. Two articles dealt exclusively with research design—one addressed research designs that might prove fruitful in English research, while the other pointed out major flaws in research designs and how to overcome them. In the "Notes and Comment" section of this first issue, Braddock made an observation and issued a challenge to readers: "In the December, 1966, issue of *College English*, George Henry maintains that research in English teaching will not amount to much until it can relate its various investigations to a major unifying theory. *Research in the Teaching of English* opens its pages to articles proposing theories for research as well as to reports and analyses of accomplished research" (1967, 91).

The first issue of the journal provided a large bibliography on research in English, and many of those cited now hold influential positions in English education today: Arthur Applebee is thanked for his assistance with compiling the bibliography. Kellogg Hunt's *Sentence Structures Used by Superior Students in Grades Four and Twelve, and by Superior Adults*, a followup to the study that gave writing researchers T-units, is cited along with an abstract on this important work. And in the bibliography is a dissertation entitled "A Comparison of the Effects of Three Types of Vocabulary Development on the Reading Comprehension and Thinking Ability of Sixth-Grade Children," written by Judith Langer. That all three of these scholars remain influential in English education research and that two of them would eventually serve as editors of *Research in the Teaching of English* should allay any concerns that research in English education "will not amount to much."

Research is no longer relegated to the ivory towers of the university. Much of today's research takes place in the classroom, a more naturalistic setting than the observation booth. In her work, Ruth Strickland provided early guidelines for teachers who wished to study their charges. By keeping careful, individualized records of her students' weaknesses, Strickland was able to chart marked improvement in her first-grade and second-grade students in the 1920s. Throughout her texts, she stated the importance of record keeping, whether it be in a notebook or on note cards or on small slips of paper: the teacher must write down observations for later reflection if that teacher wishes to help his or her students. This record keeping, coupled with keen observation skills and a desire to induce student improvement, translates into the teacher-researcher movement, as supported by such teacher-researchers as Miles Myers and Marian Mohr. "Start a research diary" is the first item in Myers's chapter-one summary (1985, 25), while Mohr speaks at summer workshops of her preference for black-and-white-speckled composition notebooks as her research journal.

Strickland's most important statement concerning teacher-researchers came at what was possibly her most disappointing moment. When she wrote to James Squire that "a program of improvement should start at the foundation, not halfway up the educational ladder" (1965a), she sounded as if she considered herself and those in executive positions in professional organizations as the foundation. That foundation, however, is not in a university system or executive office—our teachers comprise the foundation upon which educational reform must take place. Strickland knew the tremendous influence teachers had on students and ultimately on communities. Teachers, therefore, are the source of program improvement and should receive the respectability due those who hold the authority to make decisions and the resources to initiate change.

In a telephone conversation James Squire lamented that "the people [in NCTE] are more pastel today than the vivid colors of twenty to thirty years ago" (1989). Perhaps our contemporary times call for discretion, a deeper concern for political intricacies with which our predecessors did not have to contend. Or perhaps those "vivid colors" of decades past weave together into a strong fabric, one resistant to tears and absent of flaws, thus making our work, our weaving, that much easier. These vivid colors, these people who are the Council, are the intricate parts of the tapestry of English education. Ruth G. Strickland was one of those vivid colors in that tapestry, making up an integral section of the tapestry, weaving her way into our history while keeping us ever-mindful of our futures. Her research provided the bright spots, the triumphs, in her fibers, thus illuminating our present endeavors. By contributing to English education, and in such vivid fashion, Ruth Strickland leaves us with a legacy that becomes our own strand of the past, that weaves with our strand of the present, that works with our strand of the future, that helps all of us create a more complex tapestry. And we must always be mindful that our present will become the threads of the past for future English educators. Therefore, we must weave well.

Works Cited

Applebee, Arthur N. 1974. *Tradition and Reform in the Teaching of English: A History.* Urbana, Ill.: National Council of Teachers of English.

Braddock, Richard. 1967. "Notes and Comments." *Research in the Teaching of English* 1: 91.

Britton, James. 1970. *Language and Learning.* London: Penguin Books.

Corbin, Richard. 1965. Statement announcing renaming of the NCTE Distinguished Research Award as the David H. Russell Distinguished Research Award in the Teaching of English.

England, David. 1985. "Study Group 3: Language and the New Media." In *Language, Schooling and Society,* edited by Stephen Tchudi. Upper Montclair, N.J.: Boynton/Cook.

Hook, J. N. 1979. *A Long Way Together: A Personal View of NCTE's First Sixty-Seven Years.* Urbana, Ill.: National Council of Teachers of English.

Indiana Daily Student. 1948a (16 October 1948). News clipping.

Indiana Daily Student. 1948b (19 November 1948). News clipping.

Indiana Daily Student. 1949 (15 January 1949). News clipping.

Japanese Education Reform Council. 1950. *Educational Reform in Japan: The Present Status and the Problems Involved.* Tokyo: Government of Japan.

Myers, Miles. 1985. *The Teacher-Researcher: How to Study Writing in the Classroom.* Urbana, Ill.: National Council of Teachers of English.

Piaget, Jean. 1959. *The Language and Thought of the Child.* London: Routledge and Kegan Paul.

Rosow, LaVergne. "Arthur: A Tale of Disempowerment." *Phi Delta Kappan* 71: 194-99.

Strickland, Ruth G. 1938. *A Study of the Possibilities of Graphs as a Means of Instruction in the First Four Grades of Elementary School.* New York: Bureau of Publications, Teachers College, Columbia University.

———. 1943. "A Good Start in School." *Elementary English Review* 21: 241-46.

———. 1945. "The Development of Vocabulary." *Elementary English Review* 22: 9-12, 35.

———. 1951. *The Language Arts in the Elementary School.* Boston: D.C. Heath.

———. 1957. *The Language Arts in the Elementary School.* 2d ed. Boston: D.C. Heath.

———. 1960. President's Report. In the Annual Reports of Officers and Committees, National Council of Teachers of English.

———. 1961. "What Thou Lovest Well Remains." *English Journal* 50: 71-80.

———. 1962a. *Guide for Teaching Language in Grades 1 and 2.* Boston: D.C. Heath.

———. 1962b. *The Language of Elementary School Children: Its Relationship to the*

Language of Reading Textbooks and the Quality of Reading of Selected Children. Bloomington, Ind.: Bureau of Educational Studies and Testing, School of Education, Indiana University.

———. 1965a (13 January 1965). Letter to James Squire.

———. 1965b (November 1965). Statement accepting receipt of the David H. Russell Distinguished Research Award in the Teaching of English.

———. 1969. *The Language Arts in the Elementary School.* 3d ed. Boston: D.C. Heath.

———. 16 August 1977. Interview with Alfred H. Grommon.

Squire, James. 1965. (29 January 1965). Letter to Ruth G. Strickland.

———. 8 June 1989. Telephone interview with author.

Supreme Commander for the Allied Powers. 1952. *Post-War Developments in Japanese Education.* 2 vols. Tokyo: Civil Information and Education Section.

Afterword

In 1974, when NCTE published *Tradition and Reform in the Teaching of English*, there were almost no materials available about the individuals who were our professional ancestors. All that had been published were a few tributes at retirement, an occasional entry in the *Dictionary of American Biography* or *Contemporary Authors*, and brief "In Memoria" notices in *English Journal* or *Language Arts*. Politicians, literary giants, film stars, and baseball players warranted biographies, but, with a few exceptions, not their teachers.

So I turned with much interest to the essays that have been gathered together here, hoping finally to learn more about the people whose writings and actions had shaped the early teaching of our subject.

And I was not disappointed. These essays tell us much about the ideas, the conflicts, and the compromises that shaped the teaching of the language arts as we know them today, but they tell us even more about the persons behind the drama. Between the lines, and sometimes overtly in the essays, we get glimpses of the passions, the idiosyncracies, the scholarship, the strength of the women whose stories are shared here. Together, these biographies reflect both the broad spectrum of issues and philosophies that the Council has always encompassed, and the reasons that the Council has throughout its history been a leader in the movements to provide a conceptually based, child-centered, progressive pedagogy for our nation's schools.

I am grateful to the authors of these essays for helping us find our roots, and I hope that the present collection will stimulate further studies of the teachers—mainstream and minority, male and female, school and college—whose lives were dedicated to the proposition that improving the education of America's children is an endeavor in which we can all take pride.

Arthur N. Applebee
Albany, New York, March 1990

Editors

Jeanne Marcum Gerlach is Assistant Professor of Curriculum and Instruction/English Education at West Virginia University, where she teaches English methods courses to undergraduate and graduate students. She has codirected the West Virginia University Advanced Writing Project and codirects the West Virginia University Language Arts Camps. She has taught English education at all levels. A published poet, she has worked as a writer in the schools and taught creative writing to preschool students as well as senior citizens and written articles on English education pedagogy, adolescent fiction, the history of women in English education, and educational gerontology. As chair of the NCTE Committee on Women in the Profession, she has worked to promote the positive status and image of women in the Council and profession.

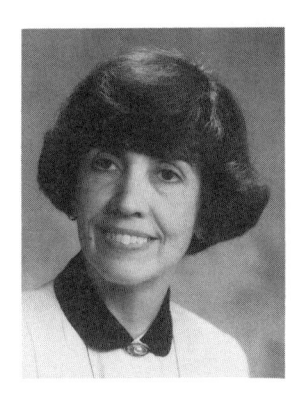

Virginia R. Monseau is Associate Professor of English at Youngstown State University, where she teaches courses in adolescent literature, children's literature, and composition, and supervises student teachers in the secondary English education program. A member of NCTE's Committee on Women in the Profession, she is also active in ALAN, the Assembly on Literature for Adolescents of NCTE, serving on its Board of Directors. Her research interests include the role of women in the history of English education, the responses of adolescents and their teachers to young adult literature, and the role of the young adult novel in the traditional literature curriculum. Recipient of a YSU Research Professorship to work on this project, she has published articles in many professional journals. She is coeditor of a forthcoming book: *Performing the Text: Reading and Teaching the Young Adult Novel.*

Contributors

Judy P. Byers is Associate Professor of English at Fairmont State College in West Virginia, where she teaches courses in composition, folk literature, and English education. A former secondary school teacher, she is a well-known storyteller in Appalachia.

David A. England is Associate Professor and Coordinator of Teacher Education at Louisiana State University, Baton Rouge. A former high school English teacher, he is active in NCTE and in the National Writing Project.

Dure Jo Gillikin is Associate Professor of English, Speech, and World Literature at the College of Staten Island, New York. One of the founders of the National Women's Studies Association, she has edited several women's journals and published extensively in the field of gender studies.

Sharon Hamilton-Wieler is Assistant Professor of Rhetoric and Composition at Indiana University–Purdue University at Indianapolis. A recent recipient of an NCTE Research Foundation Grant, she is active in national and international teacher organizations.

Betty L. Powell Hart is a teacher at Mt. Vernon High School, Evansville, Indiana. She is active in NCTE. Her publications include *Prayers in the Black Tradition* and "Alice Dunbar Nelson: Early Voices of Black Womanhood."

Sue Ellen Holbrook is Associate Professor of English and Director of the Composition Program at Southern Connecticut State University, New Haven. A recipient of two NEH grants, she has published articles on medieval literature and composition pedagogy.

Tracey J. Johnson is a doctoral candidate in English Education at West Virginia University, where she teaches in both the English and Education departments. A recipient of two fellowships, she is researching women's roles as they relate to the administration of writing programs.

Lisa J. McClure is Assistant Professor of English at Southern Illinois University at Carbondale. Formerly a writing program administrator, she now teaches in the Rhetoric and Composition program at SIU.

B. Jane West is a doctoral candidate in the Department of Language Education at the University of Georgia, Athens. She is interested in the role women have played in the evolution of English teaching.